CRITICAL MEDI
INSTITUTIONS, POLITIC

D0763720

Series Editor: Andrew Calabrese, University of Colorado

Advisory Board

Recent Titles in the Series

Floating Lives: The Media and Asian Diasporas, edited by Stuart Cunningham and John Sinclair

Forthcoming in the Series

Global Media Governance: A Beginner's Guide, by Seán Ó Siochrú and W. Bruce Girard

Continental Order? Integrating North America for Cybercapitalism, edited by Vincent Mosco and Dan Schiller

The Global and the National: Media and Communications in Post-Communist Russia, by Terhi Rantanen

From Newspaper Guild to Multimedia Union: A Study in Labor Convergence, by Catherine McKercher

The Eclipse of Freedom: From the Principle of Publicity to the Freedom of the Press, by Slavko Splichal

Elusive Autonomy: Brazilian Communications Policy in an Age of Globalization and Technical Change, by Sergio Euclides de Souza

Floating Lives

Floating Lives

The Media and Asian Diasporas

Edited by Stuart Cunningham
and John Sinclair

ROWMAN & LITTLEFIELD PUBLISHERS, INC.
Lanham • Boulder • New York • Oxford

ROWMAN & LITTLEFIELD PUBLISHERS, INC.

Published in the United States of America
by Rowman & Littlefield Publishers, Inc.
4720 Boston Way, Lanham, Maryland 20706
www.rowmanlittlefield.com

12 Hid's Copse Road, Cumnor Hill, Oxford OX2 9JJ, England

British Library Cataloguing in Publication Information Available

Library of Congress Cataloging-in-Publication Data

Floating Lives : the media and Asian diasporas / edited by Stuart
Cunningham and John Sinclair.
     p. cm — (Critical Media Studies)
    Originally published: St. Lucia, Queensland : University of
    Queensland Press, 2000.
    Includes bibliographical references and index.
    ISBN 0-7425-1135-9 (alk. paper) — ISBN 0-7425-1136-7 (pbk. : alk.
    paper)
     1. Ethnic mass media—Australia. 2. Mass media and minorities—
Australia. 3. Asians—Services for—Australia. 4. Asians—Australia—
Social life and customs. I. Cunningham, Stuart. II. Sinclair, John,
1944- III. Series.

P94.5 .M552 A 837 2001
302.23'089'95094—dc21

                                  2001019391

Printed in the United States of America

♾™ The paper used in this publication meets the minimum requirements
of American National Standard for Information Sciences—Permanence of
Paper for Printed Library Materials, ANSI/NISO Z39.48-1992.

Contents

Figures and Appendixes

Contributors

Stuart Cunningham is Professor and Head, School of Media and Journalism, Queensland University of Technology. He is an author or editor of several books and monographs on topics such as Australian media, cultural policy, global television and "borderless" education, the most recent of which are *New Patterns in Global Television* (with John Sinclair and Elizabeth Jacka, Oxford University Press), *Australian Television and International Mediascapes* (with Elizabeth Jacka, Cambridge University Press) and *The Media in Australia: Industries, Texts, Audiences* (with Graeme Turner, Allen & Unwin). He is a Deputy Director of the Australian Key Centre for Cultural and Media Policy.

Josephine Fox has extensive fieldwork experience in China, where she has been completing her PhD in History.

Gay Hawkins is Senior Lecturer in Sociology, University of New South Wales, Sydney. She has published a book on the invocation of "community" in arts policy, *From Nimbin to Mardi Gras: Constructing Community Arts* (Allen & Unwin), as well as numerous papers on television, value and difference, and transformations in public service broadcasting.

Chalinee Hirano is a PhD candidate in Southeast Asian Studies, Faculty of Asian Studies, Australian National University, Canberra.

Kee Pookong is Director of the Centre for Asia–Pacific Studies, Victoria University of Technology, Melbourne.

Glen Lewis is Associate Professor in International Communication at the University of Canberra and Professor in the Graduate School of Bangkok University. He is also adjunct Professor in the School of Communication at UNITEC Institute of Technology in Auckland, New Zealand. He is co-author of *Critical Communication* and *Communication Traditions in 20th Century Australia.*

Tina Nguyen is a postgraduate student in the Australian Key Centre for Cultural and Media Policy, Queensland University of Technology, Brisbane.

Manas Ray is a Fellow of Sociology and Cultural Studies at the Centre for Studies in Social Sciences, Calcutta. While a Postdoctoral Fellow in the Australian Key Centre for Cultural and Media Policy, Queensland University of Technology, Brisbane, during 1996–98, he researched Indian diasporas in Australia. He has authored several articles and book chapters on Indian media, cultural theory and ethics and is currently researching the making of postcolonial democracy in India.

John Sinclair is Professor in the Department of Communication, Language and Cultural Studies at Victoria University of Technology in Melbourne. His research on the internationalisation of the television and advertising industries, with particular attention to Latin America and Asia, has been published widely. His most recent books are *Latin American Television: A Global View* (Oxford, 1999) and *New Patterns in Global Television: Peripheral Vision*, co-edited with Elizabeth Jacka and Stuart Cunningham (Oxford, 1996).

Audrey Yue is Lecturer in Cultural Studies, Department of English with Cultural Studies, University of Melbourne, Melbourne. Her PhD was on postcolonial Hong Kong cinema and her current research areas include Asian media, new technology, queer theory and diaspora cultures. She has published in the *Asian Journal of Communication*, *Meanjin, Journal of Homosexuality* and *New Formations*.

Acknowledgments

The fundamental funding support for this project was provided by an Australian Research Council Large Grant, "Audiovisual Media Use for Cultural Maintenance and Negotiation by Diasporic Communities of Asian Origin in Australia", awarded for 1996–98 to Stuart Cunningham, John Sinclair and Gay Hawkins. We are pleased to record from the outset that our undertaking would have been unthinkable without such support. Ancillary funding and/or in-kind support which assisted the research was provided by Queensland University of Technology, Victoria University of Technology, the University of New South Wales and the University of Canberra.

We owe thanks to a number of people and institutions for their assistance in this project: Elizabeth Jacka, whose idea it was in the first place and who was an original applicant for the sustaining ARC grant; at University of Queensland Press, our commissioning editor, Craig Munro, and managing director Laurie Muller; the School of Media and Journalism at Queensland University of Technology and the Department of Communication, Language and Cultural Studies, Victoria University of Technology, Melbourne, which have been good home bases for our work; and Jo-Anne Clifford and Maggie Gundert for their continuing support.

Stuart Cunningham and Tina Nguyen gratefully acknowledge the vital research provided by Jo Chichester, Trang Nguyen and Jo-Anne Clifford, without which the work would have been impossible; and the help of Audrey Yue, Son Ca, Nguyen Van Khanh, Trinh Thu Lan, Tran Le Trinh, Vo Quoc Thanh and Huynh Thai Van (Jasmine). The collegial academic support and assistance provided by Mandy Thomas at the

University of Western Sydney and Ashley Carruthers at the University of Sydney have been appreciated immensely.

Manas Ray seeks to acknowledge Brij Lal in Canberra for granting a valuable interview; Satish Rai, Sashi Mahendra Singh, Nick Kumar, Saronika Pratap, Akash Hossain, Sanjoy Dello, Gabriel and Sheetal Chellam in Sydney for their assistance with the research into the Fiji Indians; Uri Themal, Firoz Khan, Taushif Khan, Raniga, Aiyasha, Sunny Prasad and Tracey Edwards in Brisbane for their assistance with the research generally; Ravi Vasudevan in Delhi and Pradip Bose, Gantam Bhadra, Moinak Biswas and Sivaji Bandhyopadhyay in Calcutta for collegial discussion and debate. Glen Lewis and Chalinee Hirano would like to thank the Thai Welfare Organization in Sydney and the Thai video rental stores, as well as the Thai communities in Sydney and Canberra whose assistance made their research possible.

Some parts of this work have been presented at a number of venues, including the International Association for Media and Communication Research (IAMCR) conferences in Sydney in 1996, Oaxaca in 1997 and Glasgow in 1998; the Communications Law Centre "Television and the Multicultural Audience" seminar in Sydney in 1995; Australian Key Centre for Cultural and Media Policy conferences and workshops in Singapore, Brisbane and Sydney in 1996 and 1997; the "Chinese in Australia" conference in Melbourne in 1996; and the Cultural Studies Association of Australia conference in Adelaide in 1998. Parts have appeared in previous form in *Media International Australia incorporating Culture and Policy, Citizenship and Cultural Policy* (eds Denise Meredyth and Jeffrey Minson, Sage, 2000), and in *New Formations.*

For the use of copyright material, we would like to thank the following: Galaxy Media Pty Ltd, ASIA Productions, Thuy Nga Productions, *Chieu Duong,* and *Fiji Times.* All reasonable efforts were made to secure permission for material used but we would be glad to hear from anyone we have been unable to contact in order to correct this for any future edition.

1

Diasporas and the Media

John Sinclair and Stuart Cunningham

This work, on the role of communication technologies in the creation
and sustenance of diasporic identities, is of profound significance.
(Morley, 1996: 330)

Clara Law's critically acclaimed 1996 film, *Floating Life*, provides
some of the key motifs of the contemporary phenomenon of diaspora,
and so has inspired the title of this book. Shot in Cantonese with
English subtitles, *Floating Life* was the first feature film in Australia
to be made in a language other than English. We adapt Clara Law's
title for this book with her kind permission. In Law's narrative of
displacement, members of a Hong Kong family have to come to
terms with their dispersal into Australia and Europe, and the
consequent experience of deterritorialisation, the psychological and
cultural dislocation of making a "home" in alien "host" lands. While
a woman goes into total social withdrawal for fear of the world
outside, her parents wonder how their prayers to their ancestors will
ever find their way back to Hong Kong. The film dramatises the
literal dis-location of culture experienced by more and more people
in the era of globalisation, "the archetypal late-modern condition"
(Chen, 1996: 490).

The concept of diaspora can be usefully applied to understanding
many of the major population movements of this century, and the
complex processes of the maintenance and negotiation of cultural
identity which go along with them. Significantly, the extent of the
population movements of recent history can lay claim to beginning
to break down the mutual identification between nation and culture
which previously was asserted to exist in classical accounts of
nationalism and the modern nation state (Collins, 1994: 382–83).

Consider mass migration from the developing world to the richer countries, such as Latin Americans in the United States, Caribbeans and South Asians in Britain, Turkish and North African *Gastarbeiter* in Europe; the resettlement in several countries of millions of refugees from Iran, Vietnam, Cambodia and the former Eastern Bloc; the declaration of "multiculturalism" as a social policy reality for Australia and Canada. If we take into account other categories of people living more or less permanently outside their countries of origin, such as business expatriates, foreign students and academics, retirees, and even long-term cultural tourists, it is clear to see that the traditional "national culture" of many major nations no longer fits (if it ever really did) substantial proportions of the people who now actually inhabit the nation. Rather, these people's cultural horizons are turned toward those they see as their kind in other nations, and (possibly) to their nation of origin, but also to the challenges of negotiating a place in the host culture.

It is not just the flows of the people themselves that are involved, but the whole "continuous circulation of people, money, goods and information" comprising the "transnational migrant [and refugee and other] circuit[s]" (Rouse, 1991: 14). In particular, flows of communication media services and contents are an integral part of what we are trying to pin down about the contemporary world when we use that buzzword of our age, "globalisation". Along with the new flow patterns of media and people he calls "mediascapes" and "ethnoscapes", Arjun Appadurai (1990), in his influential analysis, also lists flows of technologies, capital and ideas as constituting the current era. Importantly, he sees all these flows as "disjunctive"— they are occurring together, but in unsystematically related ways.

For example, whereas flows of people often have tended to be from what the world-systems theorists call the "periphery", or developing world, and towards the "centre", or metropolitan nations (e.g. Wallerstein, 1991), media flows historically have travelled in the other direction. More recently, however, there have been media flows which have developed from within centres of the periphery, such as Hong Kong, Mumbai, Mexico City, Sydney, Toronto or Cairo, which are not only thus breaking down the centre–periphery distinction itself, but beginning to define new kinds of world region

(Sinclair et al., 1996). These include "geolinguistic regions" — that is, regions across which linguistic and cultural similarities are at least as important as geographical proximity has been in forming world regions in the past. The media space of a diaspora tends to be of this kind, to the extent that it is spread throughout several of the national markets which have been the territorial unit for international media distribution in the past.

The advent of quite particular technologies, notably international satellite television transmission, but also the humble video, have been instrumental in the fostering of such international niche markets, or "global narrowcasting". At the upper socioeconomic end, business executives can check into any international hotel in the world and expect to watch CNN. At several points on the same continuum, members of diasporic groups can be dispersed widely, even into remote locations, but still pick up news from home on a satellite dish or cable in those places where they are more concentrated — or, in cases where homeland news and information transmission is underdeveloped, suppressed or radically contested, they may access video letters, Websites or special delivery orders flown in on a regular basis. Alternatively, they might rent a movie or popular television series which has come to their local store along the fine capillaries of distribution which emanate from their place of ethnic origin, or even from one of the new centres of diasporic media production now springing up in the West.

Shifting Ground

The purpose of this book is to trace the cultural significance of such global flows of audiovisual media for actually existing diasporas. This objective is pursued in the context of a number of basic theoretical paradigm shifts in sociology, population studies, and communication, media and cultural studies, to which the book is intended to contribute from a number of perspectives: from a social problem or welfare conception of the migrant to an appreciation of cultural difference; from a view of the media as an imposed force to a recognition of audience activity and selectiveness; and from an essentialist, or "heritage", to a more dynamic, adaptive model of culture. Each deserves some commentary at this point.

Migrancy as Agency

First, let's examine the image of the migrant and the settlement process. Representations of the migrant as a cultural victim have become familiar in both the humanities and social sciences over the decades since the end of World War II, during which ever-greater numbers and categories of people have, for different kinds of reasons, left their cultural homelands to settle elsewhere. Only more recently has attention been given to migration as a complex process of cultural maintenance and negotiation, or resistance and adaptation. With this attention has finally come an appreciation of the *range* of the cultural border-crossings achieved by many of the diasporas as they travel across major civilisational divides, and with it has come a new sense of what cosmopolitanism might mean now, beyond those specifically European or imperial sensibilities of the past fashioned within the grid of Western high culture. Of particular interest in this book is how diasporas make use of communications media in these dialectical processes, and how certain of the media used are thus able to create markets out of dislocated peoples, even as the diasporas redefine their cultural identities in hybrid terms, the transcendence of the dichotomy of "home" and "host".

This is not to join in the fashionable postmodernist celebration of hybridity for its own sake. Indeed, the range of actually existing diasporas studied in this book defeats any singular grid of understanding. The Chinese are part of a great diaspora which dates in Australia from the 1840s — one which is extensively cosmopolitan and lifestyle-, education- and business-oriented and which cannot be understood in terms of the liminality of recent displacement. The Vietnamese and Fiji Indian diasporas, on the other hand, are much more recent and were precipitated by direct political domination and, at least in the case of the Vietnamese, maintain an official public face as political refugees. The Thais are very recent immigrants; the reasons that have impelled movement are neither exile nor predominantly business. So the case studies in this book move around foci on the unfinished, parlous, unstable path of "cultural bifocality" which "can be a source of much psychic pain" (Smith and Tarallo, 1995: 52) as much as a condition of celebration of successful resistance and assertion (e.g. Wong, 1994), or an achieved cosmopolitanism that may render such stances of historical value only.

We seek to help shift the paradigm away from seeing the cultural adjustments of migration in dichotomous, assimilationist terms. In the corresponding policy discourse, adjustment too often has been assumed to be a problem of helping the unfortunate migrant to adapt to the clichéd dilemma of "two worlds", even in the more benign multiculturalist version which encourages migrants to retain their cultural differences at the same time as they assimilate to the language and the law of the host. It might be noted in passing at this point, as we shall return to it, that this is the version which has become institutionalised over the last two decades in Australia — the same period that has seen the term "multiculturalism" become associated with oppositional demands for social change and pluralism from and on behalf of the major minorities, rather than a project of the nation-state itself, in several other countries, including the United States and Britain (Bennett, 1998).

Using Media

Once again without lurching from one extreme to the other, there is a second paradigm shift in process which we want this book to give a push to: this is the shift from the power of texts to the power of audiences and readers to shape meaning and use of the media.

This shift is a welcome one, but media and cultural studies' moves to factor in consumption and use have rarely concentrated on cross-cultural scenarios. On the other hand, treatments of diasporic identity have concentrated on issues of representation *by* mainstream media *of* ethnic and racial identities. Not surprisingly, the conclusions reached in the numerous studies of this kind tend to be that Western mass media operate as prime filters of a hegemonic discourse "othering" minority cultures and identities. Important and necessary as these researches are, they are not sufficient to understand the productive construction of new hybrid identities and cultures by the active processes, simultaneously, of maintenance and negotiation, of an original home and a newly acquired host culture. As the field of international media studies has begun to draw theoretical inspiration from cultural studies' accounts of diasporic identity, it has begun to address media *use*, with studies of media and communications use amongst diasporic communities in Europe (e.g. Gillespie, 1994; Husband, 1992, 1998), in North America (e.g. Naficy, 1993; Srikandath, 1993) and in Australia (Kolar-Panov, 1997).

A closely related angle on this shift is to consider the strength and manner in which media can be assumed to exert influence over audiences. Since the demise of the "dominant ideology thesis" of the 1980s, with its implicit hypothesis of strong media effects being imposed on relatively passive audiences (Collins, 1990), there has been the not-uncontested rise of an alternative conception of the "active audience", accompanied by new, postmodernist theories of "decentred" individual subjectivities (Ang, 1996).

Taken to its most absurd conclusion, this new perspective would suggest that the media carry so many different meanings for so many different people that the once-assumed social impact of media messages is dissipated. However, we do not have to go that far to recognise that there are many ways in which audiences actively seek out their own media experiences, assert their preferences and critically interact with each other, as well as with the media contents they choose. This emphasis links directly to our first shift in that, throughout this book, stress is placed on the active agency of minority communities constructing a media environment through patterns of consumption and production which address needs for maintenance and negotiation.

On the other hand — and even if we also accept the postmodernist insight that individuals respond to media discourses with multiple identifications of themselves, rather than as coherent, unified subjects — there is a sense in which the media are also actively seeking out audiences. Thus, whatever collective audience preferences and desires there might be, they are still shaped commercially and ideologically as markets for certain forms and genres by media corporations. In this book, amongst other things, we want to explore the process by which the desires generated by the diasporic experience — for example, wanting to stay in touch with news and popular culture from the homeland — become transformed into demand for certain kinds of media services and products — that is, how diasporas become formed by the use of their media as global narrowcast markets.

Adaptive Culture

The third question is one of culture, "one of the two or three most complicated words in the English language" (Williams, 1976: 76) and now more problematic than ever. While the textbook "anthropological" definition of culture as a "whole way of life" — usually of a national society — became the common wisdom both inside and outside of academia during the 1980s, the notion came under attack within anthropology itself. Anthropologists recognised that the unity of the "cultures" which they studied was their own construction, "something made rather than found" (Gupta and Ferguson, 1997: 2). As the impact of globalisation has been felt right across the social sciences and humanities, and especially as the formerly assumed autonomy of the nation-state has been challenged by globalising forces, there has been a more general reassessment of the assumption that we can meaningfully think of a "culture" as the distinct and separate way of life of a given people who occupy a particular territory on the globe — as in, for example, "Australian culture". Indeed, for some time, the idea of each nation-state having its corresponding national culture had been eclipsed by the growing perception that national cultures are created in their own image by the dominant hegemonic groups in society (Morley and Robins, 1995: 48–49; Turner, 1994).

All of these developments have been calling for a redefinition of culture. The former orthodox view was that each society "has" a culture which it perpetuates, and which perpetuates it, through being passed on to each individual member. This had both consensus (functionalist) and conflict variants (Marxist, feminist) which, regardless of their fundamental differences, both took culture (or "the dominant ideology") as a thing: a kind of complexly structured essence binding society together. This could be called the quantum view of culture, as if culture is something which societies strategically allocate to their individual subjects, albeit on a differentiated basis (Bourdieu's notion of "cultural capital" is revealing here).

In this view, personal identity is a function of cultural membership. Every individual "has" a culture, or some culture, although they can lose it if it is not "maintained". Furthermore, at least in the conflict versions, not all cultures are equal — stronger cultures can dominate or "marginalise" weaker ones (as in the discourse of "cultural imperialism"). It is implied that cultures are clearly demarcated from each other, almost as if they have mass and occupy space — or at least, that they are linked to place in much the same way as nation-states mark off their territories from each other with borders. Indeed, the assumption lingers that nation and culture are coterminous. This quantum conception deserves to be criticised simply for the static and reified view of culture which it offers, not to mention its lack of relevance to a world of people on the move across increasingly porous national borders. In such a world, individual cultural identities become decentred through the same process that causes national cultures to lose their hegemony.

Jan Nederveen Pieterse (1995) argues that the older territorial conception of culture, which he calls "Culture 1", needs to be set against a more adaptive conception of culture, "Culture 2", which recognises the breadth, variety and fluidity of social relations in "translocal" culture. This broader view takes account of the phenomenon of cultural fusion, variously conceptualised by others as the emergence of "third cultures" (Featherstone, 1990), *mestizajes* (Martín-Barbero, 1993), or "creolization" (Hannerz, 1996), though all of these refer to the innovative collective responses which real people can and do make when having to negotiate between one culture and another. Repudiating any sense of culture as a closed, impermeable and unified object, and rejecting the view that cultural identity is an ideal, fixed condition which individuals seek to preserve, Stuart Hall (1995) also has argued that cultures never remain static, "pure" and true to their origin, particularly in the process of diaspora. Diasporic culture in this new perspective is thus the product of the constantly configuring process which occurs when immigrant or otherwise displaced cultures selectively adapt to host cultures, intermingling and evolving to form a regenerative "new" culture, a culture related to, but yet distinct from, both the original home and host cultures.

The master metaphor for such cultural adaptiveness and innovation is "hybridity", which — like the concepts of "culture", "diaspora" and "broadcasting" — is also based on organic growth and transformation in nature. The theorisation of hybridity is found in some lines of work from Latin America, where cultural syncretism has long been institutionalised in both national and subordinate cultures (García Canclini, 1995), but most often it is "the fashionable wing of postcolonial theory" (Chen, 1998: 22), and particularly the work of Homi Bhabha, which are cited. Bhabha views hybridity as the product of what he calls "cultural translation", in which the hybrid subject negotiates cultural difference in a performative interplay between home and host. Importantly, Bhabha's concept of hybridity as articulating between dominant and marginal discourses long associated with diasporas and other forms of postcolonial cultural contact opens up a "third space" for cultural strategies to become active forms of resistance to domination and marginalisation (Bhabha, 1994: 5–9). To simply assume this kind of role for hybrid cultural activity, however, risks a stance of postmodernist celebration for its own sake of the "subject-in-process".

Yet, in the context of this book, the most appropriate revision of all of the concept of culture comes from James Clifford, who proposes that, in order "to focus on hybrid, cosmopolitan experiences as much as on rooted, native ones" in a world of people in flux, "we rethink culture and its science, anthropology, in terms of travel" (Clifford, 1992: 101). Thus, instead of the traditional trope of culture being an organic outgrowth of a particular place, the motif of travel can incorporate all those forms of movement experienced by people today, which take them or keep them away from their real or putative place of origin. Even if they are not all travelling in the same class, Clifford's shifting of the concept of culture away from "roots" and towards "routes" instead (1992: 108) endows it with a more flexible way to deal with the many different kinds of "floating lives" which characterise our times.

Delineating Diaspora

Commenting on the revival of the concept in the late 1980s, Khachig Tölölyan has observed, "'diaspora' is now used as a synonym for related phenomena until recently covered by distinct terms like expatriate, exile, ethnic, minority, refugee, migrant, sojourner and overseas community" (Tölölyan, 1996: 10). Thus most definitions of diaspora emphasise the marginal status of those groups which, although they have settled outside their lands of ethnic origin, still maintain strong sentimental or material links with them (Esman,

1986; Sheffer, 1986). Some definitions even include irredentist consciousness as part of the concept — that is, the desire of such groups in different countries to link together and work for a return to the homeland (Safran, 1991: 83–84). Diasporas can also be very long term — even millennial — as in the archetypal Jewish case. And it is possible to claim (although this dissipates the strength of the term as one concerning minoritarian cultures) that dispersal of dominant ethnicities, such as the movements of elites and settlers emanating from the imperial powers, might also constitute instances of diaspora. The term is certainly contestable as a way of grasping all forms of dispersed peoples (see Rex, 1996; Delafenetre, 1997), but we wish to retain it in this expansive sense as it captures the dynamics of particularly cross-cultural and cross-language settlement better than terms as neutral and technical as "immigration".

Just as Benedict Anderson has definitively characterised national cultures as "imagined communities" (1991), bonded discursively by a sense of deep, horizontal belonging to an imagined common origin and a mythical past, the imagi(nations) of deterritorialised peoples — even when scattered through different lands — may be marked correspondingly by "absentee patriotism and long-distance nationalism" (Nederveen Pieterse, 1995: 49). As Anderson argues, what matters in constituting communities is not their authenticity or otherwise, but "the style in which they are imagined" (1995: 6). In this vein, William Safran (1991) points to how expatriate minority communities may be sustained by a collective homeland myth fetishised through cultural memory and (trans)national desires, and represented as mythical landscapes, invented traditions, stories and ceremonies.

Certainly, some sense of difference, marginality and displaced belonging is essential to the concept, including a strong identification with a homeland, and the corresponding resistance of diasporic groups to complete assimilation by the host nation. However, the most literal element in any definition must be that of dispersal. Etymologically, the word "diaspora" stems from the Greek *diaspeirein*, meaning "to disperse", or as *speirein* suggests, "to scatter", as of seed. "Diaspora" thus refers to a dispersion, or scattering, of people belonging to one nation or having a common culture beyond their land of origin. Archetypically, it has referred to such a dispersion of the Jews after the Babylonian and Roman conquests of Palestine in the eighth to sixth centuries BC, and later to the classical Greek and Armenian diasporas, but now, in the present era of the globalisation of peoples, the term is applied more universally. In the context of this book, it is most significant that the concept of "broadcasting" is based on precisely the same organically rooted metaphor of the scattering of seed, implying both dispersal and propagation.

Diasporic communities have thus sown themselves into several host nations, and can cover a whole world region or beyond. Still, there is a tendency to identify the diaspora phenomenon with the figure of the exile (Gandhi, 1998: 132). However, while expatriation forced by disasters, war and political and ethnic expulsion might create a diaspora, exile and diaspora are not coterminous. Exiles are not necessarily dispersed into several countries, as would occur in a diaspora, while diasporas are not necessarily sparked by cataclysmic events. Furthermore, while exiles cannot go home, some other kinds of diasporic people can and do. Contemporary diasporas include those whom current migration policy blandly labels as "economic migrants" — that is, people wanting to improve or just maintain their life-chances, and willing to go and work in any one of a whole range of countries in order to do so. (This fits the model for most of the Indian diaspora, for instance.) And there might be socio-economic conditions that give rise to very specific circumstances, such as the "bride trade" which has brought Thais and Filipinas to Australia. This displacement is not necessarily permanent — and even if it is, more successful migrants will often make pilgrimages back to their homeland, an activity of central importance to those from Taiwan or Hong Kong. So temporality is unavoidable in delineating diaspora: the liminal state of the recent shift gives way, over sufficient time, to settlement, and issues of cultural maintenance and negotiation are reconfigured. The exile may cease being exilic due to the effluxion of time or to changes in political regime or economic circumstances (while the Vietnamese diaspora of the 1970s and 1980s fits the model of exile, during the 1990s this has changed significantly with homeland changes and legal emigration).

While there is still no shortage of displacement caused by disaster and conflict, much diasporic movement today has been motivated by "flexible accumulation" (Harvey, 1989) and other such contemporary modes of globalising capital (Clifford, 1994: 331). However, it is fundamental to take into account that there are two kinds of class relation involved here, just as there was a distinction to be drawn in the historical diasporas between the entrepreneurial "middlemen minorities" and the "proletarians" (Esman, 1986: 336–37). Thus, at one level, diasporic movement is a *cause* of the globalisation of capital, in the sense identified by Joel Kotkin: "the continuous interaction of capitalism with dispersed ethnic groups — not just the staid history of financial flows or the heroic stories of nation builders — constitutes one of the critical elements in the evolution of the global economy" (Kotkin, 1992: 17). The control over both financial and industrial capital investment in Asia and elsewhere which has been attained by the "Overseas Chinese" and the "NRIs" (Non-Resident Indians) are the classic cases in point. Karim Karim (1998) suggests that we can even think of such diasporic communal networks as "a third tier of inter-regional connections", after world organisations and nation-states. Indeed, the economic output, in the early 1990s, of the 55 million overseas Chinese was estimated to be roughly equal to that of the 1.2 billion within China itself (Seagrave, 1995). This reminds us of the close interrelation of diaspora, culture and commercialism that necessitates this book being a study of the business as well as the culture of diasporic media use.

Yet, for many more people, their diasporic movement is an *effect* of global investment patterns and international inequalities — witness the current situations of Malaysian Chinese "airplane jumpers" working illegally in Japan and Taiwan (Nonini, 1997), or Indian labourers in the Middle East. Or consider the central case of the Fijian Indians described later in this book, whose nineteenth-century origins lie in a form of indenture close to, if not coterminous with, slavery. Such structured class and economic differences are in tension with mythic notions of common ethnic origins and cultural belonging. David Morley quotes Aijaz Ahmad on "the issue of post-modern, upper-class migrancy", the contradiction of people who have come from dominant-class origins in peripheral nations and become complicit in "a rhetoric which submerges the class question and speaks of migrancy as an ontological condition" (Morley, 1996: 347). While it might be true that "the rich also cry", and have their own forms of alienation, it is clearly a fallacy to identify the diasporic experience exclusively with the subaltern, and not to observe the dangers of a naive postmodernist culturalism on which we have already commented. With the partial exception, for particular reasons, of the Thais, every diaspora treated in this book is seen as a collocation of class, ethnic, origination, education, work and financial configurations, whose status as a "community" is the product of strategic unities and alliances, sometimes engendered more from without than within, rather than ethnic "essences".

A glance over the theoretical and research literature published under the rubric of "diaspora" during the 1980s and 1990s shows how the discourse itself is "loose in the world" (Clifford, 1994: 306). However, if we can set aside those works which, whatever their considerable qualities, have been written more for a general lay audience than for the research community (Kotkin, 1992; Pan, 1994), it is possible to discern a continuum ranging from social scientific to cultural studies approaches. While the former are more empirical (whether demographic, historical or comparative), such as Helweg's (1986) account of the Indian diaspora, the latter are highly theorised, though often in a diffuse manner, with diaspora serving as a universal metaphor for the deterritorialised, decentred, postmodern or postcolonial subject (Gandhi, 1998: 30–32). At its extreme, this is the idea that "we" are all nomads, although even some of the writers most associated with postmodernist cultural studies have sought to distance themselves from this romantic conceit (Chambers, 1994: 5–7). (A pertinent example of the issues that arise across the social science-cultural studies divide is seen in the critique of Kolar-Panov's work (1997) on the former Yugoslavia by Skrbis (1998).)

Area studies, comprising interdisciplinary approaches from geography, politics, history, literature and art history, could benefit from a greater sense of the mutability and adaptability of culture that cultural studies embodies. Aihwa Ong says that "[a]n essentializing notion of Chineseness continues to dog the scholarship, because the Chinese past, nation, singular history, or some 'cultural core' is taken to be the main and unchanging determinant of Chinese identity" (1999: 134–35). Terry Rambo (1987) and Neil Jamieson (1987) criticise the untoward focus on absolute origins in Vietnamese area studies: "It seems that, to many scholars in our field, knowing the origin of a thing is a sufficient explanation of its contemporary character." (Rambo, 1987: 115) And Jamieson argues, from within cultural anthropology, that a focus on diaspora communities provides the most dramatic and concrete examples of culture as a mutable, hybrid process undertaken by subjects in the process of reconstructing themselves. Nowhere is this perspective more needed than in apprehending the dynamics of contemporary *popular* media cultures — and the opposition or misunderstandings engendered about them — studied in this book.

Nonetheless, as Clifford warns, the concept of diaspora is in danger of becoming appropriated as a poststructuralist figure of speech for multiple identities of all kinds, unless it is "historicized" to affirm the distinctiveness of particular diasporas (Clifford, 1994: 319). Thus we have Paul Gilroy's (1993) remarkable study of the "black Atlantic" diasporas, impelled at different stages by slavery and free migration, and disseminating their expressive cultures in an alternative history of modernity. Yet, implicitly, this movement only makes sense in relation to the "white Atlantic", which is not just the Anglo-American "Atlantic economy", but by extension the whole diaspora of the British in their age of imperialism (Kotkin, 1992: 84–89).

To characterise the long history of British colonialism and imperialism as a kind of diaspora might seem provocative, given the very considerable extent to which the concept has become identified with post- (and anti-) colonialism. However, rather than slaves or native workers, in several countries the labour for colonial expansion involved the "proletarian" diasporas of Scots displaced by enclosures, Irish driven out by famine and transported English convicts. If it seems perverse to call these movements diasporas, it is not so much because of the concept's postcolonial associations, or even an index of the very considerable extent to which it has been racialised, but more a reminder of how much diasporas are defined by a relative lack of assimilation. Like other diasporic groups, Anglo-Celtic proletarians have had to deal culturally with displacement and longing for home, but without the same kind of exclusion from the dominant group experienced by, to take a pertinent case in point, immigrants of Asian origin in Australia. Even the great diasporas from continental European countries, notably the German, Italian and Greek, have been fairly readily absorbed into their host societies, relative to those from the postcolonial world. Ultimately, however, the value of drawing attention to the proletarian dimension of European colonisation and settlement is to underscore the point that ethnic similarities and common cultural provenance can conceal other kinds of social difference. In this instance, it is class — although Clifford (1994: 313–15) makes a similar point about gender.

Just as historicising the concept can thus tie it down in such specific — if unexpected — ways, this is also true of politicising it. Stuart Hall, while identified more with the cultural studies than the social scientific end of the spectrum, is careful to distinguish between most irredentist forms of diasporic identity, notably that of the original diasporites in their return to Israel, and progressive forms, which favour a hybrid over an essentialist conception of both culture and identity (Hall, 1990: 235). As a geopolitical imperative, Hall argues that cultural pluralism must triumph over cultural absolutism, since "the capacity to *live with difference*" is "the coming question of the twenty-first century" (Hall, 1993: 361). The theoretical corollary is that, to the extent that globalisation presents more and more people with the experience of difference and displacement, the diasporic experience becomes not so much a metaphor as the archetype for the kind of cultural adaptiveness which our era demands. Hall is worth quoting at length on this:

> the new diasporas which are forming across the world ... are obliged to inhabit at least two identities, to speak at least two cultural languages, to negotiate and "translate" between them. In this way, though they are struggling in one sense at the margins of modernity, they are at the leading edge of what is destined to become the truly representative "late-modern" experience. They are the products of the cultures of hybridity. This notion of hybridity is very different from the old internationalist grand narrative, from the superficiality of old style pluralism where no boundaries are crossed, and from the trendy nomadic voyaging of the postmodern or simplistic versions of global homogenisation — one damn thing after another or the difference that doesn't make a difference. These "hybrids" retain strong links to and identifications with the traditions and places of their "origin". But they are without the illusion of any actual "return" to the past. Either they will never, in any literal sense, return or the places to which they return will have been transformed out of all recognition by the remorseless processes of modern transformation. In that sense, there is no going "home" again.
>
> They bear the traces of particular cultures, traditions, languages, systems of belief, texts and histories which have shaped them. But they are also obliged to come to terms with and to make something new of the cultures they inhabit, without simply assimilating to them. They are not and will never be unified culturally in the old sense, because they

are inevitably the products of several interlocking histories and cultures, belonging at the same time to several "homes" — and thus to no one particular home ...
They are the product of a diasporic consciousness. They have come to terms with the fact that in the modern world ... identity is always an open, complex, unfinished game — always under construction. (Hall, 1993: 362).

This sense of cultural adaptiveness, innovation and hybridity which, along with the notions of dispersal and unassimilated difference, is at the heart of the concept of diaspora, has held a fascination for generations of social scientists interested in the dynamics of modernisation. In the 1930s, Robert Park wrote of the "marginal man" who arose when cultures were thrown together, living in "two worlds", taking "the role of the cosmopolitan, and a stranger". Thanks to his "wider horizons", he is a "more detached and rational ... civilized human being" (cited in Rogers, 1969: 147n). A similar affirmative evaluation was given by Everett Rogers to the quality of "cosmopoliteness", which was not so much universal civility as "the degree to which an individual is oriented outside his immediate social system", particularly through communication media. This was a key variable in motivating social change (Rogers, 1969: 147). In these sociological formulations, the common element was the triumph of modernity over tradition, or the value of more "global" perspectives, however minor, being brought in to transform "local" social settings. Notwithstanding the limited scope of their ideological blinkers, these writers provided a positive way of conceptualising minority status and of exposure to difference as the mediation of knowledge of a world beyond.

However, in more recent times, the notion of cosmopolitanism has become rather fraught, to the extent that it has become associated with the worldview of privileged castes in the West (Hannerz, 1990; Robbins, 1992). Against this tendency, several writers have sought to rework it — for example, Homi Bhabha with his "translational cosmopolitanism" (1996: 204) — or otherwise reclaim it — for Kotkin (1992: 4), diasporic populations are "today's quintessential cosmopolitans". Similarly, for Hannerz (1996: 90), the "real" cosmopolitans are those who "are in the nation, but not of it", yet Hebdige (cited in Lash and Urry, 1994: 309) draws attention to the way in which tourism and the media, as vehicles of consumer culture, have made cosmopolitanism less elite and more "mundane", at least in the West.

Once again, it is Clifford who provides an historical, comparative and class- and gender-sensitive formulation of the concept, with his notion of "discrepant cosmopolitanisms". This employs his metaphor of culture as travel, yet also takes into account the dialectic of cultural maintenance and negotiation, home and host, margin and centre: "what is at stake is a comparative cultural studies approach to specific histories, tactics, everyday practices of dwelling *and* traveling: traveling-in-dwelling, dwelling-in-traveling" (1992: 108).

In other words, not all diasporas are created equal: the cosmopolitanism of diasporas is historically variable, and also relative to the quite different experiences of individuals within the same diaspora. As with Stuart Hall, we are exhorted here to get down to the observation and analysis of particular, empirically grounded diasporas, and that is what this book presents. It will deal with the abjection of exile and displacement, but also the commercial businesses — from the modest middleperson who arranges for some videotapes to be shipped on a weekly plane flight from Bangkok to Sydney, to imposing international concerns like Hong Kong's TVBI, one of the five largest program distributors in the world — whose product is used to constitute markets for cultural maintenance. It will chart the imperative of hybridity and the cosmopolitan mentalities it engenders without celebrating such cultural expression as an achieved state in the abstract.

Constructing a Research Object

Just as in the 1960s, when there were social researchers who sought to bridge the "middle range" between the rarefied heights of "grand theory" and the dense depths of untheorised empiricism (Rogers, 1969: 44n), the task today is to construct a valid object of knowledge in the absence of the now discredited "grand narratives" of even the recent past, and with regard to the new-found relativism and reflexivity of research methods. Like the Marxist and feminist versions of the "dominant ideology thesis", the positivist idea of an objective world in which the facts almost select themselves for researchers to observe, measure and report upon is one which is well and truly discredited, but alternative epistemological paradigms are still in the process of formation. Methodologies cannot be taken for granted, to the extent that the "findings" of a piece of research are an artefact of the theoretical framing of its problematic, and the design of the research itself.

Just as anthropologists now have become aware of how much their ethnographies are a product of their own preconceptions, researchers in media, communication and cultural studies need to be reflexive, in the sense that they know they are constructing their own object of research when they set out to investigate something. Ien Ang's advocacy for a "radical contextualism" which can bring to light "the articulation of world capitalism with the situations of people living in particular communities" in the context of "the progressive transnationalization of media audiencehood" is to begin to construct an object we would like to align ourselves with in this book (Ang, 1996: 81).

All of the particular communities examined in this book are contextualised in this way, as members of worldwide diasporas who happen to be located in certain cities of Australia. The studies strive to bring to awareness not only the global character of these diasporas, but also the very local nature of how diaspora is experienced, which includes the use of media at both these levels. The researchers self-consciously seek to ground their work in the middle range, between the theoretical and the empirical, the macro and the micro. While there are several contributing authors in this book, it is not a conventional edited volume. Each of the four case studies (which form the basis for the chapter divisions) seeks to address our central research question: how are media — audiovisual media in particular, such as video, music video, television and music — drawn on in opening up a cultural space for negotiation between the demands for positioning within the dominant host culture and the desire for cultural maintenance? This question is pursued through attention to the businesses that service Asian diasporic communities; the communities' responses to media produced for the communities or otherwise consumed by them; and the nature of the material produced for and consumed by the communities. Each chapter addresses the specifics of its methodologies and local variations within the book's methodological "template".

Consideration of some direct models of media studies' engagements with media use by diasporas provides a useful guide for how we might proceed. Hamid Naficy's (1993) study of what he calls the "exilic" television produced by Iranians in Los Angeles in the 1980s is a model for how communications media can be used to negotiate the cultural politics of both "home" and "host". Largely Shah-supporting exiles from the Islamic revolution of the late 1970s in Iran, this community was able to fashion a wholly advertising-supported cable television presence redolent with longing, nostalgia and fetishisation of an irrecoverable homeland displayed in both low-budget fiction, variety show and information formats. Naficy provides a detailed account of cable television production by Iranians in Los Angeles during the period since the overthrow of the Shah and the so-called "Islamic revolution". He explores the political economy of this production, examines the program texts broadcast, and theorises the consumption and production in terms of the dialectic of diasporic hybridity:

> On the one hand, Iranian exiles have created via their media and culture a symbolic and fetishized private hermetically sealed electronic communitas infused with home, memory, loss, nostalgia, longing for return, and the communal self; on the other hand, they have tried to get on with the process of living by incorporating themselves into the dominant culture of consumer capitalism by means of developing a new sense of the self and what can be called an "exilic economy". (Naficy, 1993: xvi)

By incorporating the industrial as well as the narrative features of the television services and program genres developed by the Iranian exile community, Naficy shows the relationship between the transnational experiences of displacement and migration (enforced in this case), and strategies of cultural maintenance and negotiation within the liminal slipzone between "home" and "host", as seen on TV. His study is useful for our purposes as it combines the strengths of media studies — with its emphasis on political economy and media production processes and outcomes — and cultural studies — with its emphasis on social and identity formations informed by psychoanalytic and textual methodologies.

Marie Gillespie's (1995) study of "the microprocesses of the construction of a British Asian identity among young people in

Southall [West London], against the backdrop of the emergence of
"new ethnicities" in the context of post-colonial migration and the
globalisation of communications" (1995: 205) also sets a benchmark
in its detailed audience ethnography and the need for different
methodologies to capture consumption of different media formats
(mainstream soaps, news, advertising, and community-specific or
narrowcast media such as Hindi television and film).

The same attention that Naficy pays to the liminal experiences of
the exile from a broken national community is seen in Dana Kolar-
Panov's *Video, War and the Diasporic Imagination* (1997). Like
Naficy's work, Kolar-Panov's study goes "below" the level of
consumption of mainstream media in capturing the role played by
video "letters" used as news media by overseas citizens of the former
Yugoslavia as their country breaks up during the early 1990s. The
politics of intercommunal discord in the homelands as they are played
out in the diasporas, and the textual alterity of "atrocity videos"
which perform the role of virtual palimpsests of the "real time"
destruction of the homelands are relevant features of Kolar-Panov's
work for our purposes.

These media studies models do not allow us to forget that hybrid
cultural expression is a struggle for survival, identity and assertion,
and that it can be a struggle as much enforced by the necessities of
coming to terms with the dominant culture as it is freely assumed.
And the results may not be pretty. The instability of cultural
maintenance and negotiation can lead, at one extreme, to being locked
into a time warp with the fetishised homeland — as it once might
have been but no longer is or can be — and, at the other, to
assimilation to the dominant host culture and a loss of place within
one's originary culture. It can involve insistent reactionary politics;
extreme over-commercialisation (Naficy (1993: 71) cites a situation
in 1987 when Iranian television in Los Angeles was scheduling over
40 minutes of advertising per hour) due to the necessity to fund
expensive forms of media for a narrowcast audience; and textual
material of excoriating tragedy (the (fictional) self-immolation and
(actual) atrocity scenarios played out in some, respectively, Iranian
and Croatian video).

Australia as a Situated Research Field

Australia is one of the most "multicultural" nations on earth, with 40 per cent of its population born elsewhere, or at least one parent born elsewhere. In 1947, the Australian population was 7.6 million, of which only 9.8 per cent were overseas-born. Of these, 90 per cent were from Great Britain and Ireland. According to the 1991 Census, 24 per cent of Australia's population were immigrants and some 40 per cent of Australians were born overseas or had at least one parent born overseas. More than half of Australia's post-World War II population growth was driven by immigration, with the proportions changing from overwhelmingly British and Irish to migrants from eastern and southern Europe and, since the 1970s, Asia, Africa, the Americas and the Middle East. The relaxation of a race-based immigration policy around 1966 and the subsequent abolition of the "White Australia" policy in 1973 has greatly diversified the cultural composition of Australia's resident population. By the late 1980s, more than half of its total immigrant intakes were originating from Asia. A recent estimate by Kee and others (1994) suggests that there are now over a million Australians of Asian descent. As a result, for example, Chinese has become the second largest language group in wider Sydney and is expected to replace Italian as the second most commonly spoken language in Australia by 2000.

In response to this, since the late 1970s, Australian governments — at least until the mid-1990s — have constructed an official policy of multiculturalism and organised an impressive array of state support for this policy, including the Special Broadcasting Service (SBS), which is both a TV and radio broadcaster, one of the few major public broadcasters in the world dedicated to not only the reflection, but also the propagation, of multiculturalism.

However, while Australia is, in proportional terms, the world's second largest immigrant nation next to Israel, the relatively low numbers of any individual group have meant that a critical mass of a few dominant non-English Speaking Background (NESB) groupings has not made the impact that Hispanic peoples, for example, have made in the United States. Further reasons for this include the fact that the largest immigrant groups have been historically British and Irish; the sheer variety of immigrant and refugee/humanitarian communities (at present, over 150 ethnic groups speaking over 100 different languages); and that immigration has occurred in several distinct waves over a period of 50 years (some earlier groups successfully negotiated their resettlements more than a generation ago, while many Asian groupings have only just begun the process). Nor do Australians experience "strong" cultural diversity through policies of official multilingualism (such as in Canada); nor the considerable cultural intermixing caused by the sheer contiguity of the major imperial languages in Europe; nor the significant accommodation in the daily life, the polity and the public rhetorics of those societies with a critical mass of indigenous persons, such as New Zealand.

In addition, the history of direct subvention to multicultural cultural forms from government arts bodies has tended to focus on the folkloric and the literary rather than the most popular cultural forms such as video and popular music. Typically, then, with the exception of zones of "official" contact like the SBS, community radio and the like, the media's, and most mainstream cultural institutions', embrace of cultural diversity goes little beyond a sort of mutual distance and monolingual incomprehension. As a recent study (Jamrozik et al., 1995) put it, the bulwarks of monocultural power in Australia have not yet been fundamentally challenged.

No one non-Anglo-Celt ethnic group has therefore reached "critical mass" in terms of being able to operate significantly as a self-contained community within the nation. For this reason, Australia offers a strategic site for the examination of a number of themes in the theory and policy surrounding diasporas, and the cultural industries supporting them. As subsequent chapters show, theories of diaspora need to be "de-essentialised", adapted to conditions where ethnicities and sub-ethnicities jostle in ways that would have been unlikely or impossible in their respective homeland settings or where long and sustained patterns of immigration have produced a critical mass of singular ethnicities. It is important to focus on the gaps and slippages between policy and practice in a country that has an official policy of multiculturalism — albeit one currently under great stress. The lack of critical mass also means that expensive Australian-based electronic media production for such small numbers is very underdeveloped. The book thus concentrates on an aspect of globalisation often neglected in the rush to write up the latest exploits of the American, British, European or Japanese world-spanning multinationals. This is the diasporic ethnoscape and the truly global but ethno-specific media flows that are to a significant extent its condition of existence. Both the policy focus and the lack of critical mass come together in the focus on the relations between broadcast media and diasporic narrowcast media, which often, in debate, concentrates on the role of the SBS.

The SBS as Social Change Agent?

It is worth spending a moment at this stage on the SBS, as it "quite simply is the most outstanding expression of multiculturalism as policy" in Australia (Jakubowicz, 1994: 136) and thus acts as a major lightning rod for NESB communities' expectations about the state's and the society's commitment to cultural diversity. In recognition of the political power and skills of the "ethnic lobby" reflected in elections during the 1970s, the Fraser conservative Coalition government decided to set up a multicultural television service in the late 1970s. In contrast to grassroots ethnic radio, what became SBS-TV was a creature of government initiative.

Over time, this distinction has consolidated: SBS-TV markedly differs from multilingual radio services, which are found both within SBS and in the community-based sector. The model for television centres on the employment of broadcasting professionals rather than community representatives and volunteers. Further, there is a policy that virtually all material is subtitled in English, the national *lingua franca* which is assumed to be the common linguistic denominator uniting disparate ethnicities. Also, there has been an expectation that the programming schedule would not be too radically different from the "norm", especially with broad-appeal material being broadcast in prime time, and that the core programming of the service — its news and current affairs — would be English-language based.

While SBS radio allocates broadcast time to language groups largely on the basis of their numerical representation in the community, there has always been an arguably necessary disparity between community languages and SBS-TV programming. Programming centres on that which is of conventional "broadcast standard" — thus omitting much that communities watch as diasporic video, and instead running programming from the major non-English language film and television industries which can be afforded within the SBS's very limited budget. Indian films are often too expensive; French, German, Brazilian or Swedish films and television long-form drama are very over-represented (according to these language groups' numerical place in Australian demographics) because these are the product of experienced export industries which can sell some of their material cheaply. Programs are chosen on the basis of their ability to address, within the discourse of multiculturalism generically, potentially all Australians, rather than address specific language groups. Added to this is the effective displacement of SBS's original charter of multiculturalism by contemporary notions of "cultural diversity" (where sexual orientation, or age, or physical disability becomes as valid a marker of cultural difference as ethnicity) during the last decade in SBS's policy discourse, as the service has moved to seek a broader base (Jakubowicz, 1994; O'Regan, 1993).

It is therefore easy to see how the service could be perceived as a general-interest station for cosmopolitan taste cultures rather than a social change agent for those marginalised by language and (non-British, Irish or broad European) culture. This has been the major criticism the service has had to field in the 1990s, and it has come from high-ranking politician and senior representatives of ethnic communities, as well as from critics and journalists (see Lawe Davies, 1997). So it is refreshing to see that there can also be a spirited defence of the SBS in its catering to cosmopolitan taste cultures (Hawkins, 1996; Hartley, 1992). As the discussion of the use of SBS's news services in Chapter 2 makes clear, this approach assumes a high level of global cosmopolitanism inherent in the reality of diaspora, whether the migrant is working class, middle class or "middle classing", thus displacing the debate about whether SBS exists basically for an internationalising Australian middle class or a cosmopolitan world citizen, or should exist for a marginalised lumpenproletariat defined by an essentialist ethnicity.

As might be expected, assessing the role and functions of the SBS — precisely because of its enthusiastic uptake of its charter responsibility to not merely reflect multiculturalism but actively proselytise for social change — has engaged critics, broadcasters, policy-makers and its public in large-scale debates of social and cultural power and representation. In a concerted critique of the power of established media to resist social change, Jakubowicz et al. (1994: 136, 14) argue that "multiculturalism as a policy has not achieved significant change in the commercial media" and that the creation of a special multicultural service has "allowed the television industry in general to remain largely unaffected by the cultural changes wrought by migration".

This is a debate endemic to any large-scale project of programmatic social change conceived in an era of greater state intervention. The problem with it is that it is largely a debate which is insoluble inside the structural constraints of channel scarcity in a terrestrial free-to-air environment. The SBS simply cannot successfully program to meet the diverse and incommensurate needs of Australia's multifarious communities within the constraints of a single-channel service. The changing demographics of multicultural Australia also need to be considered, particularly the middle-classing of a core SBS demographic, based on the post-World War II waves of southern and central European immigrants. The structural conflicts between the established European ethnic lobby and the emerging influence of the 1970s and 1980s waves of migrants and refugees which have had increasing components of Asian origin make the ground of debate a shifting one. It is also a debate about class, overlaid on the combustible rhetorics of race and ethnicity, especially Asian ethnicity.

Asia-in-Australia

If we are concerned, at the broadest level, with cultural diversity and its articulations to the media, and if there are communities of particularly southern European non-English speaking background which are larger and longer established in Australia, why the focus on Asia? Despite fluctations in the rhetorics surrounding Australia's "Asian future" (from Paul Keating's "a peaceful multicultural nation in Asia" to John Howard's overly cautious withdrawal from any direct identification as part of the region), and in particular economistically driven concerns about the region's financial health, the focus of this book underlines the ongoing and inescapable interpenetration of "Asia-in-Australia" and charts some of the cultural dynamics and policy implications that flow from this. We seek to contribute to the maintenance of this country's focus on its regional identity through a period of political, economic and policy drift, but great cultural dynamism.

The inescapable importance of Australia's Asian context has resulted in an increasing focus on the representation of Asia and Asian-Australians by mainstream Australian media (e.g. Bell, 1993; Jakubowicz, 1994) and on the opportunities for audiovisual export to the region (DITARD, 1994; Cunningham and Jacka, 1995). However, much of the public rhetoric about cultural export is one-sided. Australia's population originating from Asian countries is the basis for more importation *from* the region than there has been scope up to the present for export *to* the region. Audiovisual import, mainly in the form of Hong Kong movies and videos, other Chinese-language material, and Special Broadcasting Service (SBS) imports, and the pay rates for them, at present outweigh export figures to the region by a significant amount. But traffic in non-English language programs need not be seen only in these terms. Treating the multicultural composition of the country as the basis for a long-term regionally oriented audiovisual strategy should be part of any focus on the economic benefits of "productive diversity" (Kalantzis and Cope, 1997).

The present realities of audiovisual media use by Asian-originating diasporic communities in Australia represent a noticeable absence, both in current research and in public discourse about this country's "Asian future". While there have been significant advances in our understanding of Asian immigrants' cultures, literatures and print media dynamics (e.g. Gunew, 1993), very little is known about such diasporic communities' audiovisual media use. Those few studies that have been done (e.g. Bednall, 1988) provide valuable data from questionnaire-style surveys, but fail to interrogate the dynamics of cultural maintenance and negotiation. Additionally, while SBS-TV stands as the major single contribution to serving the broadcasting needs of Australia's multicultural society, there is little publicly available research into SBS's relations with Asian-language communities.

Public "Sphericules" and Policy Scenarios

If we eschew a singular focus on diasporic imagination as an "ontological condition" occupied by the migrant subject, in what sense is the diasporic a series of public or civic cultures, particularly as they exist in a transnational, global space, and what (national) public policy challenges do they continue to pose?

The public sphere, in its classic sense advanced in the work of Jurgen Habermas (1974), is a space of open debate standing over against the state as a special subset of civil society in which the logic of "democratic equivalence" is cultivated. The concept has been regularly used in the fields of media, cultural and communications studies to theorise the media's articulation between the state/government and civil society. There are those for whom the contemporary Western public sphere has been tarnished or even fatally compromised by the encroachment of media, particularly commercial media and communications (Schiller, 1989), while there are those for whom the media have become the main — if not the only — vehicle for whatever can be held to exist of the public sphere in such societies. Such "media-centric" theorists within these fields can hold that the media actually envelop the public sphere:

> The "mediasphere" is the whole universe of media ... in all languages in all countries. It therefore completely encloses and contains as a differentiated part of itself the (Habermasian) public sphere (or the many public spheres), and it is itself contained by the much larger semiosphere ... which is the whole universe of sense-making by whatever means, including speech ... It is clear that television is a crucial site of the mediasphere and a crucial mediator between general cultural sense-making systems (the semiosphere) and specialist components of social sense-making like the public sphere. Hence the public sphere can be rethought not as a category binarily contrasted with its implied opposite, the private sphere, but as a "Russian doll" enclosed within a larger mediasphere, itself enclosed within the semiosphere. And within "the" public sphere, there may equally be found, Russian-doll style, further counter-cultural, oppositional or minoritarian public spheres. (Hartley, 1999: 217–18)

Hartley's topography has the virtue of clarity, scope and heuristic utility, even while it remains provocatively media-centric. We will complicate that topography by suggesting that minoritarian public spheres are rarely sub-sets of classic nationally bound public spheres, but are nonetheless vibrant, globalised but very specified spaces of self- and community-making and identity (see, for example, Husband, 1998). We will strongly agree with Hartley, however, in his iconoclastic insistence that commercial and public/state-supported spheres of activity are closely related and interdependent. We will also be stressing another neglected aspect of the public sphere debate developed by Jim McGuigan (1998: 92) — the "affective" as much as "effective" dimension of public communication, which allows for an adequate grasp of entertainment in a debate dominated by ratiocinative and informational activity.

Todd Gitlin has posed the question of whether we can continue to speak of the ideal of *a* public sphere/culture as an increasingly complex, polyethnic, communications-saturated series of societies develop around the world. Rather, what might be emerging are numerous public "sphericules": "does it not look as though the public sphere, in falling, has shattered into a scatter of globules, like mercury?" (Gitlin, 1998: 173). Gitlin's answer is the deeply pessimistic one of seeing the future as the irretrievable loss of elements of a modernist public commonality. In contrast, we argue that the emergence of ethno-specific global mediatised communities suggests that elements we would expect to find in "the" public sphere are to be found in microcosm in these public sphericules. Such activities may constitute valid, and indeed dynamic, counter-examples to a discourse of decline and fragmentation, while taking full account of contemporary vectors of communication in a globalising, commercialising and pluralising world.

Hartley's *Uses of Television* (1999) is also perhaps the most sophisticated account of the constructive (civic, educational) role audiovisual media play in contemporary societies. For him, these media have a "permanent" and "general", rather than specific and formal, educational role (1999: 140) in the manners, attitudes and assumptions necessary for citizenly participation in communities. It is clear that the ethno-specific minoritarian public "sphericule" is a special exemplification of Hartley's account of television as general education. Epistephilic desire, that heightened need for information about the homeland and others within the diaspora, suggests a concentrated sense in which the information–entertainment dyad of popular media is more strongly blurred in the diasporic setting. It should be stressed that much of the diasporic media traced in this book constitutes displaced broadcast television — displaced from its original moment of transmission by satellite retransmission, video piracy or Web-based consumption.

There is another sense in which information–entertainment distinction — usually maintained in the abundance of available media in the dominant culture — is blurred in the diasporic setting. As there is typically such a small diet of ethno-specific media available to these communities, they are mined deeply for social (including fashion, language use and so on) cues, personal gossip and public information, as well as singing along to the song or following the fictional narrative. Within this concentrated and contracted informational and libidinal economy, "contemporary popular media as guides to choice, or guides to the attitudes that inform choices" (Hartley, 1999: 143) take on a thoroughly continuous and central role across the information and entertainment divide. Hartley's allied claim for the media's role in promoting "do-it-yourself" (DIY) citizenship is even more strongly borne out in the case of the minoritarian sphericule. The "permanent" and "general", rather than specific and formal, education (1999: 140) in the manners, attitudes and assumptions necessary for citizens' participation in communities spread across the world brings its "DIY" nature into sharp focus.

Multiculturalism, Arts and Media Policy

Our emphasis on the public nature of diasporic cultures and their relation to nation states and the public sphere raises issues of policy. Do multicultural policies need to take account of popular culture dynamics amongst diasporic groups to a much greater extent than hitherto? Are government apprehensions of Asian-Australian culture bound to inadequate notions of tradition and folklorics? To what extent are the current broadcasting and video industries, and future expansion within them, serving the cultural needs of Asian-Australian communities?

This focus on the "public sphericules" of diasporic communities goes below and beyond state-supported programs of multicultural production, which are characterised by their being typically traditional "high" cultural forms (such as literature and the visual and performing arts) or residual folklorics practised firmly within the boundaries of the nation state even as they draw on cultural traditions established elsewhere. It goes below such forms in its concentration on vastly popular cultural practice, such as Vietnamese music video, Hindi cinema (widely known as "Bollywood", based as it is on Mumbai, once known as Bombay) and Hong Kong action films. It goes beyond in the sense of focusing on the dynamics of ethno-specific narrowcast mixed entertainment and information media which, while they may originate in specific locales, are consumed globally.

In doing this, we also raise questions about the focus and effectiveness of multicultural policy. State multiculturalism can be criticised as cooptative insofar as it offers a space for cultural maintenance, respect and tolerance while requiring conformity to liberal democratic practices and acquiescence in the hegemonic position of the dominant (British–Irish) cultural formation. Culture can thus be deployed as a safety valve, essentialised and made largely manifest as language, food and ritual. In defensive response to opponents of migrant intakes of certain sizes and compositions, it can also lead to situations where the greatest stress is placed on economics to the effective exclusion of the challenge of genuine cultural apprehension. In the United States, for instance, "when the refugees from Indo China first came in 1975, the United States government was more concerned about their self-sufficiency and employment than about their cross-cultural adjustment and communication" (Nguyen, 1987: 100).

However, since 1996, concerns with the limitations of state multiculturalism have been overtaken by the re-liminalisation of "Asian-Australian" ethnicities by the overt racism of the notorious Pauline Hanson and her One Nation party. This, together with a barely covert desire on the part of the current Liberal–National Party federal government to displace and de-fund multiculturalism, officially Australia's policy on the management of cultural and linguistic pluralism for more than two decades, makes it imperative that it is defended vociferously, even as its limits are explored. Acknowledging that the basic assumptions of Australian multiculturalism are distinctly better than other policy frameworks which could be conceivably won politically in the climate of our times marks out our stance from those strong critiques of the policy such as Ghassan Hage (1998), Jon Stratton (1999) or Charles Husband (1994).

The area of state-supported arts practice, while it has been subject to significant democratisation for a generation (with clear examples such as the Community Arts Board of the Australia Council), remains some considerable distance from the popular media activity documented in this book. This disparity between state-supported programs and the popular culture of minorities is an international phenomenon. The National Endowment for the Arts (NEA), the major federal arts funding body in the United States, has found it very difficult to attract minority applicants, "so profound is their alienation from organs of governance, which are seen to police them, and service others" (Miller, 2000, citing Gilmore, 1993: 159). The organs of arts, audiovisual and cultural support, pre-eminently the Australia Council and the Australian Film Commission at the national level and the various arts bodies at the state and territory level, have developed policies of targeting NESB groups for special support programs in various ways. However, through inconsistent attention to ethnic/cultural diversity objectives in recruitment, selection and appointment policies, and through these policies being historically "narrowly conceived as the folk practice of a disadvantaged minority" (Stevenson, 2000: Ch. 7) and latterly being grafted on to pre-existing precepts of "excellence" (Castles et al., 1994), the relevance of state cultural support to the popular media production and consumption canvassed here is distant at best.

The key issue for media policy raised by this study is the need to structure screen services for both majoritarian and minoritarian populations in the interests of equity, access and the acquisition of social and cultural capital. Mass market, free-to-air, mainstream television will rarely meet all the needs of culturally pluralistic societies. To place stress, therefore, on other forms of media is by no means to absolve the mainstream of its responsibilities for implementing, at the very least, the codes of advisory practice, Equal Employment Opportunity (EEO) policies and anti-discrimination and racial vilification laws that are specific industry standards and general legal prescription that may see a greater representation, both behind and before the cameras, on Australian screens and related media. As the chapters that follow detail, while mainstream media are in most instances consumed widely amongst Asian communities (subject to people's degree of comfort with the dominant *lingua franca*), their expressed dissatisfaction with the effect of the *mono*cultural maintenance it achieves is equally widespread.

Stronger community-based media are necessary to meet the needs currently serviced through diasporic cinema and video circuits and the other methods outlined through this book (see, for example, Husband, 1992; Thussu, 1998); these need to be better controlled by minoritarian communities themselves but supported by the state to a greater and more creative degree than currently is the case almost anywhere in the world. However, the future for enhanced community broadcasting services is complicated strongly by the increasingly complex mix of technologies, and subscription-based as well as free-to-air terrestrial services emerging in most countries, with Australia being no exception.

From where we write in 1999, the strongest developments in minority broadcasting in Australia are occurring in subscription (pay) television. With about a million households (now close to 20 per cent of total households) signed up, and reasonable expectations of further growth, and with more than 60 channels available on one or more of the services (Foxtel, Optus, Austar), there is corresponding growth in languages other than English (LOTE) and ethnic-specific programming. The Optus subscription package in the largest cities offers up to seven non-English language channels and many of these offer programming specifically designed to address interests not catered to by SBS. However, there will remain for the foreseeable future real volatility in subscription-based specialist services. The marginal financial position of such services will not improve until the costs of delivering specialist and narrowly themed channels are driven much lower.

The costs of production, distribution and consumption are each keys to the growth of viable ethnic minority audiovisual media, and while there are viable models elsewhere, the lack of critical mass amongst any one community group in Australia makes the costs of distribution a key inhibiting factor. At least in the medium term, Australian broadcasting policy on the introduction of digital platforms will drive this scenario further out of reach, with its adherence to digital television being focused on the production of high-definition television formats rather than on the proliferation of channels that may compete with the established mainstream broadcasters for advertising share.

Around the world, there is significant evidence that ethnic communities themselves place significant store on the development of their presence on specialist, community and non-mainstream audiovisual formats. For example, British Independent Television Commission research on ethnic minority viewing preferences and perceptions shows that Asian and African-Caribbeans are "far more positive about cable and satellite channels, and their hopes for the future probably lie here, where there is greater scope for specialist programming" (Hanley, 1995: 17).

World Citizens?

In conclusion, then, we see that accepted models of citizenship as identification with and participation within single nation states, and of a binary divide between public and commercial cultures, are tempered by the forms of Asian diasporic cultural citizenship traced in this book. In the mainstream media, we hear the term "global citizen" usually attributed to the Rupert Murdochs and Ted Turners of this world. But perhaps the term should be made equally available to those whose *civitas* connects communities in dozens of countries, while also embracing their situatedness in this one. These lines from "Buoc Chan Viet Nam/The Footsteps of Vietnam", from the ASIA Productions music video *Tinh ca 75–95 Chon Loc* (Selected Love Songs 75–95), in which vivid rememorisation of the abjection of exile are tempered by confident community assertion, and thankful ensconcement within a host country by cosmopolitanism, captures what we want to say:

Thanks America for your open arms
Grand merci la France pour vos bras ouverts
Big thank you to France for your open arms
Thanks Australia for your open arms
Merci Canada pour la liberte
Thank you Canada for liberty

Ngay nao con day ngo ngac
The day when we were still bewildered
Tung tieng noi xa la
Every language foreign and distant
Nhin duong phang phiu ngut xa
Looking at the smooth road far away
Nghe long tuoi than tung buoc
Hearing the pity in our hearts at every step
Nho doi day nang lui toi
Owing to a life of frequent coming and going
Thanh men pho quen duong
We grow to cherish and become accustomed to the streets
Ban be vai muoi sac dan

Friends from several tens of ethnicities
Nuoc rieng nhung than phan chung
Different nations but together the same conditions

Ta tham thia tu sinh, cuoi buoc nhuc nhan
We are penetrated with life and death, bowing, we step in disgrace
Ta niu anh binh minh giua con tu sinh
We cling to the light of dawn amidst the flush of life and death

Doi du phon hoa lap lanh
Although life is prosperous and sparkling
Long van nho que nha
Our hearts are missing our homeland
Me hien trong cho rat ngong khi troi nua dem ve sang
Gentle mother awaits when midnight comes dawn
Doi du buon vui van the, dung gay them chia lia
Though happy or sad life is still so, don't cause further separation
Lac loai la mot noi dau
To be lost and astray is an aching pain
Thay nhau hay tin con nhau
Seeing each other, believe that we still have each other

Khap noi tren dia cau
Everywhere throughout the globe
Gio in dau buoc chan Viet Nam
Now is stamped with the footsteps of Vietnam
Nhung doi chan miet mai dang vuon toi duoi anh ban mai
The footsteps of devotion are reaching towards the light of the early morn

Lau nay ta lang thinh, hai muoi nam ngai ngan
For a long time now we have remained silent, twenty years of hesitation
Song giua an va oan, muon hat len doi lan
Living between gratitude and resentment, wanting to sing up a few times.

2
Chinese Cosmopolitanism and Media Use

John Sinclair, Audrey Yue, Gay Hawkins,
Kee Pookong and Josephine Fox

The patterns of Chinese migration represent one of the world's most impressive and complex cases of the phenomenon of diaspora. At least in the sense of forming a potential television audience on a global scale, we can think of the worldwide diasporic communities of Chinese as an extension of "Greater China" — a virtual "imagined community" or common cultural region united either through the "time–space compression" of satellite broadcasting or, where this is not the case, then instead by the portability and reproducibility of video (Sinclair et al., 1996).

In most countries of the world, both public and commercial television networks within the national boundaries continue to assert their traditional role of generating a sense of national belonging and identity. And in Australia, people of Chinese origin can be expected to be attending to such national media to a greater or lesser extent. However, they also can use media to maintain their links and orientation to a whole cultural world outside their nation of residence by means of "narrowcast" channels for specific markets, such as Chinese-language services on pay television, and other media forms such as video rental and cinema distributed from the Chinese-speaking nations.

It is the questions produced within this tension between the national and the diasporic, the local and the global that motivate the research outlined here. How are audiovisual media, especially television and video, used in the everyday lives of diasporic communities such as the Chinese in Australia? By what processes can and do these people maintain cultural connections with the Chinese world while negotiating a place within the host culture? How are they able to maintain access to Chinese-language audiovisual material? As well as ethnographic investigation, this research incorporates a mapping of the sources of production and the systems of distribution of audiovisual products and services which emanate from the nations comprising Greater China (Mainland China, Taiwan and Hong Kong), so as ultimately to assess the actual patterns of consumption against the political economy of production and distribution.

In order to trace the entire process from local consumption to global production and distribution of Chinese-language media products and services, various lines of investigation were pursued, drawing on a selective mix of methodologies. Institutional studies were made of the main narrowcast television networks, and the actual use of these services was investigated through direct viewer research. Trade research traced the complex entrepreneurial connections between the television programs, films and videos available to Chinese-speakers in Melbourne, and the corporate provenance of this material in Greater China. Finally, consumption in the home of these and other communication media products and services was studied via a two-stage approach involving a household survey linked to more specific, qualitative ethnographic case studies.

The Chinese in Australia: Global Diaspora in Microcosm

Size and Composition of the Chinese-origin Population

From the point of view of how immigrant communities can use communications media, whether to maintain their cultural identity or to adapt to a new environment, the Chinese in Australia provide a valuable case study, as they present a microcosm of both the past and present Chinese global diaspora. In recent decades, major immigrant communities from Mainland China, Hong Kong, Taiwan, Malaysia, Vietnam, and smaller groups from Singapore, East Timor, Indonesia, Cambodia, Papua New Guinea and other parts of the world have settled in various cities of Australia, particularly Melbourne and Sydney. Many have come not directly from Chinese nations, but from the "Nanyang" countries of Southeast Asia to which their ancestors migrated during the century prior to World War II, and where over 15 million "Overseas Chinese" still live (Esman, 1986; Kee, 1995). There is also a large local-born Chinese population which has developed from earlier immigration, comprising a relatively high proportion of third- and even fourth-generation Australians of Chinese descent (Kee and Huck, 1991). The 1991 Census found 261 466 Chinese-speaking persons out of an estimated 400 000 people of Chinese ancestry in Australia (Kee, 1997).

The sources, socioeconomic backgrounds and circumstances of Chinese immigrant arrivals in Australia have been much more diverse than those of Chinese communities in the other great contemporary immigrant-receiving countries such as the United States, Canada, Britain and New Zealand, or earlier immigrant-receiving countries in Southeast Asia, South America, Europe and Africa. The first Chinese migrants, especially those who came during the Gold Rush of the latter half of the nineteenth century, were predominantly from the Cantonese-speaking *Sze Yap* (Four Districts) of the Pearl River Delta in Guangdong province, but their numbers were drastically decreased by the immigration restrictions against non-Europeans enforced for the first half of the twentieth century — the "White Australia" policy. With the eventual abandonment of such a race-based immigration policy from the late 1950s onwards, and particularly with the progressive "multiculturalism" policy phase of the 1970s and 1980s, Australia has attracted relatively large communities of Chinese from Malaysia, Singapore and Hong Kong, including many who previously had studied in Australian universities. Those from Malaysia in particular enjoy high levels of education and have become concentrated in the professions (Kee, 1995).

By contrast, large numbers of Chinese with relatively few formal qualifications, limited English-language skills, and no prior familiarity with Australia's still predominantly British values and institutions were admitted in 1978, for the first time in the twentieth century, when the Fraser Coalition government began to accept Indochinese from refugee camps in Southeast Asia. This began a process of diversification that has been extended and consolidated in a quite different direction since the 1980s by the Business Migration Program, which has seen a rapid growth in the numbers of Chinese coming from Taiwan. Whereas many of the Indochinese came with the skills and some also with the capital, which enabled them to set up small businesses, the Taiwanese as a group are much more affluent, and have a low participation in the labour force. This is partly because of the number who continue to travel back to Taiwan to conduct business there — the so-called "astronaut syndrome", which is very much a part of the contemporary diasporic experience for this type of migrant. The Taiwanese are mainly speakers of Hokkien and Mandarin, unlike their predecessors from Southeast Asia and Hong Kong who mostly came speaking Cantonese and were also fluent in English (Kee, 1997). Importantly, the advent of these business migrants, from Hong Kong as well as Taiwan, gears Australia into the "essentially stateless" business networks of the Overseas Chinese (Langdale, 1997: 307), the powerful informal links underpinning Chinese capitalism, not only in the Asian region, but throughout the diaspora (Kotkin, 1993; Ong, 1997).

Beginning later in the 1980s, an intensification of efforts to attract overseas students into Australian universities led to the resumption of a steady flow of new settlers from the Chinese Mainland, a movement that had terminated earlier in the century, not just as a result of the "White Australia" policy, but also the great political upheavals in the People's Republic of China (PRC). Prior to the Hawke Labor government's granting of residence to those PRC nationals who were here before the Tiananmen Massacre in June 1989, and even to a substantial number of those who arrived afterwards, Chinese immigrants in Australia had originated very much from the periphery of China — although, as noted, many were children or grandchildren of earlier Chinese emigrants from Guangdong, or were themselves secondary migrants from China. The new Mainlanders have come mostly from Beijing, Shanghai and Guanzhou. Although the student population of more than 30 000 at the core of the Mainland community has greatly increased the number of Mandarin speakers, and those from Shanghai have added yet another dialect to the varieties of Chinese spoken in Australia, the Cantonese of the earlier groups continues to be predominant (Kee, 1997).

While more favoured with education and creative talent than the great bulk of contemporary Chinese society, the PRC nationals in Australia still reflect Mainland values and behaviour — albeit in highly variable ways, given the differential impact of the cultural, social and political transformations set in play by the Communist Revolution of 1949, the Cultural Revolution of 1966–76 and the more recent socialist market reforms. In contrast, the communities of Chinese in Taiwan, Hong Kong, Malaysia and Singapore have adhered more closely to the traditional forms of Chinese values and practices. Confucian codes of conduct, Buddhism and folk beliefs have influenced the worldview and behaviour of these Overseas Chinese to a greater degree than their counterparts from the Mainland. Nevertheless, with the significant exception of the Indochinese refugees, the Chinese who have come to Australia generally have high levels of education, as well as a secular outlook. Many are also affluent and well-travelled, and much more cosmopolitan than most other communities which have been formed as a result of postwar immigration. They are predominantly urban, with the Mainlanders, Taiwanese and those from Hong Kong favouring Sydney, while those from Malaysia and Indochina are proportionately better represented in Melbourne (Kee, 1995). However, in Melbourne and the surrounding state of Victoria, where a quarter of the Australian population lives, Mainland China has replaced Vietnam as the main source country of immigrants of Asian origin, with Hong Kong a distant eighth (Department of Immigration and Multicultural Affairs, 1997). Like other world cities with an appreciable Chinese-origin population, Melbourne and Sydney both have a Chinatown in their central business districts, dating from the mid-nineteenth century; there are also clusters of suburbs with a high proportion of recently arrived migrants, as well as more settled — or just more affluent — Chinese-origin families sprinkled throughout their metropolitan areas.

In short, Chinese groups in Australia present a microcosm of the differences within the Chinese diaspora: differences in countries or regions of birth, socioeconomic status, languages, dialects, religions and degree of "de-sinicisation" of values and behaviour. As such, they provide an excellent opportunity for the study of diasporic cultural identities, specifically of the factors which shape the identities of people of Chinese descent on a more universal scale.

The Meaning of Chineseness

Within the Chinese imagination, "China" *(zhong guo)*, as the Middle *(zhong)* Kingdom *(guo)*, has always glorified itself literally as the centre of the world, designating all non-Chinese as "barbarians" or "red-haired devils". Such constructions manifest China's paradoxical relationship to the West, a relationship which is at once negative and affirmative, signifying both fear and desire. In the (imperial) Western imagination, "China" exists, on one hand, in the terms of Edward Said's discourse of Orientalism, as a primitive, eroticised and exoticised Other. On the other hand, it is also worshipped as the Great (Other) Civilisation, one is that is the opposite, yet equivalent in status, to its Western counterpart. As a postsocialist paradox, China is thus both "empire" and "victim", caught between the forces of "First World" imperialism and "Third World" nationalism. In more recent times, the exotic homeland myth of China has produced an Oriental form of Orientalism, with the East appropriating the instruments of the West to fantasise itself and the world. Chen Xiaomei (1995) terms this creative discursive practice "Occidentalism", a process whereby the Chinese Orient obverts the Western construction of China into a Chinese construction of the West.

Within the diaspora, the imaginary homeland of "China" has tended to become the absolute norm for "Chineseness", against which all other Chinese cultures have to be measured. Discursive concepts such as "Mother China", "the motherland", "the fatherland" or "the ancestral land" evoke a nostalgic emotional reverence. Consistent with the mythologised image of traditional China in the critically acclaimed Fifth Generation Chinese films, postcolonial feminist Rey Chow (1991) has argued that Chinese from the Mainland might be seen as more "authentic" than those who are from Taiwan or Hong Kong because the latter have been "Westernised". Yet such an essentialised concept of "authenticity" implies both an abundance and a lack. Depending on where one is situated with regard to the boundaries which mark out nations as "homes" and "hosts", it is conceivable that either privilege or disempowerment could be constituted by such notions as "too Chinese" or "not Chinese enough".

Cultural theorist Ien Ang (1992) offers an autobiographical staging of her own "Chineseness" as a strategy to illuminate the precariousness of diasporic identity, highlighting the very difficulty of constructing a position from which one can speak as (an "Overseas") Chinese. Originally a speech in English at a Chinese symposium in Taiwan, her essay, aptly entitled "Not Speaking

Chinese", maps a strategic positioning which calls to task the indeterminacy of "Chineseness" as a signifier for "identity". Tracing the discursive otherness and the incommensurabilities of her life as an Indonesian-Chinese, Peranakan, Dutch-speaking and educated woman living in Australia, Ang argues against the hegemonic condition that "not speaking Chinese" signifies the loss of "authenticity". She puts the case for the recognition of a heterogeneous "Chineseness", the meaning of which is not pregiven and fixed, but constantly renegotiated and re-enunciated, both inside and outside China.

A similar argument is articulated by Aihwa Ong and Donald Nonini (1997), who find that the heterogeneity of Chineseness apparent in the emergent cultures of Asian modernity manifests a new Chinese identity that displaces and de-authorises China as the centre of the world. In this perspective, diasporic Chineseness is constituted by deterritorialised Chinese transnational practices operating across all recognised borderlines.

If, on one hand, Mainland China is too often mythologised as the "real" China, Hong Kong can be seen as a kind of Chinese diasporic centre for cultural reformulation, being a hybrid of East and West, as well as one of the world's largest production centres for films, comparable to Hollywood and Bombay (Mumbai). The Chinese communities of Asia, Australia, Europe and North America form a "geolinguistic region", or worldwide audience for the Hong Kong film industry. Its hybrid cinematic aesthetics fuses different genres and creates a syncretism analogous to the constitution of hybrid personal identities. Its narrative preoccupations, particularly prior to 1997, which centred on such postcolonial themes as exile, displacement and migration, offer their own kind of ethnography of the Chinese diaspora, and resonate with the diasporic sensibilities of loss, deterritorialisation and incorporation. Clara Law's *Floating Life* (1996), the first-ever foreign-language film to be made in Australia, provides an excellent illustration of such narratives of displacement, not unlike the stories of some of the respondents who participated in this research.

In Australia, in the name of an immigration and settlement policy which aims to protect the rights of immigrants to keep their cultural differences, the official discourse of multiculturalism ironically almost obliges them not just to "have" a culture, which they come with, but furthermore to maintain it. This rhetoric valorises an essentialist concept of "culture", largely manifest as language, food and ritual. Whereas the Chinese of the Southeast Asian and Indochinese countries are accustomed to living in societies which, while not necessarily tolerant and harmonious, at least give them some experience of cultural pluralism and sense of difference, this is not true for the Taiwanese, nor for the Mainlanders. Thus, apart from the likelihood that these latter groups have not been prepared by their culture of origin to know how to respond to the "discovery" of their own racial and cultural difference, Australian officialdom, even as a benevolent host, can also make them acutely aware of their "Chineseness". Furthermore, since 1996, having to bear the role of Chinese subject ascribed by the official though benign discourse of multiculturalism has been given a darker side, to the extent that all Asian ethnicities have been very publicly racialised by the notorious Pauline Hanson and her One Nation party.

In the context of international power relations, Taiwanese Chinese now resident in Australia have their own reasons again for relating to the host society and the media in a state of awareness of their Chinese ethnicity. The public political culture of Taiwan, in which Taiwan is set off ideologically against the PRC and the Communist Party as the sanctuary and the guardian of Chinese culture, arguably leads to Taiwanese migrants carrying with them an already acute, if overdetermined, sense of Chineseness as a dutiful burden. Thus, due to both their characteristic collective historical experience and the shifting features of the new social environment with which they must deal, they are likely to continue to occupy the position of "Chinese subject", much as they would have done in Taiwan. In the case of the Mainland Chinese, by contrast, few of them leaving China in recent years are likely to have identified themselves with the position of "Chinese subject" as promoted by the government of the PRC, being rather more influenced by the "leave-the-country fever" *(chuguore)* prevalent after Tiananmen (Yang, 1997: 305).

Narrowcast Institutions: SBS and New World

Broadcast television in Australia is a mixed system, with a private sector comprising three national commercial networks (Channels 7,

9 and 10), while the Australian Broadcasting Corporation (ABC) provides its national network out of public funds, and the Special Broadcasting Service (SBS) delivers a "multicultural" service to the main population centres, funded by a combination of sponsorship and government allocation. Within its wide range of foreign-language news and entertainment programming, SBS provides daily news services in Chinese (both Mandarin and Cantonese), and screens occasional films from the nations of Greater China. In addition, there are low-power "community" channels in Sydney and Melbourne, where the *Asian Community TV* program is broadcast, having been prepared by volunteers from the Asian communities.

As well as programs, cultural products such as television services attest to the formation of transnational networks of media circulation and (re)production between "home" and "host" sites, the technological means for cultural maintenance and negotiation. In this context, new services such as New World TV, an Australian Chinese-language subscription television channel, can be regarded as a form of specifically diasporic television because the "global Chinese" of Melbourne and Sydney are targeted as the sole audience for this kind of "narrowcast" service. Both SBS and New World were therefore of great interest to this study from the viewpoint of their sources of programming and its timeliness, relative to the countries of origin.

Within the diverse complex of media used by Chinese viewers in Australia, narrowcast television services have a special place. While broadcasting is driven by the logic of maximising audiences across difference, by the production of an abstracted "mass", narrowcasting fragments the audience using niche media targeted at minority publics or markets. While broadcasting generally denies difference, narrowcasting exploits it, often fetishising a notion of a singular or "special" identity determined by a fundamental essence: ethnicity, race, sexuality or whatever. There are, of course, other forms of narrowcasting which service various taste markets or restricted localities, but for diasporic Chinese viewers in Australia, it is those television services that speak directly to their Chineseness — that invite various forms of diasporic identification — which are the most significant. As the marketing slogan for New World TV, a Chinese-language subscription channel, used to declare: "Intimacy is to speak your language."

For Naficy (1993), narrowcasting remains an under-appreciated discourse. He argues that the processes at work in the specialisation and fragmentation of television demand more thorough attention. This is not simply because these developments are important evidence that the media imperialist and global homogenisation theorists are wrong, but also because ethnic narrowcasting is a manifestation of the emergence of new media sites that address the experience of hybridity, migration and diaspora, speaking to the disruptive spaces of postcolonialism. Narrowcast media, then, provide one example of a growing third or multiple cultural space where various "othered" populations are creating sites for representation, where all kinds of "resistive hybridities, syncretism and mongrelizations are possible, valued" (Naficy and Gabriel, 1993: x). Implicit in this valuation is a fundamental opposition between broadcasting as the heartland of nation and family, and narrowcasting as the space of the migrant, the exile, the refugee. But the space of narrowcasting is not simply a space of representation: it is also a space of consumption, a space where otherness circulates as a commodity. How, then, should the distinctive cultural economies and topographies of desire shaping narrowcast television services for Chinese viewers in Australia be understood?

The crucial point, Naficy argues, is to recognise the various ways of being narrow, to understand the specific dynamics of inclusion and exclusion ordering minority media. This is the reason why two Chinese-language narrowcast services available in Australia have been investigated: in order to track patterns of similarity and difference in their institutional and cultural logics. By looking closely at the Chinese programming of SBS, Australia's unique free-to-air (but advertising-supported) public-service multicultural channel, and at a cable subscription, or "pay TV", channel — New World TV — it is possible to see the complexities and variety of narrowcast television.

The other reason for singling out these two services is that they provide the main source of audiovisual news for Chinese audiences in Australia. As many studies of the migrant experience have shown, news from or about "home" has special status and value. It is a privileged form, watched avidly and intently and often in a state of what Naficy (1993: 107) terms "epistephilic desire". News generates strong demand: all services programming Chinese news in Australia report intense viewer requests for more, which confirms the strength of demand apparent across all groups in our household interviews, to be detailed later. So, in the maze of diverse textual forms available to Chinese audiences, news is distinctive not just in terms of the way that it is watched, but also in the symbolic value it holds as a source of direct access to and information about homelands. News generates very specific relations in space between here and there, because of the way it mediates the play of separation and connection in time, then and now. By contrast, in the absence of any referent in real space or time, purely fictional texts function quite differently in the kind of longing they work upon.

Thus, in focusing on these two services, SBS and New World TV, the intention is to examine the nature and meanings of their narrowcast organisation through the specific example of news. In this way, it will be possible to not only understand how news is implicated in particular forms of diasporic identification, but also how differently two narrowcasters use news to establish distinctive relations with Chinese viewers.

Special Broadcasting Service

SBS Television was established in 1980 with the mandate to be both multicultural and multipurpose. The channel has to service various special communities (ethnic, indigenous, minority), reflect multiculturalism to all Australians, and increase diversity in the broadcasting system. As a public service broadcaster, SBS is unique in the world. Established as a key institution of multicultural social policy, it is charged with the dual tasks of representing and maintaining different identities and adding quality and innovation to the Australian television landscape. The complexity of SBS's mixture of objectives adds up to a bizarre and pleasurable heterogeneity. To scan its program guide on a given day is to encounter a strange collection. For example, one evening during the research period included the previous night's news bulletin from Beijing in unsubtitled Mandarin; the *OUT Show* (a local gay issues program then current); a studio debate about cultural diversity in Australia; an *avant garde* animated film; and a movie from Turkey. This heterogeneity means that SBS has several different logics of narrowcasting at work within the one service, unlike exilic TV or other single-purpose niche TV services.

At the simplest level, SBS is a narrowcaster because it imagines the nation as a series of fragments, a multiplicity of constituencies produced through various axes of difference — often those very differences that broadcasters are unable to see in their obsession with maximising audiences. In fragmenting the nation, SBS also recognises its members' connections with other places, and acknowledges identities constituted through relations of movement and longing across national boundaries. Programs in languages other than English, programs imported from outside the dominant Anglo-American nexus, implicitly disrupt narratives of national cohesion. Most significant here is the example of *WorldWatch*, SBS's morning news service, which broadcasts satellite-delivered national news bulletins from around the world.

WorldWatch began on SBS in 1993 with screenings from 6.30 a.m. onwards of daily news services from CCTV (China Central Television) Beijing in Mandarin; France 2 Paris; Deutsche Welle Berlin; the Russian News, *Vreyma*; and two current affairs programs from public broadcasting stations in the United States. These services were generally picked up the night before by various satellites to which SBS had access, taped and then broadcast unsubtitled the following morning. Access rights were free, so the cost of the services has been negligible, while allowing SBS to assume a role in providing timely news to an impressive variety of niche audiences. Since its inception, *WorldWatch* has steadily increased its representation of nightly news or weekly current affairs magazines to include bulletins from Italy, Indonesia, Japan, Hong Kong, Lebanon, Spain, Hungary, Chile, Poland, Greece and the Ukraine.

The significance of *WorldWatch* on SBS is that it is evidence of its capacity to establish a particularist or minority stance within a broader multicultural framework. While most non-English shows on SBS are subtitled in the interests of national access, in not subtitling *WorldWatch* (a decision predicated on cost and time pressures), SBS addresses migrant and diasporic audiences without symbolically "assimilating" them into the nation. However, the absence of subtitles also means these bulletins are subtly marginalised within the overall institutional politics of the network, in that SBS remains primarily a broadcaster, albeit of a very particular kind. Thus prime time is the privilege of multicultural programming accessible to all, rather than minority or narrowcast programming.

SBS's CCTV4 news in Mandarin is one of its most controversial services, generating a significant number of letters and phone calls protesting that the service is nothing more than a propaganda exercise. Once again, this is consistent with the train of comments made about it in the household study, to be presented later in this chapter. CCTV is Mainland China's national broadcaster, and Channel 4 is its international service, aimed at diasporic audiences and able to reach almost every part of the globe.

CCTV4 leases satellite capacity around the world, and SBS has an agreement with it to access the service without charge via the PanAmSat private satellite network. SBS's only costs are infrastructural, as a dedicated downlink and encoder are necessary to pick up PanAmSat. Beijing authorises SBS's use of this service through a special code and pin number, although this authorisation is never completely assured. For example, SBS has wanted to develop a Taiwanese service on *WorldWatch*, but fears that Beijing may revoke its licence to CCTV4. SBS initially picked up CCTV4 via the Russian satellite, but the service is now more sophisticated and has moved to PanAmSat which has far wider reach and digital transmission. CCTV4's 9.00 p.m. (China time) news, which SBS picks up at midnight, tapes and screens at 7.55 a.m. the next morning, is more outward looking than its 7.00 p.m. service. It has shorter domestic stories and a slight orientation towards international issues.

Screening directly before CCTV4 on *WorldWatch* is *Hong Kong News*, aimed at balancing the Mandarin service with a Cantonese one coming from outside the Mainland. *Hong Kong News* was picked up as a direct result of community demand, and helps SBS avoid accusations of bias or special privileging of one section of the Chinese audience over another. These sorts of delicate negotiations and accommodations are not peculiar to SBS's Chinese programming, but occur across many different languages. They reveal the difficulties in assuming any sort of coherence within categories like "Chinese viewers" or "the Chinese community". They also reveal the potential within narrowcast services to fragment audiences into ever more specific niches.

Hong Kong News comes from Asia Television Limited (ATV), one of the two commercial free-to-air broadcasters in Hong Kong that provide programs domestically in Cantonese, Mandarin and English. The Cantonese language bulletin on SBS is primarily produced for audiences in the United States. It is commissioned from narrowcast channels in the United States and Canada, and compiled using large segments of content from the ATV domestic news bulletin for Hong Kong. As the satellite signal from Hong Kong is available only on a hemispheric northeast beam to northern America, the SBS pictures travel to the west coast of the United States first before being re-routed via the same satellite to Sydney.

The significance of the Chinese and other non-English language news services on *WorldWatch* is that they represent a very unique and innovative form of public service narrowcasting within the overall context of a multicultural free-to-air channel. While SBS is without question a niche service, its political rationality has historically favoured rhetorics of access and tolerance in the name of serving "all Australians". This has been evident in the symbolic economy of English subtitling, which has functioned to make all shows in whatever language accessible in the interests of national coherence and the promotion of intercultural understanding and tolerance. Yet, by switching on *WorldWatch* in the morning, the monolingual English speaker can have the interesting experience of exclusion — of confronting what Benedict Anderson (1983) aptly describes as the vast privacy of language. In this moment, non-subtitled Chinese and other news services disrupt the hegemony of the singular national language; they manifest a form of narrowcasting that is militantly particularist, and that implicitly contests multicultural rhetorics of national unity across difference. The absence of subtitles on *WorldWatch* could mean forms of identification unmediated by the obligations of multiculturalism, diversity without access and difference without nation. Perhaps it even prefigures a new form of postnationalist or even postmodern public service television.

New World TV

The example of SBS is extraordinary because of its singularity. Here is a free-to-air public service channel offering an impressively diverse array of narrowcast programming from *avant garde* video for yuppie taste markets to unsubtitled news bulletins for diasporic, migrant and refugee communities. In contrast, pay TV operates within a quite different set of cultural and economic dynamics. For a start, it is fundamentally demand-driven in its relationship with the subscriber base. This means that it is not necessarily committed to increasing media diversity: more channels does not mean more variety or difference in program types or sources. Pay services still tend to be driven by competition for big audiences, hence the favouring of mass-appeal shows. The genuinely narrowcast channels that pay does offer exist on the margins, and there remains a certain reluctance to provide them, on the assumption that so much television viewing still seems to be habitual rather than discriminating. There is obviously a fear that too much targeting of niche audiences could undermine the search for a big and therefore broad subscriber base.

Narrowcast channels on Pay are thus relatively scarce in Australia and exist as tiered add-ons to subscription packages. This was notably the case with New World TV (NWTV), a Chinese-language channel available to subscribers of Australis Media's Galaxy pay TV service for an additional monthly fee. NWTV began transmission in Sydney and Melbourne in 1994. By 1998, when the service ceased with the collapse of the Australis Media company, it was transmitting 24 hours a day to all capital cities except Hobart and Darwin, using a mixture of MDS and satellite. Programming was put together in Sydney, nearly all of it being imported from three main sources: Television Broadcasts International (TVBI) which offered satellite news, variety, movies and specials in Cantonese; Chinese Television Network (CTN), also from Hong Kong, but in Mandarin, with two channels, one on news and finance updates (the Chinese version of CNN), the other focusing on lifestyle and infotainment; and Television Broadcasts Superchannel-Newsnet (TVBS-N), a popular cable channel from Taiwan in Mandarin. A small minority of drama and documentary programs came from Radio Television Hong Kong (RTHK), the government-owned service in Hong Kong. There was negligible "local" — or, more specifically, Australian-made — content on New World TV: only around ten minutes per week.

The sources of programming reveal the strong links which NWTV had with Hong Kong, the centre of Chinese languages audiovisual production and export. They also show the sense in which NWTV could be classified as a form of diasporic narrowcasting. This almost complete reliance on imported content is a product of economic and policy factors. Australian pay TV regulations do not demand local content on narrowcast or non-drama channels. In contrast, Canada has foreign content rulings on pay which mean that 40 per cent of programming on Chinese channels has to be locally produced. There were no such obligations on NWTV and this had significant implications for the overall feel of the channel, for its sense of place — or perhaps placelessness. Studies of free-to-air broadcasting have noted the crucial role of links, station identifications and promos in generating a sense of audience loyalty and identity that is place-based. These televisual forms work to localise the channel even though it may be part of a network. This strategy was not crucial to the operations of NWTV, which had a constantly shifting array of links, modes of address and promos in which the local was absolutely marginal. Viewers were rarely addressed as members of an imagined community known as the "Australian Chinese", linked by their common location in Australia and common pleasure in NWTV. Instead, they were internally fragmented with a service that spoke to diverse forms of Chineseness and diverse senses of homeland.

If there was any location that did give NWTV some sense of place, it is Hong Kong. Most of the news, financial reports, forums and movies came from there, as well as the very distinctive and popular soaps. This Hong Kong-centrism reflects its history of long-established dominance in media production, and the way in which Hong Kong has come to stand for what could be described as an Asian version of Hollywood. For not only do Hong Kong media companies engage in aggressive distribution to Chinese markets overseas, but they have also been central in providing the spaces where narrations of East–West relations are negotiated. Hong Kong stands as a key signifier in this relation, the New York of the East: the site of consumerism and upward mobility. Hong Kong's domination in media exports to Overseas Chinese is also linked to hierarchies of Chinese identities, and to the complex politics of inclusion and exclusion in Overseas Chinese communities, with Hong Kong Chinese having higher socioeconomic status and better social connections *(guanxi)* than, for example, Mainland or Vietnamese Chinese.

News services were a major component of NWTV's schedule. Audience surveys conducted by the channel consistently revealed a strong demand for news. This was always rated as the most desired content, but this desire was qualified by demands for very particular types of news. CTN's global orientation, its address to the "global Chinese", was not valued nearly as much as local news bulletins from the homelands, synchronised as closely as possible with the country of origin. In order to satisfy this demand, NWTV was picking up the nightly news bulletin from TVBI in Cantonese on a satellite feed via PanAmSat2, taping it, then immediately screening it. Taking into account time differences, this meant that the TVBI news went to air at about 11.30 p.m. in Australia — too late for many viewers — so it was repeated at 7.00 a.m. the next morning. The only news service that was broadcast live — direct via PanAmSat2 — was CTN's Zhong Tian News Channel in Mandarin, which was basically used as filler between 1.30 and 6.30 a.m. TVBS-N's midday news from Taiwan in Mandarin was fed to Hong Kong for satellite re-broadcast internationally. It was going to air on NWTV at 4.35 p.m. on the same day.

With the demise of the Australis service in 1998, Optus Vision was left with the only available pay channel in Chinese. This effectively is no more than a package of the Hong Kong CTN feed formerly seen on NWTV, and the Mainland CCTV service, already available free-to-air on SBS, as previously discussed. The pay market leader, Foxtel, has not sought to fill the vacuum created by NWTV's disappearance, suggesting that the complexities of providing a satisfactory range of programming for the substantial but diverse communities of Chinese in Australia do not warrant the returns to be gained, particularly where there are free-to-air programs on SBS.

Yesterday's News

Indeed, the variety of Chinese news programs available on SBS's *WorldWatch* and formerly on NWTV provides evidence not only of the diversity of viewers, but also of the special status news holds for diasporic communities. While other genres such as movies or soaps may be enjoyed by Chinese audiences from different backgrounds and countries of origin, news does not generally function in this way. Naficy's (1993) account of epistephilic desire reveals the intensity of longing for specific information about "home" — the desire for immediate, simultaneous access to knowledge about "there". Domestic news bulletins from countries of origin are the key form sought out to satisfy this longing. This very distinctive use of news shows how crucial this genre is — probably more so than any other — in mediating senses of liminality, and in providing a space where the movement of separation and connection, of ambivalent and unstable points of personal and national identification, are negotiated.

There are several reasons why news occupies this role beyond the obvious fact that it is a major source of information and national imagining. Studies of the relationship between television and everyday life point to the central role of news bulletins in ordering the lived experience of time. For Paddy Scannell (1996), the structuring principle of broadcasting is "dailiness": the processes through which radio and TV retemporalise time via institutional regimes like the schedule and audience viewing rituals that are shaped in relation to this. News is crucial in this process because of its location in the schedule as a marker of each day passing and because of its textual principle of liveness, of specifying what is going on rather than what has been, what marks the particularity of this day. Broadcast television news, then, is central to how senses of home and the everyday are both ritualised and temporalised.

What then of news bulletins on narrowcast media, screened out of the context of a national television service, and in a different time zone and frame? How are these experienced by viewers? Chinese audiences for SBS and NWTV watch yesterday's news. They wake in the morning and switch on last night's bulletin from Hong Kong, Beijing or Taipei. These minority audiences access evening news from home (with all the temporal effects that are associated with news as a summation of the nation's day) the following morning. This temporal dislocation may appear insignificant. After all, narrowcast television channels are still satisfying the fundamental desire for access to homeland news services. There can be no doubt that, for these audiences, narrowcast news generates a double imaginary of time, a sense of being in two temporalities: here and there, then and now. Scannell's argument about dailiness applies more to the national rhetorics of broadcasting. In the cultural and economic logics of global narrowcasting, the schedule has a quite different function and generates correspondingly different audience rituals and temporalities. In interviews, Chinese viewers of these news services described how they delayed going to work in the morning in order to find out what happened at "home" yesterday. They needed this information, this sense of ritualised summation of the day over there, even if it was experienced in another place and another temporal order.

One Taiwanese family interviewed had a distinctive set of news-viewing practices. This family subscribed to NWTV because of the mother's strong desire for access to the TVBS-N news service, which she had watched daily in Taiwan. News was the main form of content that the family watched on NWTV. The father watched the TVBI service in the mornings on a semi-regular basis for business reasons, but he had problems with the incomplete subtitles because it was in Cantonese, and he also found its Hong Kong-centrism very frustrating. His preference was for news in Mandarin, and found subtitles a major disincentive on television news, so often preferred to read a newspaper. It was a similar story for the two daughters still living at home in this family. They occasionally watched CTN's lifestyle channel, Dadi, for gossip about the Hong Kong film and pop industry, but generally were not home during the day for the TVBS-N service direct from Taiwan.

The most avid news watcher was the mother, who watched TVBS-N daily. A significant value of this service to her was that it was being screened close to real time in Taiwan. This is the same service that she and the father used to watch in Taiwan over lunch, and now could watch in Melbourne later in the afternoon. For the mother, this service generated intense epistephilic pleasure, not just because it provided information, but because it was a domestic service, not one re-edited for an international market. It provided a strong sense of temporal and spatial connection with home — as she said herself, it made her feel "very close to home". This was definitely not yesterday's news, unlike all the other news services that were then available on NWTV. It could be argued that, with this service, the mother was able to maintain a sense of dual dailiness, a doubling of time that allowed her to remain connected to experiences of everdayness, both here and there.

Also of interest were the family news-viewing rituals in this household. Every evening over dinner, everyone watched the ABC news. The daughters often had to translate, but there was generally a lot of discussion, especially about the ABC's coverage of Taiwan. This repeated a domestic practice from Taiwan, where the family would watch the government news at 7.00 p.m. daily. Here, too, is another sense of dailiness produced through the maintenance of a ritual, and the ways in which evening news bulletins are incorporated into family interaction. ABC news is of a quite different order textually, and was much more connected to the family's sense of location in Australia. For the daughters especially, knowing about "here" was highly valued. These complex and various patterns of news viewing are, of course, open to disruption. When there is a major event in Taiwan or elsewhere in Greater China, every available news service is devoured, such as was the case with the events of Tiananmen Square. Significant events generate another sort of temporality that disrupts the sense of a daily summation or a never-ending flow of information, as they have a quite distinct temporal existence and duration.

Uses of narrowcast news services by Chinese audiences in Australia are complex in that they are intricately connected to questions of time, to the relation between the distinctive temporalities of televisual news which privilege presentness — the live — and a ritualised marking of the immediacy of each day — the phenomenological time of viewers. The mother's use of the TVBS-N service, which explicitly was not a global news service structured around a 24-hour flow of never-ending information, but a national domestic service structured around the daily ordering of information and events marking the particularity of each day in Taiwan, raises interesting questions about the significance of the temporal and the pleasures of double time for such diasporic viewers.

Distribution of Chinese-language Video and Film in Australia

In order to bring to light the circulation flows and distribution circuits of non-broadcast media products (film as well as video) which connect the countries of origin of such material with their diasporic markets in Australia, the audiovisual media consumption of diasporic audiences in Melbourne was investigated through a series of interviews with video store traders and a film distributor. More particularly, the purpose of interviewing video store traders was to obtain inside information and opinion on the organisation of the Chinese video business, including the relationship of video store owners to the distributors; and to collect the traders' observations of the characteristics of the market for Chinese videos: its dynamics, its demographics and any segmentation it might exhibit. As well, information was obtained on the Chinese cinema circuit, and the integration of cinema exhibition and video distribution, using both interviews with individuals involved and printed material from business and trade journals, and from secondary sources.

While videos from their home or culturally proximate countries are an important medium for diasporic viewers, it should be appreciated that they do not rely necessarily or exclusively on commercial distribution through video stores as a source of their videos. Some of the respondents in the household interviews did not rent videos from local stores at all, but did watch them occasionally when tapes were circulated amongst their informal kinship or other social networks. Videos are constantly brought into Australia by diasporic viewers themselves — some of whom are frequent travellers, as we have seen — or by visitors from their home countries, and then passed throughout such networks.

Furthermore, videos and other audiovisual products such as karaoke tapes are not just imported in a single, direct flow from the home country to Australia. Sometimes, they are involved in a lateral distribution circuit — for example, Hong Kong videos might first circulate in other parts of the Chinese-speaking world, such as Singapore, Malaysia or China, before being brought to Australia. In other words, some of our household respondents in Australia, particularly Southeast Asian ones, would have acquired Hong Kong tapes from such other countries, but not so much from Hong Kong. In some instances — especially when the tapes are acquired in Singapore — the original Cantonese vernacular is dubbed into Mandarin: in Singapore, Hong Kong material in Cantonese is not allowed to be distributed, so it is all dubbed into Mandarin.

In fact, this language difference — Cantonese being the language of Hong Kong and Mandarin of Mainland China and Taiwan — turned out to be a decisive determinant in the structure of the video business. The Mainland Chinese and Hong Kong video industries effectively run in parallel, each with its separate producers, distributors, rental outlets and customers, with very little crossing over to the other side. This is for linguistic rather than business or political reasons. Thus, because Taiwanese videos — like those from the Mainland — are in Mandarin, they are also available in stores which rent Mainland videos. The subtitling of Hong Kong as against Mainland Chinese and Taiwanese videos does allow for some crossing over, since the written language is much the same.

Videos of cinema releases carry subtitles in Chinese characters, so that Chinese who do not speak Mandarin can follow a Mainland or Taiwanese film, and Chinese who do not speak Cantonese can follow a Hong Kong film. Some film studios, certainly those in Hong Kong, also give English subtitles to their cinema releases. However, it is interesting to note that television series and variety programs produced for domestic viewers in Hong Kong, China or Taiwan, and then marketed as videos, are not subtitled — the expectation being that television product is less tradeable across national borders within the Chinese-speaking world than is film.

Distribution Circuits

Apart from its geopolitical position on the threshold to the "motherland" of China, its central location within the networks of Overseas Chinese, and its mythical status as the metropolis and global disseminator of Chinese popular culture, Hong Kong is in fact prominent in television production and distribution in Asia, based on its older pre-eminence in cinema production and export. Television production is based on the two networks which dominate the domestic market, TVB and ATV.

TVB (Television Broadcasts) is controlled by Sir Run Run Shaw and the Malaysian-Chinese entrepreneur Robert Kuok. Through its international arm, TVBI, it exports most of its domestic production — around 5000 hours annually — in various forms and in several languages, but principally to diasporic markets. As well as having its own video outlets in Southeast Asian countries such as Malaysia, it also has cable subsidiaries in the United States and Canada, and a satellite superstation aimed mainly at Taiwan, TVBS. These are its major overseas markets, from which it was deriving over 15 per cent of its income by 1995 (Chan, 1996; Langdale, 1997; Lovelock, 1995; To and Lau, 1995).

As well as its vertical integration of television production and distribution on an international scale, TVB is horizontally integrated with Shaw Brothers (Hong Kong) Limited, a major distributor of cinema (Lent, 1990). After these, the next largest companies in Hong Kong active in media exports to diasporic and other overseas markets are built on similar vertically integrated models to TVB and Shaw Brothers, but are not related. These are the television network ATV and Golden Harvest, which is a major exhibitor as well as producer and distributor of films, well known in the West through one of its principals, Jackie Chan ("Hong Kong Films Conquer the World", 1997). In 1998, it was announced that Golden Harvest would issue shares to Rupert Murdoch's News Corporation, as well as to Robert Kuok and the Hong Kong communications entrepreneur Li Ka-Shing. Also at that time, Australian cinema distribution and exhibition company Village Roadshow had more than a 16 per cent share in Golden Harvest, and a joint venture with it in building cinemas in Southeast Asia (Mathieson, 1998).

As for Mainland China, television production and distribution — both for the domestic and international markets — is centralised under CCTV (China Central Television), which commenced a global service for the Chinese diaspora in 1995 (Langdale, 1997: 315). There are also significant provincial and municipal stations in Shanghai, Guandong and Sichuan. According to Chan (1996), all of these are active in program exports, both in their own right and coordinated through the export agency CTU (China Television United). Films are marketed overseas through the Beijing Film Export Corporation. Thus Mainland China, as well as Hong Kong, is active in pursuit of audiences of diasporic Chinese.

Our research in Australia has found that there are direct links between the many small neighbourhood Chinese video stores and the major distribution corporations of both Hong Kong and Mainland China. These same global distributors also supply films to the specialist Chinese and cult cinema circuits, as well as the narrowcast broadcast television services which have been mentioned, evidencing how the patterns of horizontal and vertical integration in which they structure themselves in their domestic markets also extend out into their diasporic markets.

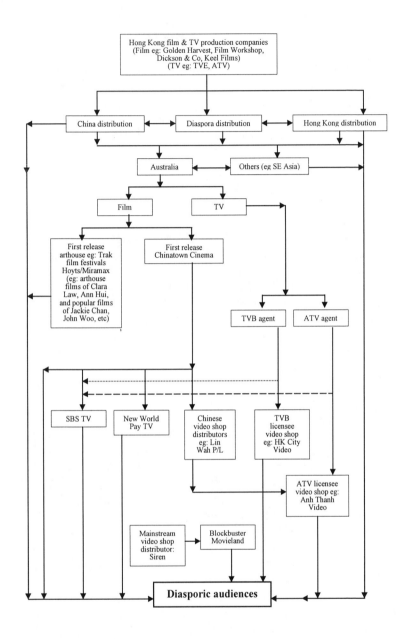

Figure 2.1: Flowchart of distribution of Hong Kong film, TV and video in Melbourne

Video

To take video stores first, our research discovered that, in line with the market segmentation by language noted above, a video store would stock either Mainland Chinese videos in Mandarin (most are CCTV serials, in fact), or would be tied to one or the other of the two Hong Kong major distributors by licence agreement, and so stock either ATV or TVB Cantonese product.

Although traders in both kinds of store were suspicious of the project and gave evasive or reluctant answers, we were able to establish that the Hong Kong video stores in Melbourne sign contracts with TVB or ATV, but not both: each distributor requires that a store deal with it exclusively. The contract with the distributor typically runs for a year, and can cost at least $100 000. In exchange for this fee, the trader has access to TVB or ATV's entire past and present stock, which includes movies and all television genres, for the term of the contract, which may then be renewed with another fee. However, video store owners cannot choose from catalogues, but must take what the distributor offers — a practice obviously advantageous to the distributor, particularly where distribution is vertically integrated with production. The trader is always given only one master copy, but authorised by the contract to make as many copies as necessary from his or her own blank tapes.

The Mainland Chinese side is organised on principles that generally follow the Hong Kong pattern. To quote one video store manager in an inner suburb: "There's a distributor in Melbourne. We sign a contract with a distributor each year who deals with all the Chinese state-owned TV serial producers. We give the distributors their fee each year and they give us a package. We can't choose." This store dealt only with the one distributor. Another trader named a distributor in Sydney, Tangfeng, and said he dealt only with them.

While the Hong Kong stores are tied to either TVB or ATV, some do stock videos from other sources as well. For example, Anh Thanh Video is one of the biggest Chinese video chains in Melbourne. It has shops in the City (Chinatown Midcity Arcade), and those suburbs which have an above-average proportion of people of Chinese descent, namely Richmond, Footscray, Springvale and Box Hill. Anh Thanh Video stocks not only ATV programs and shows (including game shows, infotainment, music and variety shows, television serials and news), but also a similar range of Mainland Chinese Mandarin-language programs and shows; popular Japanese material (such as television serials, *mangas*, music and variety shows); and popular Taiwanese television programs, serials and shows in the hybrid dialect Minnanhua. Anh Thanh Video is exceptional in that it has a "parent" company called Lin Wah P/L with which it shares premises and a phone number. Lin Wah P/L is the licensee and main distributor of Chinatown Cinema videos to Chinese video stores in Melbourne, distributing Chinatown Cinema movie videos to both Anh Thanh and Hong Kong City TVB Video.

Chinese video shops are organised differently from mainstream video shops. Usually, there is a counter in the front of the shop, on which are several clear folders and photo albums of movie posters, surrounded by walls that are covered with handwritten lists, and more movie posters. Customers make their selection from the lists, posters, clear folders and photo albums, rather than browsing around and picking up copies of empty tape covers like in the mainstream chain outlets such as Blockbuster and Movieland. More often than not, customers will have already heard of the video they are after before going to the video shop. The trader usually charges customers about $30 (refundable) for membership, which entitles them to rent tapes which cost from $2 (old releases) to between $4 and $5 (new releases). There are no specific overnight loans because the number of days that one is allowed to keep the tapes is dependent on the number of tapes borrowed. For example, if a customer rents seven tapes, they are returnable in seven days' time.

From this system, it follows that traders will usually want to make numerous copies of latest releases, as customers are allowed to keep them for over a week — hence more copies to accommodate slower turnover. Also, there is an incentive to re-record new titles over tapes of old ones when their popularity ebbs, so our questions about which types of videos did the traders find were in higher demand and which they had the least stock of were irrelevant, because if traders found that they had higher demand for a particular tape, they would simply make more copies, and when their popularity faded, they would recycle the tapes for the next blitz of popular new releases. This practice is one reason for the extremely poor quality of the tapes, a matter on which most respondents in the household interview study made comment.

In these circumstances, piracy might become an issue, concerning whether or not the store owner has continued to copy and rent out videos once the term of the contract that covered them is over, and the broader issue of whether or not the film or television producer's copyright has been infringed by the contract between the distributor and the video shop. Because, under the terms of the Berne Convention, action against infringement of copyright must be initiated by the possessor of the copyright, the copying of Hong Kong videos in Australia passes without attention from the film and television producers in Hong Kong, who neither need to nor wish to spend money and time on small claims in Australia, and who, for the bulk of the content available, are also vertically integrated with the distributors in any case.

China is not a signatory to the Berne Convention, but piracy in the Mainland sector is alleged to come about through unauthorised taping of Chinese television programs in China directly from broadcast television, then exporting them. It was not possible to tell from looking at the tapes on the shelves in the three Mainland Chinese video shops visited whether they had been released under licence by CCTV or not. Some were in sleeves with printed titles, indicating a master tape released to the trader under licence, but most were in sleeves with handwritten titles. This meant that they could have been pirate tapes, or they could have been copies that the trader was authorised to make from the distributor's master tape under contract.

Cinema

Chinese-speakers in Melbourne can see first-release Cantonese-language Hong Kong films at the Chinatown Cineplex on Bourke Street, part of a national chain owned by Winston Leung. Tickets cost approximately $8 for a double-feature, one being a first-release main feature; the other usually a re-run. These are the popular films many diasporic viewers would watch in their "home" countries, and those able to travel back there for business or to visit do also watch such films when they have the opportunity.

There are also alternative arthouse cinema and film festival or other special-event circuits which screen films from *auteur* Chinese directors like Clara Law and Wong Kar-wai, films which the Chinatown distribution circuit will not show — at least unless they prove popular on one of the other circuits. Chinatown's resistance can be attributed in part to the international (that is, non-Hong Kong-tied) nature of their funding, production and distribution, as well as to the off-beat character of the films themselves (that is, commercially risky compared with proven genres).

For example, Clara Law's *Autumn Moon* (1992) was a Hong Kong film, but partly funded by a Japanese consortium. It was released in Cannes and picked up by the film festival circuit, and then distributed via the arthouse cinema circuit. Wong Kar-wai's masterpiece *Fallen Angels* (1996) was not circulated via Chinatown Cinemas and its video outlets, but released in Melbourne and other capitals via the national arthouse group Palace Cinemas' Cine7 event.

It is interesting to note the cultural and commercial exchange which occurs between the arthouse and the Chinatown circuits over these Chinese *auteurs*. Because they are acclaimed and "approved" by international arthouse audiences, their most recent films tend to bypass the Chinatown circuit altogether, and go straight into the arthouse/film festival circuits. The response to this is for Chinatown then to screen their earlier films as popular cult reruns. A similar process occurs with films which fail with Chinese audiences but go on to enjoy international critical acclaim in the "West". *Sex and Zen*, *Naked Killer* and *The East is Red* are good examples of films that enjoyed very successful queer or film festival screenings, were picked up by the international arthouse circuit, and only then were screened by Chinatown.

Finally — at least over the last few years — there is the mainstream distribution circuit, in which the West has become infatuated with the kinaesthetic martial arts comedy style of Jackie Chan. Of late, most of his films have been repackaged and re-released in the West via mainstream cinemas and cult-fanboy specialist venues. In Melbourne, for example, *Rumble in the Bronx* (when bought, re-packaged and re-released by the multinational consortium, Miramax) was released (dubbed in English) through the mainstream national chain Hoyts in 1996. John Woo is another example. Having migrated to the United States from Hong Kong and become involved in joint productions with American companies, Woo's first American-produced film, *Broken Arrow*, was also released via the national chains in 1996, soon to be followed by his *Face Off*.

As a footnote, it is interesting to note that some films enjoy laser-disc release status before they are released even in Chinese cinemas overseas. Some interview respondents affirmed this when they revealed that they had already seen some Chinatown movies from laser-discs that they had rented. The researchers' experience is that traders sometimes do pass the latest not-yet-released films, such as *Fallen Angels*, over the counter to their customers.

From Chinese Cinema to Mainstream Video

Since about 1995, local video stores in Melbourne belonging to the major English-language chains, notably Movieland and Blockbuster, have been stocking a regular supply of popular Hong Kong films. It transpires that a local company, Siren Entertainment, has purchased a licence from Winston Leung, the owner of Australia's Chinatown Cinema chains, to become the official distributor of Chinatown cinema movies to mainstream video stores. Siren gets rights to distribute a film on video only after its initial release through Chinatown Cinema (which holds the rights for the first twelve months), and then its video distribution to the Chinese-language stores, namely through Chinatown's licensee, Lin Wah P/L (which holds joint rights with Chinatown Cinema for the next twelve months).

The recent success of particular Chinese films with mainstream audiences — both cult/arthouse and popular — and the advent of Chinese videos in mainstream stores would seem to demonstrate that appreciation of Chinese culture is not restricted to the Chinese and their descendants. Rather, it becomes diffused into the host society, and appears particularly attractive to those whom we could call, without prejudice, "cosmopolitan". That is, Chinese media products, if made accessible to non-Chinese-speakers via dubbing or subtitling, can appeal not just to "communities of difference", but also to "communities of taste" (Hawkins, 1996b). Second-generation Chinese, for their part, respond to these products in the context of whatever assimilation they would have received into the mainstream culture, so their media experience is hybrid, or "cross-cultural" in the best sense.

Results of Household Interviews (Survey Phase)

A household study was chosen as the best means by which researchers could speak to respondents in the "natural" setting in which they made use of the audiovisual products and services to which they had access, and because the household as a site for this kind of predominantly qualitative research has become so thoroughly theorised in the literature (Gillespie, 1995; Morley, 1992; Silverstone et al., 1992). In particular, a theoretical linkage has been established between the micro world of the household and the macro context of institutional structure, conceived at both levels in terms of space and time (Giddens, 1979). As well, a range of available research techniques has been developed around such an "ethnographic" approach, and its focus on the household setting (Silverstone et al., 1991; Sinclair, 1992).

The purpose of using such a household-based ethnographic methodology is:

> to understand relationships in space and time: relationships with the physical geography of the home ... relationships to the networks of friends and kin (which extend and transform the boundaries of the household beyond the physical); relationships with the past and with the future, in the appropriation of images and identities and in the expression of hopes and fears (Silverstone et al., 1991: 206).

There were two phases of household study. First, semi-structured family interviews were carried out with a constructed sample of households in which all the major Chinese-origin groups were equally represented. Then, in contrast to such a relatively broad-based survey approach, more truly ethnographic follow-up visits were made to the small number of households that were willing to provide the considerable level of cooperation which such research requires. For brevity, these will be referred to as the *survey phase* and the *ethnographic phase*. Taken together, they provide both an overview of media usage as found in selected sectors of Melbourne's Chinese-origin population, as well as a more closely observed account of how media are integrated into the lives of specific households.

A target sample of 50 households was decided upon, composed of a quota of ten households for each of the five major Chinese-origin groupings in Australia: the People's Republic of China, referred to here for brevity as Mainland China (MC); Southeast Asia, namely Indonesia, Malaysia and Singapore (SA); the Republic of China, better known as Taiwan (TW); Indochina, comprising Vietnam, Cambodia and Laos (VC); and Hong Kong (HK). Households were defined to include both unrelated adults living together as well as families and, as far as was possible, they were interviewed when all members could be at home together. Researchers were able to conduct the interviews in Mandarin, Cantonese, other dialects of Chinese, or whatever combination householders felt most comfortable with.

The semi-structured interview schedule used in this survey phase was designed for both adult and adolescent members of the household, asking them about their television viewing habits and preferences, though with particular attention to Chinese-related material. It also asked about their filmgoing and use of video, radio and other domestic information and communication consumer goods such as karaoke units and computers. Further questions were used to elicit socioeconomic status indicators such as occupation and education, as well as country of origin, citizenship and sense of cultural identity.

Mainstream Broadcast Television

When asked about the programs they regularly watched on television, there was quite a large number and wide range of programs mentioned, and without significant differences between groups, as Figure 2.2 shows. Programs in all genres were mentioned, from sport (the Atlanta Olympic Games were on during the period of some of the interviews, of particular interest to Mainland Chinese) as one might expect, to game shows, movies, series and serials, ranging from Australian soaps like *Neighbours* to thoroughly global programs such as *The X-Files*. News and current affairs programs of all types received frequent mention.

Mainland China	Southeast Asia	Taiwan	Indochina	Hong Kong
44	57	49	49	57

Figure 2.2: Number of English-language television programs named (all types)

Bearing in mind the sample size, the figures do suggest that the groups most fluent in English — those of Southeast Asian and Hong Kong origin — named slightly more programs in English. However, the number of times television programs in English were mentioned across the board by all survey respondents suggests that language is not so much of a barrier as might have been thought in watching mainstream television, even for the most recently arrived group: Chinese from the Mainland are every bit as likely to watch the news, or slightly less so a movie in English, as Chinese originating elsewhere.

Entertainment

On the other hand, the Mainland respondents' remarks about their actual comprehension of television entertainment in English are illuminating, and suggest that television is often used as a means of access to mainstream language and culture. One (MC 9) said about *The Oprah Winfrey Show:* 'The English is fairly familiar and informal, that's why I've started to watch chat shows. I keep up with things watching them. I don't watch regularly though." That is, the accessibility of the English spoken on the show was a reason for this respondent to watch it, though she seemed aware that the program would be considered trivial by Anglo-Australians with her level of education.

Some of the Taiwanese respondents' remarks about television (and about video and film) displayed a similar concern with comprehension, but also with informing themselves about culture — and in surprising ways. One 19-year-old Taiwanese respondent (TW 8) said about a national variety show, *Hey! Hey! It's Saturday*, that: "It gives Australian news and humour. Trying to assimilate into Australian culture — that's an indicator of how much you understand the language and the humour." About *Seinfeld*, he said: "You watch and you learn quite a bit about Western culture, the way friends speak with each other sometimes." Another respondent (TW 2) said, with a better sort of alibi: "Last month's women's group at La Trobe [University discussed] why *Melrose Place* attracts a female audience. Wanted to know why it's so popular."

News and Information

The parochialism of news and current affairs on Melbourne television was a regular cause of complaint from respondents of all national origins. For example, regarding the Channel 9 news in particular, one Mainland respondent (MC 1) said: "News content not bad but pays more attention to British, Anglo-Celtic people." A Cambodian-born respondent (VC 5) had a slightly more generous view of news: "They have very good news except that they are very limited, to Australian current affairs only. It would be better worldwide." A Singapore-born respondent (HK 4) thought that: "In international news they're very poor. Australia is very poor in terms of geographical and political awareness of the region." A Hong Kong respondent (HK 5), asked whether there was enough coverage of events of concern to Chinese people on the Channel 7 news, said: "I wouldn't say so. If I know something particularly is happening in China or Hong Kong, I will turn to the SBS news." Similarly, a Mainland respondent (MC 4) said about the Channel 10 news: "The international news on Channels 7, 9 and 10 isn't as good as on ABC or SBS. They [the commercial channels] have more Australian news."

The ABC news fared a little better, though it did not escape criticism. A Malaysian-born respondent (SA 9) said: "[It] gives you more substance to the facts, more of a world view." A Mainland respondent (MC 2) thought the ABC news was "All right. [It has] a bit more [on China] than the commercial channels. They have their own correspondent in Beijing." An Indochinese respondent (VC 1) said it was: "Better [than the commercial channels], still mainstream, not analysis." Asked if there was enough news on Chinese topics on the ABC, a Southeast Asian respondent (SA 5) said: "No. Slightly better than commercial news format. News is presented too short and snappy to get the full picture."

The SBS news was best regarded for its international scope, but attracted different and sometimes contradictory charges of political selectivity. One Taiwanese respondent (TW 3) said it was "All right. Better than Channels 7, 9 and 10, because it's broad in scope. The other channels have more Australian news." A Southeast Asian respondent (SA 8) thought it was: "Very international. News mainly on Yugoslavian civil war lately but they had a comprehensive report on the flood situation in China. I prefer it to news focused on local content."

However, while the global scope of the SBS news was valued, there were criticisms of the way in which news from China was framed. Another Southeast Asian (SA 5) said, with some theoretical knowledge: "Chineseness is constructed as other, exotic and different." Yet another (SA 3) said it was: "Politically correct in Western terms — for example, the Dalai Lama; anti-Chinese, pro-Western standpoint." A Taiwanese respondent (TW 8) said: "The materials they present are very selective. They try to avoid sensitive topics. Even if they're concerned with something that could affect the Australian government, they just give a very brief story on it." Another (TW 2) thought it: "Always portrays how people are fighting in Taiwanese parliament. Not OK, don't like that way. Don't really deal with what is happening." One other (TW 9) was more concerned with the host audience: "It lets me know how Western people look at my country."

Specialised Television Services

Unfortunately, in the whole sample, there was only one subscriber to the Chinese-language New World pay TV service discussed earlier in this chapter, and disappointingly few viewers of the Chinese programs on community television (Channel 31), a fact attributed by several to poor reception in the suburbs further out. Nevertheless, what those few viewers did say points suggestively — if rather insubstantially — towards an analysis of Channel 31 use based on country of origin or, more specifically, on whether or not there is or has been an established, institutionally based discourse of ethnic identity and of inter-ethnic relations in the countries from which the respondents have come.

Of the fourteen respondents who watched Channel 31 at least sometimes, five were from Indochina, five from Southeast Asia, three from the Mainland and one from Hong Kong. All the Southeast Asian and Indochinese respondents who watched the Asian community TV program counterbalanced their criticism of its poor production standards with the belief that Channel 31 is a valuable social asset that should be maintained. Although widely separated in socioeconomic terms, one thing Southeast Asian and Indochinese respondents do have in common is that they come from a part of the world where ethnic Chinese are in the minority. "Chineseness" was (and is) an issue of potentially great personal seriousness in both Malaysia and Vietnam in a way that it has never been in China. In countries where such minority Chinese communities exist, there are ethnically defined Chinese community organisations which fulfil both practical and spiritual functions at the local level, in a situation where state institutions are indifferent, actively hostile or just not equipped to perform such functions, and which mediate between the Chinese community and the government. It may be that the Southeast Asian and Indochinese respondents' experience of these organisations as a form of civil society leads them to identify themselves with the Asian program on Channel 31, much as they do with their community ethnic organisations such as the Chinese Association of Victoria and the Indo-Chinese Ethnic Chinese Association of Victoria. VC 7's view summed up this attitude: "It's important that there should be such a service."

We have noted that, in addition to its evening news program in English, SBS broadcasts a number of news services in other languages, including Mandarin and Cantonese, in morning timeslots. This is the *WorldWatch* programming examined earlier. Figure 2.3 shows the numbers of households who watched the Chinese-language services on *WorldWatch*. By comparison, there were only five households which regularly watched the SBS news in English, one in each of the groups in the sample, although — as noted — many more across all groups watched news in English on the other channels.

Mainland China	Southeast Asia	Taiwan	Indochina	Hong Kong
6	2	4	3	4

Figure 2.3: Households regularly watching SBS Chinese-language services

The respondents' comments reflect a continued close engagement with the unfolding of events in East Asia, and irritation at the difficulty of staying adequately informed — reminiscent of, in another context, Naficy's (1993) observations of the "epistephilic desire" found in his study of the Iranian exiles in Los Angeles. Several respondents

— and not only those from the Mainland — complained of the pro-Communist Party character of the SBS Mandarin news, the national daily news broadcast of the Chinese state television network syndicated to SBS. One (MC 2) described it as: "Not great. We just want to see what's going on. It's not the same as Australian news. A lot of propaganda." One Southeast Asian (SA 1) said: "Comes from Communist country, can't expect it to be impartial. Haven't given it [its adequacy of cover] much thought from the Australian perspective." The Cantonese news was thought to be rather tame and insubstantial, however. One Mainlander (MC 4) said: "Because it's almost 1997 the Hong Kong news doesn't have much to say about China any more." Two Hong Kong respondents (HK 1 and HK 2) said it was too short.

SBS entertainment programming also drew some comments. Asked about her favourite type of program on television, a Mainland respondent (MC 1) said: "Movies banned in China that you can see here." When asked for her opinion on SBS programming, she said: "Sometimes SBS shows movies that are banned in China. SBS should do this more often instead of Hong Kong fighting movies. People in Australia think Chinese are stupid because of what's on TV and films in Chinese." This is a point of sensitivity to be found also with regard to cinema and videos: an anxiety that media representations of Chineseness will create undesirable impressions within the mainstream culture.

Non-broadcast Audiovisual Media

Video and Film

An apparent trend with regard to video and film use is that people from the Mainland watch appreciably less video material in English than people from any other origin, although there is no significant difference with film, as Figure 2.4 shows.

At first sight, this is probably best understood as a reflection of the significant fact that the Mainland Chinese tend to have been in Australia for the shortest time, and to be the least fluent in English. However, one important qualification to be made about the data in Figure 2.4 is that the Mainland sample is composed entirely of adults over the age of 30, while all the other samples include teen-agers and people in their early twenties, who are heavily represented as viewers of English video and film, as they went (or go) to school here, and participate in the usual social life of young people in Melbourne, which includes watching videos and going to films.

Videos				
Mainland China	Southeast Asia	Taiwan	Indochina	Hong Kong
3	8	13	8	17
Films				
Mainland China	Southeast Asia	Taiwan	Indochina	Hong Kong
7	9	10	9	

Figure 2.4: English-language films and videos named as being watched

What about going out to films and renting videos in Chinese? Among residents of Melbourne of Chinese origin, those from the Mainland appear slightly more likely to go to the effort and expense of going out to see a film or renting a video in Chinese. This does fit the common wisdom that Chinese from the Mainland are rendered more marginal socially than others in Melbourne because of their relatively poor level of English, combined with their relatively shorter length of stay in Australia and usually impoverished circumstances; because of this, they tend to continue to involve themselves in Chinese rather than Australian cultural consumption, as much by force of language as by personal choice.

However, there is also an additional factor, suggested by some of the Mainland respondents' comments about films, that should be considered. One Mainland respondent (MC 2), when asked what he thought of the range and quality of Chinese films screened in Melbourne cinemas, said: "The Mandarin films here are mostly new and not bad in quality. You can see films that are banned in China here." An additional angle is provided by one other Mainland respondent (MC 8) who, when asked if there was any category of Chinese video he thought was over-represented in Melbourne video shops, said: "Ones that talk about how backward China is. We don't like them, even if they win awards overseas."

For these respondents, watching a Chinese film is an act that carries political implications. Their interest in Chinese politics is conscious, and they tend to speak readily and with some force about the positions they continue to take. On the other hand, even while continuing to speak as informed critics of the Chinese government, some respondents expressed resentment against those films which gave an impression of China as totalitarian, medieval and poor. Perhaps distance also affects political convictions, but these respondents' unease may be attributable to a feeling that, in terms of the renewed debate about multiculturalism, they are somehow responsible for China, as its subjects.

Other Audiovisual Media Use

Radio

There are Chinese-language radio programs on the SBS AM station in Melbourne and the FM community service 3ZZZ, but these were listened to regularly in only a fraction of households overall, while several listened to no radio at all. However, those that did listen were concentrated in the Mainland and Indochinese groups. Most respondents tended to listen to mainstream music format radio, either classical, contemporary rock or "light", depending on personal taste and age.

Of the respondents who listened to Chinese radio, only one (TW 1) was aged under 30, and her attention to 3ZZZ was due to her having worked there. She was critical of the standard of the 3ZZZ Chinese broadcast, describing it as "not very good in content or skill, not professional". A Mainland respondent (MC 2) commented more kindly: "It's a volunteer program, and not very standardised. We can understand that." VC 6 didn't know it existed. Another Taiwanese respondent (TW 10), also once a volunteer with the station, said she no longer even listened to 3ZZZ because the content was not sufficiently interesting for young people, hinting again at the significance of a generational factor in media use. However, there was also a political cause in this case, as she thought 3ZZZ favoured the PRC.

More appreciative comments about Chinese radio included: "We miss a lot when we listen to the English news. There's also more detail on China on SBS and 3ZZZ." (MC 2) Another said they listened: "Because it broadcasts on Australian situations that concern Chinese people in particular, like immigration laws and policy changes. It also broadcasts Chinese news that isn't broadcast in China, like *Voice of America.*" (MC 4) Another's reason was: "To understand the news. I can't follow it in English. To understand a bit more about Australia." (MC 7) Another said simply: "I like Chinese songs", but disliked all "talk" shows (VC 2).

The Mainland respondents' comments are in line with certain characteristics that they displayed when talking about television and film: their close engagement with events in East Asia and an epistephilic desire to seek out information; an acute awareness of the implications of their Chineseness; and an uncertain grasp of English. Related to the last of these is their rather lateral use of Radio for the Print Handicapped, which appears as often for them as SBS radio as a source of linguistically accessible useful information. In the words of MC 7: "I listen to 3RPH sometimes. They read very slowly. I can pick up a word here and there." Another (MC 10), couldn't name the station, but also liked the way they spoke slowly.

Karaoke

Only one of the Mainland households (MC 8) had karaoke at home. The respondent reported that his family enjoyed singing karaoke and they brought it out when friends came. Two of the other Mainland respondents said they liked karaoke but only took part in singing when invited by friends. The others were uncommitted, in two cases expressing positive dislike for it. One such respondent (MC 5) said: "I really hate it. It's Cantonese trash, or Japanese." Of the Southeast Asian respondents, only one had karaoke at home, two reported occasional social use and the others either never used it, or in one case (SA 3) only used it when on holiday overseas (perhaps when feeling "more Chinese").

Of the Taiwanese respondents, four had karaoke at home, three of whom reported also using it when out socially, including one real enthusiast. There was also one harsh critic, but another respondent in that group who did not use karaoke made no criticism of it as such, but said only: "I can't sing" (TW 3). Five Indochinese respondents had karaoke at home, though two of these said they didn't enjoy karaoke much and didn't use it often, and two without their own karaoke equipment said they sang sometimes when out with friends. Of the Hong Kong respondents, five had their own karaoke at home and a similar number reported that they took part in it when out, at least "sometimes".

In general, karaoke looks like something that Chinese-speaking people resident in Melbourne tend to acquire with length of stay and economic security, yet karaoke singing appears as much a social duty as an individual indulgence. There was one respondent (SA 9) who did not own karaoke equipment but said: "I've hosted a couple of CAV (Chinese Association of Victoria) karaoke evenings. I viewed it as community work" and proceeded to explain how she avoided having to sing. The low frequency of ownership and use among Southeast Asian respondents, even though they tend to be well off, is interesting and suggests that the karaoke fashion is less established in Indonesia and Malaysia than in Taiwan or Hong Kong, with the respondents from the latter two countries of origin appearing to show more genuine enthusiasm.

Computer

Computer ownership was high across all the sampled groups: all ten of the Southeast Asian households had a computer of some sort — nine of the Taiwanese, and eight of each of the others. This is around three times the national average at that time, when less than a third of all Australian households had a computer, and just 262 000 of them were connected to the Internet (Bogle, 1996). When asked about use, most said that they used their computers for study, work or letter writing without being more specific. Some respondents (all male) reported that they experimented with programming or generated graphics.

Concerning the Internet, there were six Taiwanese households with connection to the Internet, three Southeast Asian, two Hong Kong and one of each of the others. Of these, three of the Taiwanese households mentioned keeping contact with friends and relatives overseas as one of their uses, as did a similar number — indeed all — of the Southeast Asian households. Interestingly, SA 3 mentioned that he used the Internet to access a number of Southeast Asian newspapers.

On this evidence, computers are much more of a priority than karaoke for people of Chinese origin in Melbourne, particularly for those of Taiwanese background, although it is likely that there is a strong socioeconomic factor at play also, just as there is in the population at large, with regard to connection to the Internet.

The Identity Question

A good deal of the media-related behaviour and attitudes observed amongst the different groups of respondents can be explained in terms of the patterns of difference and similarity regarding the sociopolitical orientation and linguistic skills which they bring from their homelands, and the socioeconomic status and generational experience which they accrue over time in Australia. At this point, it is possible to sum up some of the differences in media use between the groups which the survey phase brought out. Thus the Mainland respondents are less likely than all other categories to go to English language films and rent videos in English, though they are almost as prone as the other groups to watch broadcast television in English. They are more likely to see films and rent videos in Chinese. The Southeast Asian respondents are less inclined than all other categories to go to karaoke bars. The Southeast Asian and Indochinese respondents are the most disposed to watch Channel 31, while the Mainland respondents are most likely to choose the deliberate English of Radio for the Print Handicapped and the broadcasts in Chinese on the SBS or 3ZZZ stations.

Although we can account for such differences in terms of pragmatic adaptive and sociological factors, rather than any conscious effort by these groups to preserve their various versions of Chineseness in Australia, some respondents did refer explicitly to Chinese culture and their relationship to it when talking about themselves and their media use. It has been suggested already that these respondents' concern with "culture" is influenced by the established discourse of multiculturalism in Australia and by the position of "Chinese subject" that they find themselves required to take. However, first of all, Chineseness and Chinese culture are meaningful and consequential concepts in Mainland China, Taiwan, Hong Kong, Malaysia and Vietnam, although with different constellations of forces at work in each case, so it is this prior cultural identification against which the discourse of multiculturalism positions them.

When householders were asked directly whether they considered themselves to be Chinese or Australian and, if Chinese, what they meant by that, differences became apparent between the various groups, just as there had been in their media use. Eight of the Mainland households regarded themselves as Chinese, while the other two could give no definite account of what they were. None of them seemed at all defensive or uneasy about calling themselves Chinese when asked the question "When considering your identity, do you regard yourself first of all as a Chinese or Australian person?" However, they did express two fairly clear and explicable ethnic concerns when asked about their media use. One was anxiety about their language proficiency and the degree to which they were informed about Australia, and the other was a sensitivity about the impression given by Chinese and Hong Kong films about what kind of place China was.

In the latter regard, some demonstrated that they understood the negative implications of "Chineseness" then current in Australia. It is worth recording that the interviews took place at the time when public debate about ethnicity, immigration and settlement policy had been rekindled by the provocative maiden speech of independent federal House of Representatives MP Pauline Hanson, though well before the launch of her party, One Nation. This debate — and even public behaviour towards anybody of Asian appearance — manifested a strongly racialised, rather than merely "ethnic", definition of Chineseness, as alluded to at the beginning of this chapter. Without prompting, several respondents mentioned the Hanson syndrome, and some had their own very strong reactions to it: "That bitch ought to be shot," said one.

In spite of such an intense atmosphere being generated by this debate, and in contrast to the declared Chineseness of the Mainlanders, the Hong Kong respondents showed negligible concern for national identity. In some of their households, members could not agree amongst themselves on precisely what nationality they were. Individuals in six households defined themselves wholly or in part as Australian, more than in any other group. It could be inferred from this that Hong Kong's ambiguous and soon to be foreclosed status as a country at the time of the survey encouraged these respondents to think of national identity as a matter for conscious choice. However, for others, national identity did not seem to be an important issue, in the sense that they were comfortable with Hong Kong's cosmopolitan version of Chineseness. The Hong Kong respondents' overall lack of interest in the local Asian Community TV program on Channel 31 and their preference for English media except as a source of news from East Asia were in line with this.

The Indochinese respondents' ideas of their national identity were as varied as those of Hong Kong origin, and they had the next highest incidence of individuals identifying as Australian. However, it was noticeable that the Indochinese respondents thought the most about national identity, and gave the longest and most complex and ambiguous answers, especially in contrast to the Hong Kong respondents, whose answers tended to be confined to a word or two. These respondents' intense concern with the topic of national identity was reflected in their involvement with Channel 31, as discussed elsewhere.

The Taiwanese respondents' views on national identity appeared to be dominated by the issue, of entirely Taiwanese rather than Australian derivation, of whether Taiwan is really China or not. The Taiwanese respondents' views of their own identity appeared to reflect a markedly Taiwan-centric view of the world, in the same way as some of their comments about media use.

The Southeast Asian respondents tended to say they were Chinese rather than ascribe themselves to Malaysia, Indonesia or Singapore, though some of them added significant qualifications to their national identities. In their tendency to define themselves as Chinese even although they had been born and lived in non-Chinese countries, the Southeast Asian respondents resembled the Indochinese, though the former's responses to the question on national identity tended to be brief and low key in comparison, and sometimes to convey a kind of flippancy which none of the Indochinese could quite manage.

Some Conclusions from the Survey Phase

There is a commonsense level at which patterns of media use are matter-of-fact and pragmatic, not at all difficult to explain. Chinese people in Melbourne watch English media if their English is fluent, and watch Chinese media if their Chinese is much better than their English. As we have noted, they also make creative, selective and adaptive use of both mainstream and specialised media. At this pragmatic level, their choices of television programs, films and videos are affected neither by their own ideas of identity, nor by official or unofficial Australian perceptions of their identity. For example, the manifest preference for non-fiction television, and for "serious" and not "escapist" film and video, that was apparent — especially amongst Mainland and to some extent Taiwanese respondents — gives an impression of people who use audiovisual media deliberately to improve their English, and to provide themselves with factual information and cultural insight which they might use in negotiating a place for themselves in a new society.

The impression of the ethno-political dimension of audiovisual media use, as provided by the household interview respondents, is that they tend to remain closely interested in events in East Asia, find themselves out of the way of things in Australia and wish to stay informed, even though they would not conceive of this continued engagement as "cultural" according to any theoretically essentialist or multiculturalist definition. "Cultural negotiation" in this light includes negotiation of the particular difficulties of migrating to a country in which "culture" is thus fetishised and foregrounded, and which can stand as a cipher for race. This means consciousness of difference is heightened in the search to satisfy culturally and circumstantially given needs for information and entertainment, including the phenomenon of epistephilia, seen in wanting more news than the mass media are prepared to give about the outside world, especially of these respondents' former part of it.

Results of Household Interviews (Ethnographic Phase)

Ethnographic interviews

After the survey phase had been concluded, return visits were made to a limited number of households for more detailed interviewing and other qualitative observation and data collection. This we have called the ethnographic phase. As well as answers to more detailed and unstructured questions about respondents' different kinds of media use than was possible in the survey phase, the extended interviews conducted during the ethnographic phase were able to elicit more personal background information, and more on the diasporic life-style of individuals and how they negotiated their cultural identities.

Given the inherent difficulties in winning the confidence of respondents and asking to be given both access to people's homes and a claim on their time, households were recruited into the sample through *guanxi:* principally the personal contacts of the researchers, with some obtained through community organisations. Four households were revisited for the ethnographic phase: one was Taiwanese, one Indochinese, and two were of mixed Southeast Asian and Hong Kong origin. Thus the whole sample has no claims to be representative, but nevertheless is able to present data from a wide and systematic selection of households, as well as more fine-grained observations from particular households. Sampling and participant observation issues raised by this mode of research are given further consideration later in this section.

Together with the interviewers' own observations of the layout and presentation of the household, the return visit interviews also yielded some insight on what Silverstone et al. (1992) have called the "moral economy" of the household: the sense of what kind of household its members see themselves as being. During these "long conversations" on the return visit, householders were also asked to provide "network diagrams" of their relationships to other family members living outside the household and their geographic location, along with lists of all the communication and information devices in the household, and their personal "mental maps" of the household's interior space (Silverstone, et al., 1991). The interviews were conducted during May and June 1997.

Household VC 2: "I say I'm Chinese."

This household consists of a married couple in their fifties, a son at university, and a daughter at the point of marrying and moving out. Another adult daughter is in California, living with the wife's family, and there is another son in Sydney. Their modest 1960s-style suburban house is distinguished inside by framed calligraphy scrolls on the walls, and a huge home theatre system in the living room, indicative of this household's involvement in media. The parents are both executive members of AsiaTV, the group responsible for producing the Asian community TV program on Channel 31, the low-power community channel in Melbourne. They also present a program on the community access FM radio station, 3ZZZ.

The father, the almost exclusive spokesperson in both the initial and the longer interviews held in the home, is in fact an internationally recognised diasporic Chinese writer. However, far from being one of the cosmopolitan celebrities of postcolonial literature now lionised in the West, a professional "diasporic subject" (Kaplan, 1996: 122), he is not well known in Australia, even though he is published and has won awards there as well as in Asia. He also works as a journalist, contributing to Chinese-language newspapers in Australia and in Taiwan. The wife writes as well, but is more distinguished as an opera singer. She meets weekly with a karaoke group to sing Cantonese opera, and has her own new laser disc karaoke unit in the living room.

The father comes from a family with ancestors who were originally feudal landowners in China, but with the Communist Revolution of 1949 they fled to Vietnam, where they became successful in a range of businesses. One of his books tells the story of the family's subsequent exodus from Vietnam in 1978, when the victorious government closed down all business. His parents and brothers went to Germany, while he, together with his wife and children, found their way to Australia amongst the first "boat people".

Although born in Vietnam, the father says he has always identified culturally as Chinese, but now feels himself to be the Australian citizen that he has become:

> When I arrived in Australia, people ask me if I'm Vietnamese, I say I'm Chinese. Now, I can't imagine I have any other homeland than Australia. But sometimes when I hear about Pauline Hanson ... small groups of people are discriminatory. It hurts the heart. It's no good, a person like her. Big damage to the Australian country.

With her family in the United States and Singapore, and his in Germany, both husband and wife travel from time to time — for example, he has been to Germany five times since 1979, and they both had been to Singapore not long before the interviews. This cosmopolitan orientation to travel was reflected in their comments on media use, as were their language skills. Thus, while he prefers to watch the *WorldWatch* Chinese-language news services on SBS (which they also like for its Chinese movies: "SBS is a very good channel. Even Australians think so"), he says that when he is in Germany, he watches CNN because it is in English. In Melbourne, the couple both also watch Channel 31 and listen to 3ZZZ, because of their personal involvement with these very local media, and listen to Chinese-language programs on SBS radio.

The five videos which they had rented in the previous month were all English-language mainstream, as was the film which they had most recently gone out to see at a cinema. Interestingly, however, they had also been to see *Floating Life*. While the father often rents videos (never Hong Kong action movies, which he holds in contempt), the university student son is also influential in the household's choice of video and film. As well, he is the member of the family most oriented towards communication and information technologies. It was the son who had installed the home theatre system, and who was the main user of the only computer in the house. This he has in his room, along with his own television set and VCR.

The house has one fixed telephone line (the daughter's former own line having been disconnected in view of her imminent departure), a fax and two mobile phones, which are used by the son and daughter. Telecommunication is important in keeping this diasporic family in contact — they speak to relatives in Germany and the United States at least once a week, including the daughter in California, as well as the son in Sydney. The wife calls her sister in Singapore about once a month.

HK 4: "All Chinese come from China"

Although they live in one of the more "Asian" suburbs of outer Melbourne, this is one of the more "Australian" of the families interviewed in this phase. The father, originally from Singapore, studied in Melbourne from 1957 to 1964 under an educational aid scheme, the Colombo Plan, and — like many of his peers — came back to live in 1980. The mother came from Hong Kong in 1974, although the rest of her family subsequently remigrated to Singapore, Canada and the United States. Both the parents work as accountants, she on a part-time basis.

They have two teenage children living at home: a son at university and a daughter finishing secondary school. An older daughter recently has gone to live in Singapore. All the children are "ABCs" (Australian-born Chinese), or "half-baked potatoes", to use the father's terms: they speak with marked Australian accents, although they are not really accepted by Anglo-Celtic Australians, he says.

Raising these issues prompted a robust discussion about Pauline Hanson, with the mother saying: "She's like the frog in the well, like the Chinese proverb. That's the extent she can see."

In both the interviews, although the father spoke the most, the mother took an active part. With some encouragement, so did the son. When they all proffered their "mental maps" of the house, the father's did not extend beyond the living room where he said he spent most of his time, watching television. This sparked a caustic remark from the mother about her responsibilities in the rest of the house. While he was devoted to the large new television set there (complete with Foxtel pay TV cable and VCR attached), the karaoke was hers. For his part, the son also had a television in his room, and a new computer.

The father still sees Singapore as his homeland, while the mother asserts that, whether from Southeast Asia, Indochina or wherever, ultimately "All Chinese come from China". The son values his Chineseness and, although "Australianised" enough to resent perceived preferential treatment at the university for Asians, he had taken time to learn Mandarin — this in addition to the Cantonese which he had learned at home, along with his sisters. He also showed himself as knowledgeable as his father on a certain point of Chinese folklore which came up in a discussion of a Jackie Chan film.

While there were some predictable generational differences in television viewing preferences — the children named favourites such as *The Simpsons*, while the father liked the *Asian Business News* on cable and the Cantonese *WorldWatch* service on SBS as a "bit of nostalgia" — more striking was the cosmopolitan orientation of the family as a whole, even in their Chineseness. Both parents used the phrase "pretty international" to describe the range of their selections from the World Movies channel they liked on Pay TV, which is similar to how they described their social mixing ("We mix internationally — with Australians, English, Indians, Greeks"). In like vein, the son listens not just to Chinese but also to Latin American and Indonesian programs on 3ZZZ, for the music. They all enjoy the "atmosphere" of going out to the Chinatown Cinema, and the father recalled with pleasure a Singapore–Hong Kong co-produced video series which they had recently rented — reflecting the family's own diasporic origins.

This also is a family used to travel. The mother had been to the United States and Canada twice in the previous four years ("In Toronto lately, it's like a small Hong Kong. One can earn a living without speaking one word of English," she reported), while the father visits Singapore every other year. The children have travelled in their own right as well as with the parents. Patterns of telecommunications use coincide: the mother calls North America each week, while the father speaks to his mother and the daughter in Singapore with similar frequency, and the son is in daily contact with overseas friends via email at university.

HK 6: "I'm Australian. My wife too."

In this household, there is a young nuclear family. The father migrated to Australia in 1977 when he was nine years old, together with all of his immediate family. The mother came from Malaysia in 1985. Both of them grew up in the new outer suburban area where they now have their home. They have become Australian citizens, and both of their children, a boy of six and a girl of four, were born in Australia. They are not currently involved with any local community of Asians.

He works as a telecommunications consultant, she as an accounts clerk, on a part-time basis. The wife had not been at home for the initial survey visit, and did not participate in the interview on the return visit. The contact was made through researcher Audrey Yue, who had worked with the respondent a few years earlier in AsiaTV, the association involved with community television.

In the lounge, three Taoist statues look across to an enormous wall cabinet with a television, VCR, laser-disc karaoke unit, stereo and huge speakers. To one side is a work station with a Pentium computer, with which the children played during the interview.

In terms of his television news-watching habits, the respondent doesn't watch the SBS *WorldWatch* services, nor the SBS evening news, but prefers the ABC. He had neither time nor interest for *Asian Business News* on Foxtel, and let his subscription lapse. Regarding entertainment, however, he wanted to see more popular programming from Asia on SBS, and enjoyed the Hong Kong videos

("TVB stuff"), which he would borrow from his mother when she rented them. There are three televisions in the house, each with its own VCR.

Although Australian by citizenship, and appreciative of the standard of living, he says he still considers himself Chinese, and "sometimes" would like to go back to resettle in Hong Kong. He has visited there four times since 1977, but says there's no real reason to, in that all his closest relatives are in Melbourne. He has also been in Malaysia several times with his wife and children, but "can't stand it" for political reasons.

This household has a fax and Internet modem as well as a regular line with three phones. Although both the respondent and his wife call family members in their homelands, they do so much less frequently than in any of the other households studied in this phase. However, they also use fax and email for this purpose, the latter being used on a daily basis, and actually have their own family Web page for the benefit of the relatives overseas. Thus they appear to have taken advantage of what these newer technologies can offer extended families living in diasporic circumstances, rather than just using the telephone.

TW 1: Living like "astronauts"

Like the other households in this phase of the study, this one consists of Australian citizens, but they are the most recently arrived and the most diasporic in the sense that the parents at least are frequent travellers back to their nation of origin, not really having settled into Australia as their "home". They could also be said to be the "most Chinese", both in the kinds of cultural habitus or domestic environment which they have created around themselves, and in the legal sense that they all have retained their Taiwanese citizenship under dual arrangements. This is the same "flexible citizenship" discussed by Ong, and exemplified by the Chinese businessman who avers: "I can live anywhere in the world, but it must be near an airport." (cited in Clifford, 1997: 257)

From the outside, their two-storey brick house in a desirable leafy eastern suburb is distinguished by its double carved wooden doors flanked by flowerpots, in keeping with *feng shui*. While the researcher was received in a Western-style drawing room, she also saw a prayer room and another drawing room with an ancestral Buddhist altar. This and the dining room were furnished with antique inlaid rosewood furniture which had come as part of two container-loads from Taiwan. They showed their appreciation for the researcher's traditional visiting courtesies, and she noticed from the style of interaction within the family that the Confucian code of respect for elders was being followed. On the first visit, when the father was home, he was always the first to respond to questions, whether or not they were directed to him, while the mother participated on her own behalf but also mediated responses from the three adult daughters.

At the time of the second visit, the father was in Taiwan, where he spends weeks or months at a time, three or four times a year, for business reasons, while one of the daughters, the 29-year-old eldest, had taken a job in her field of business computing in Sydney. At the time of the first visit, this same daughter had just come back from Taiwan, via Singapore, where she had visited the second-eldest 27-year-old daughter who has been working there since 1996 as a food technologist. The next daughter, aged 25, is a social worker who says "Melbourne is my home" but has been back to Taiwan twice, as has the youngest, 23-year-old daughter who is doing an Arts Honours course.

The mother enjoys travelling, and visits Taiwan two or three times a year, spending up to three months at a time there. She also schedules visits to the daughter in Singapore on these trips, and brings home foodstuffs, clothes and CDs from Taiwan. Significantly, the family still maintains a house in Taiwan, where they also have many relatives. The mother says she is hopeful of the youngest daughter getting a job in London, to have a further base.

Yet, for all her jet-setting lifestyle, when it comes to media use there is an apparent generational difference between the mother and the two daughters still at home. As has been discussed in an earlier section, the only news which the mother watches is the service from Taiwan on Pay TV, while the daughters — who seem much more reconciled to their lives in Melbourne — show a more cosmopolitan sense of themselves in their choice of news. In explaining their preference for the mainstream news on SBS, one said: "SBS news is international, and we feel we are a part of this international world … We don't see ourselves as migrant, but someone who's really concerned with the world, with international affairs." However, the whole family shuns the *China Television News* on SBS *WorldWatch*, even if it is in Mandarin. It gets them "upset and angry" because of its PRC point of view, so they all remain very Taiwanese in that regard. When it comes to entertainment, there is also a consensus in favour of the general Chinese-language programming which they receive on New World — so much so that this family hardly ever hires videos, but uses their VCR only to record programs from the television.

Like two of the other households in this phase of the study, some members are actually involved in Chinese-language community media. In this case, it is the two youngest daughters still living at home, who research and present a youth-oriented program on the community access FM radio station 3ZZZ. This consists of talk about young people's concerns, Taiwanese popular music and a folk-tale segment, in which they actively seek to include stories from the various non-Han Chinese ethnic minorities. Of this involvement, they say: "That's the time you feel all Chinese."

This family has only two television sets, both in family areas, but four telephones (one a cordless, but no mobile), and a fax machine with its own dedicated line. Given the dispersal of the family, the mother and one of the daughters at home "regularly" use the fax to send collective family faxes to the distant daughters, and to the father when he is in Taiwan, as well as to other relatives there. The mother also speaks to the Sydney and Singapore daughters two or three times a week on the phone when he is away, and about once a month to other relatives in Taiwan. The daughters at home use the phone mostly for local calls to friends and for personal business, but both also have access to email outside the home. As well as for academic and professional purposes, the two sisters use email to stay in contact with friends in Taiwan — and each other, when there are matters that they can't talk about at home.

Methodological Issues

While household studies have the advantage of allowing researchers to engage with respondents in the actual setting where their domestic media consumption takes place, such research cannot help but intrude upon the private space of the home. Experience with the population at large has shown how difficult it is to obtain cooperation even for a survey at the front door on such matters (Sinclair, 1992), let alone to win the confidence of an entire household for an extended interview inside the home. Since sampling sufficient households for the survey phase had proved difficult enough, it would be understood that return visits really only could be made to those households where one or more of the researchers was known already to the householders, whether personally, by reputation or both. For example, Professor Kee Pookong, associate researcher with the project, was known in three of the households visited in the later phase, and two were the families of friends of Audrey Yue, a researcher and a principal author of the project who conducted the actual visits. Both researchers are of Southeast Asian Chinese origin. While this mode of selection of households via individual contact introduced an obvious source of bias from a formal sampling point of view, it also meant that the researchers could find their way to households in which members were for the most part interested and articulate about media, some even being personally involved in Chinese-language media in Australia, and who were also living or had lived the "floating lives" of the contemporary diasporic experience of the Chinese.

In the fieldwork, ethnographic observation included the noting of styles of family interaction, and the domestic culture of the households (such as the spatial arrangements of photographs, objects and furniture) in the rooms to which the researcher was given access. Interactive techniques enabled respondents to give their own account of their media use and familial relations, including the local, interstate and transnational routes of their telephonic and electronic communications. Participant observation took place in chatting about current events, and sharing joint experiences of migration and resettlement.

Such informal, discursive evocation of commonalities and connections was enabled only because Audrey Yue, an ethno-specific researcher carried out this part of the project. She provided the cultural capital, linguistic skills, personal experience and *guanxi* needed to gain entry to an otherwise inaccessible minority culture. Because of her "insider" and "unofficial" knowledge of this culture, she could actively mediate in the discursive interplay between the observations required for the research, and identification with the narratives of diaspora proffered by the "subjects".

In this sense, the researcher was bringing to this project the privileges and the partialities of her different subject-positions as a diasporic Chinese person in Australia. She shared with most of her interlocutors the commonalities of their different experiences of migration, and the syncretic, postcolonial, multilingual fluidity of the English language, infused with variously accented forms of Mandarin, the Taiwanese hybrid Minnanhua, and other Chinese dialects such as Hokkienese, Teochew and Cantonese. Inscribed upon her immigrant memories was the social power of her education that strategically allowed her to implement the tools of the coloniser. As the unauthentic native from Singapore caught between the legacies of Western imperialism and the autocratic regime of a neo-Confucian sovereignty, her "Chineseness" was also acknowledged as an experience constituted by a particular diasporic reality.

In this sense, the relationship between the Chinese interlocutors and the researcher, in her curious objectified subject-position of the native informant as ethnographer-observer-observed-translator-transcriber, is discursively framed by the contingent meaning of ethnicity (Wilson and Yue, 1996). Following Rey Chow's suggestion (1993) that part of the task of articulating diaspora is to undo the submission to one's ethnicity as the absolute signified, it can be argued that the methodology in this chapter begins from the assumption that "Chineseness" is not a given, but something to be tactically mobilised.

Floating Lives

The ethnographic phase of the study brings out the particularities of individual households in their moral economies and modes of adaptiveness to the experience of diaspora. When contrasted with the relatively anxious and socially isolated Mainland Chinese respondents who, as revealed in the survey phase, are closer to the rather traditional image of the immigrant as a perplexed victim seeking to cope in an alien culture, the households in the ethnographic phase show how very different the experience of diaspora can be. In the first place, it seems clear that, at least for some families, diaspora should not be taken to be synonymous with immigration, and certainly not with exile. One thing the ethnographic households have in common is the ability to travel — to visit and revisit the homeland or, even if not there (as in the case of VC 2, the family from Vietnam), to visit relatives who have spread into other parts of the world.

Most striking are the parents in the Taiwanese family (TW 1), who, in a cultural sense, have never really had to leave Taiwan, yet can savour the benefits of both home and host countries on a rotating basis — the "astronaut" way of life known in Taiwan as *tai kung fei jen* (Kotkin, 1992: 168). The portability of their Chineseness provides a luxurious example of Clifford's argument that "culture" has as much to do with travel as it has with being rooted to a particular place (Clifford, 1997: 24–25). For the mother in particular, being able to access the same Taiwanese news service whether she is in Melbourne or Taipei offers some centredness and routine to her mobile existence.

Even in the other, much less ostentatiously diasporic, households, travel to the homeland or to relatives overseas every few years is an established part of the style of life they have made for themselves in Australia. Perhaps it is even a priority, given the particularly strong sense of family traditional amongst Chinese, but in a mood of matter-of-fact adaptation to the realities of diaspora, rather than any sense of enforced loss or displacement.

The active use of telecommunications seems to be pursued in a similar vein. The only one of the ethnographic households which did not report making phone calls to relatives overseas on at least a weekly basis was the one which instead used email for this purpose every day, and also maintained its own Web page with family news and photos for the homeland relatives (HK 6). While the telephone is the traditional mode of communication which sustains social relationships of all kinds, through not just diasporic but most forms of both permanent and temporary displacement, there seems to be a generational shift towards email, at least in these households. Apart from the young adults in the household just mentioned, the users of email in the other households were the teenage son in HK 4 who communicated daily with friends overseas, and the daughters in their twenties in the astronaut household who used email not only for that same purpose, but also to communicated with each other.

The households all have a strong orientation towards media as well as telecommunications use. While this is explicable at one level as the epistephilia of the diasporic home, it is also indicative of the outward-looking, cosmopolitan ethos which forms a major part of the cultural capital and moral economies of these households: the writer with the home theatre system who watches news in Chinese on SBS when he is in Melbourne, and CNN in English when he is in Germany is the clearest example (VC 2). Significantly, he and his wife were active in the community television association AsiaTV, as the man in the household with the Web page also had been, while the daughters in the astronaut household ran their own program on community radio. It is worth remembering that it is media-oriented cosmopolitans such as these people who form at least part of the audience for SBS and other more specialised services. While it might be objected that the selection of such people is a distortion due to the sampling procedure, it is worth remembering that even the most recent immigrants of Chinese origin tend to be more educated than those from other sources — and in any event, as Clifford (1997) observes of anthropological "informants":

> A great many of these interlocutors, complex individuals routinely made to speak for "cultural" knowledge, turn out to have their own "ethnographic" proclivities and interesting histories of travel. Insider–outsiders, good translators and explicators, they've been around. (1997: 19)

3

Popular Media of the Vietnamese Diaspora

Stuart Cunningham and Tina Nguyen

The Vietnamese diaspora is arguably unique in this study, because of its historical roots in refugee-exile circumstances. Being originally refugees and only lately immigrants makes the Vietnamese peoples in the Western world very aware of the pull between maintaining their original cultures and adapting to their new host cultures. They are thus most similar, of any Asian-Australian group, to Naficy's (1993) Iranian exilic community. They contrast in the recency of their diasporic history with, for example, the Chinese community in Melbourne. They also contrast with the Chinese and Indian communities in their part-reliance on non-Vietnamese audiovisual media, because the Vietnamese industry is very small and there is a negligible export dynamic, but most importantly because most overseas Vietnamese reject the output of the "homeland" as fatally compromised by being produced under a communist regime.

The Vietnamese is by far the largest refugee community in Australia. For most, "home" is a denied category while "the regime" continues in power, so media networks — especially music videos — operate to connect the dispersed exilic Vietnamese communities. Small business entrepreneurs produce low-budget music video mostly out of southern California, which are taken up within the fan circuits of America, Australia, Canada, France and elsewhere. The internal cultural conflicts within the communities centre on the felt need to maintain pre-revolutionary Vietnamese heritage and traditions; find a negotiated place within a more mainstreamed culture; or engage in the formation of distinct hybrid identities around the appropriation of dominant Western popular cultural forms. These three cultural positions or stances are dynamic and mutable, but the main debates are constructed around them, and we will use them as a way of organising our analysis of the cultural and media environment.

This chapter will treat the media businesses that specifically service the Vietnamese diaspora; the media consumed; and the active appropriations made of media. Between 1995 and 1999, business interviews were conducted at the headquarters of the main Vietnamese music video production companies in Westminster, Orange County and some of their distribution representatives in Bankstown, New South Wales; several video store proprietors in Brisbane; and with newspaper editors in Sydney. Interviews with several performers and other artists who make a living from live and recorded performance and music video activity (discussed in "Vietnamese Diasporic Video", below) were also conducted in person in Southern California, Sydney and Brisbane and by email.

For audience response, the "affinity group" methods used were appropriate to tracking forms of fan and less intense consumption of the central media. This involved the research team establishing initial contacts through professional and community associations, workplaces and personal relationships, and then working out from these by "referral-on" to establish an adequate base of diverse consumption patterns and relations to media. Semi-structured interviews with community leaders and in households; focus groups assembled through community associations and through a special school for recent migrants; and participant observation of festivals, concerts, celebrations and karaoke sessions, together with television and video viewing in homes in Brisbane, Sydney and Westminster, were all used in the course of the research.

The most detailed audience response research, in Brisbane, was conducted with two families who were first-wave refugees and whose members held some responsible positions in the community; a brother and sister (and their regular clientele in the coffee shop) who are extremely well-informed fans and who run a grocery store and an adjacent coffee shop where karaoke and music video are played; a large group of recently arrived teenagers on the family reunion program assembled through their school; and a working class group of youth, many of whom were unemployed and who had had limited education. We will use the term "respondents" or "informants" in most cases when referring to activities undertaken or insights offered. Sometimes this will be supplemented by a description of the social location of the respondent(s). In a few cases, we will use the actual names of people who have engaged very strongly with the project, providing richly textured responses and insights that they were happy to share publicly.

Basic Demography

The Vietnamese have had a long history of migration within their immediate region, but a very limited history of migration outside of Vietnam. By 1975 only about 100 000 Vietnamese were living outside Vietnam. Australia's earliest record of Vietnamese migration goes back to August 1920, when a group of 38 Vietnamese aboard a ship transporting labourers blew off course and ended up in Townsville. Australia next encountered Vietnamese in the country as part of the Colombo Plan from the late 1950s. By 1975, 335 Colombo Plan students were attending Australian universities along with some 130 private school students.

However, from 1965–75, during the height of the Vietnam (or "American") War, over half of Vietnam's population was displaced internally, and now the Vietnamese diaspora numbers something over 2 million Vietnam-born throughout the world. (The current population in Vietnam is 76 million, whereas in 1975 it was estimated that the population of Vietnam was 60 million.) To this, of course, should be added the second generation — those born to Vietnamese parents in the host countries — whose numbers are notoriously not reliable because census data collection in several countries follows widely variant protocols, but are estimated at at least half a million.

About half of the total diaspora is domiciled in the United States, with significant population centres in Orange County, San Jose, Texas, Minneapolis, Washington and Houston. Other major host countries include France, Canada, Germany and The Netherlands, as well as Australia. The 1996 Census figures show a little over 151 000 Vietnam-born people in Australia, to which numbers should be added a substantial second generation. Given the fraught history of the treatment of refugees in the immediate East Asian and Southeast Asian region, it is not surprising that there are very few Vietnamese resettled in the country's immediate region. Overall, there are about 70 population centres across the world with some Vietnamese presence outside the "homeland".

It is a small diaspora but one which has had a very high profile internationally because of the implication of major Western countries in the conditions which led to the creation of the group: the US and French involvements in Vietnam, together with the crucial nature of the Vietnam War for the course of international relations and ideological alignments in the 1960s and the 1970s. Also, the nature of escape — particularly by boat — from the homeland in the late 1970s and early 1980s constituted one of that period's ongoing international media events. The acceptance of Vietnamese refugees, including the so-called "boat people", during this period was the first major test of Australia's liberalised, post-"white Australia", immigration policies, and arguably its major humanitarian project in response to war and refugee displacement since World War II (Thomas, 1997: 274–75).

It is also a very recent diaspora, with virtually the entire overseas refugee and immigrant population resettlement occurring since 1975, and the median period of residence in Australia in 1995 being nine years (Viviani, 1996: 83). There has been an exceptionally high level of attention paid in the media to the Vietnamese population in Australia, despite the very small size of this population:

> The strong profile of the Vietnamese population in the broader Australian community is partly due to their relatively spatial concentration in our largest cities, high unemployment rates and comparatively low levels of English proficiency. There is, however, a danger in stereotyping the attributes of the Vietnam-born, as a superficial examination of their dominant socio-economic features can mask the more complex nature of spatial mobility and status differentiation ... it has become clear that, among the Vietnam-born, there is a persistent pattern of accelerating socio-economic diversity, along with important class, status and ethnic differences. (Thomas, 1997: 275)

Further indicators of the specialness of the group are brought forward by Viviani (1996). The Vietnamese are over-represented in university attendance, with twice as many of those born in Vietnam at a university than the Australian-born population, but they are also over-represented in gaols, with longer sentences for more serious crimes. The rate of consumption of and reliance on video and television is to some extent related to rates of under- and unemployment (Viviani, 1996: 111).

It is widely known as an exilic diaspora, although the proportion of the overseas Vietnamese who began their resettlement as refugees has declined all through the 1990s as the Doi Moi (Renovation) policies of the Vietnam government have permitted structured legal emigration since 1989. In the mid-1990s in Australia, only around 30 per cent of the population were originally refugees (Viviani, 1996: 83). The Vietnamese have arrived in Australia (from 1975 to the present) in four main waves. The first two, in the mid- and late 1970s and the early 1980s, were refugee intakes, including the so-called boat people. The latter of these refugee movements was predominantly of the ethnic Chinese, whose small-business interests were specifically targeted by the communists for expropriation and nationalisation. The last two major waves, in the mid-1980s and early 1990s, were mostly immigrant intakes, predominantly under Australian government immigration policies of family reunion. When the Australia-born group is added (in 1995, there were about 180 000 Vietnam-born or second generation), it becomes clear that the proportion of the population who were refugees/exiles is rapidly declining. Also, since the 1986 Census, there has been a dramatic rise in older age groups due to family reunion, and thus a growing difference between recency of arrival (older age groups and relative lack of English proficiency) and generational difference (the young are predominantly Australian-born and have experienced greatest acculturation to the host country).

Over 30 per cent of the Vietnam-born population claim Chinese ancestry (the ethnic Chinese) and, while it is not readable from Census data, there are sizeable proportions of the population who have undergone double and triple migratory experiences, having migrated internally from the north to the south or central regions as a result of Ho Chi Minh's Communist assumption of power in 1954 and then moved again out of the country during the 1970s. Thus there are significant differences along axes of generation, ethnicity, region of the home country, education and class, and recency of arrival and conditions under which arrival took place amongst this small population.

"Structured in Dominance": The Vietnamese Media Diet

The Vietnamese media diet is "structured in dominance": while mainstream media offer little of relevance and can be perceived as, in one respondent's calmly diplomatic word, "unfriendly" in the way they portray the community, there are therefore of necessity a range of alternative media that in varying degrees service community information and entertainment needs and desires. So, with an emphasis on agency in media use, the study of the interpretative community at work might start with those forms which Vietnamese audiences have least access to and control over — dominant broadcast and print media — move to specialist broadcasters and to language-specific print forms such as ethnic newspapers, but stress those electronic media which embrace both information and entertainment and which are engaged with most strongly as indicators of popular cultural capital: Hong Kong video product and Vietnamese live variety shows and music video — the latter a form unique to the diaspora as audiovisual media made by and for the diaspora.

The Televisual Mainstream

Most of those respondents who worked full-time asserted that they were too busy to watch broadcast television regularly; and of those who did watch (mostly under- or unemployed and school-aged young people), it was game shows, soaps and daytime talk shows that were most regularly mentioned as broadcast television fare. Substantial survey-style research has been done on ethnic minority preferences and viewing patterns which report largely negative outcomes for broadcasters' service to these communities. In spite of the development of various "Advisory Notes", including one on Cultural Diversity, by the Federation of Australian Commercial Televisions Stations (FACTS) since 1994, there is strong, ongoing evidence for television and commercial radio to be perceived as a distinctly hostile, and at best benignly neglectful, environment for Asian-Australians.

While studies of the mainstream press indicate a broader range of representation, and a greater possibility of stories with positive representation (Pittam, 1993; Pittam and McKay, 1991), these are based on content analysis and cover both soft and hard news genres, with "human interest" stories demonstrating the most positive representations. Studies exclusively of hard news genres are uniformly critical of mainstream coverage of Vietnamese-Australians (Loo, 1994; Thomas, 1996). The work of Hartley and McKee on the "Indigenous Public Sphere" — which constructs as strongly positive an account of Aboriginal agency in the Australian mediascape as possible — opens up importantly innovative avenues in a depressingly predictable field, but even in this work there is a recognition that soft news has been more open to real cultural diversity than hard news genres (Hartley, 1999a; Hartley and McKee, 2000). The field of mainstream media remains virtually a no-go area for Asian-Australians in terms of directly inclusive invitations to identification and engagement.

Perceptions studies (rather than content analysis, either quantitative or qualitative), which seek opinion from representative groupings within the minorities, tend also to produce uniformly critical outcomes. The most extensive of these in Australia is *Nextdoor Neighbours, A Report for the Office of Multicultural Affairs on Ethnic Group Discussions of the Australian Media* (Coupe et al., 1993). Findings from studies of this type are replicated in similar research elsewhere — for example, in the mid-1990s by the Independent Television Commission (ITC) of the United Kingdom, which found large percentages of ethnic minority groups in Great Britain arguing that mainstream television was biased against ethnic minorities and their religions and in favour of the police force. Seventy-six per cent of Asians, 88 per cent of African-Caribbeans and 52 per cent of the "main" (ethnically undifferentiated) sample agreed that "all too often television portrays negative stereotypes about different ethnic minority groups". The research concluded that "the overwhelming impression … is that viewers from ethnic minorities consider terrestrial television to be 'white' television" (Hanley, 1995: 17).

The key mediating institution between the mainstream and specialist mediascapes is SBS. We have considered the broad structural position of the SBS in Chapter 1, and also the significant role its *WorldWatch* programming plays in Chapter 2. The structural limitations of SBS Radio, and other community-language radio stations in the community broadcasting sector, are that they can provide very small windows for each separate "community" language and are locked into the problems and politics of limited time and resource allocation in a regime of spectrum scarcity. As information sources and language maintainers, SBS and community radio continue to play significant roles for mostly older age groups. However, in 1999, with an estimated four hours per week on community radio, one hour per day on SBS radio, and about 1.5 hours a week on C31, the community television station (if the signal is receivable), community broadcasting barely begins to address the media needs of the Vietnamese community in western Sydney, the largest in the country. A representative of the Vietnamese Women's Association in Queensland told us that:

> About 90 per cent of older Vietnamese listen to Vietnamese radio or hear about news and views in the community in Queensland and the other places in Australia. SBS Radio serves a very important role in the community, people always listen. 4EB [the community radio station in Brisbane] is good but not enough, only one hour at inconvenient time. SBS TV too is very good but also good for many Australians. The people watch SBS movies to read English because it is easier than to hear it.

The adequacy of Vietnamese representation on SBS-TV brings into sharp relief the structural limitations of the service and the politics of particularly refugee diasporas discussed in Chapter 1. In the period 1992–97, only nineteen Vietnamese-language programs were screened, or were purchased to be screened, by SBS. Most were single-episode documentaries, with the rare exception of a feature film such *The Scent of Green Papaya*. SBS points out that the country has a very underdeveloped production base; there is negligible emphasis on program export (as the Vietnamese language diaspora, compared with the Chinese or the Indian, is opposed to the consumption of homeland material); and there are quality control concerns regarding program suitability for Australian broadcast standards (Edols, 1995; Webb, 1997). Overall, though, the predominating SBS position is that there are structural constraints on programming and purchase policy governed by its charter commitment to multicultural programming for the whole Australian population, not specific sections of it.

The size of the corpus, though tiny, can still attract strong criticism of the screening of many items on the basis that they are barely-disguised "propaganda" for the regime. Documentaries such as

Vietnam Church and State (screened in 1993) and *Women, the Strength of Vietnam* (screened in 1996) attracted criticism for this reason. While a feature such as *Cyclo* (screened in 1996), by Paris-based expatriate Tran Anh Hung, was "acceptable" to those overseas Vietnamese who may have watched it insofar as it portrays the desperation of the contemporary Vietnamese underclass, an acclaimed international art feature such as *Indochine* can be suspect. First-wave refugee Trinh's political criticism of this feature was that it centres on narrative justification for the emergence of Vietcong resistance to the French occupation and, because its narrative ceases at the point at which communist anti-colonialism can be regarded as undeniably progressive nationalism, valorises the origins of the regime from which the refugees ultimately had to flee.

Of course, the charter of SBS-TV, as discussed in Chapter 1, does not address language and cultural maintenance as such, so it is hard to imagine a scenario within the parameters of its single-channel service where the situation described above could change significantly. On the other hand, community newspapers are largely defined by their cultural maintenance role (albeit with significant variations), and are major established media formats designed specifically and exclusively for the community.

Community Newspapers

The first cultural position — that of heritage maintenance — is primarily centred on the ideological monitoring role of maintaining the salience of the anti-communist originary stance foundational to the diaspora. Community-language newspapers are to a large extent controlled by established figures of the first and second wave who were refugees and members of the South Vietnam power elites. As such, they remain powerful voices maintaining the currency of the originating acts and reasons for separation from the homeland. It is not surprising, therefore, that the readership of community language newspapers is generationally skewed towards the older, original refugees and the less English-proficient segments of the population.

The Vietnamese community press, like most print media serving more recent immigrant groups (the most comprehensive analytical study of the ethnic press is Bell et al., 1991), is characterised by an editorial model of strong, often strident partisanship. In effect, many community newspapers contribute to the continued liminalisation of everyday life for their readerships. In this respect, they work on a press model followed normatively by most newspapers up to the end of the nineteenth century, and which continues in many European countries. The development of normative objectivity as a governing principle for professional journalism ("Our reporters do not cover stories from their point of view. They cover them from nobody's point of view." — CBS News President from the 1970s, Richard S. Salant, quoted in Cunningham and Miller, 1994: 35) is meant to supplant the partisan model — and it has done so to some extent in ethnic newspaper production in Australia for those communities which are well established over several generations, typically the southern European communities (Kissane, 1988: 32).

As a mark of the partisan model of the press, there is a plethora of ethnic community newspapers in Australia, and the Vietnamese press is no exception. In Australia, from the early days of the Colombo Plan through to the present, there is estimated to have been a total of 92 different types of Vietnamese print publication with some claim to a broad readership (Tran, 1995). While a sizeable proportion of readers expect the newspapers to reinforce the rationale for escape and exile from the homeland, and to provide an information base to facilitate cultural maintenance in Australia (Tran, 1995), there has been differentiation of editorial focus and emphasis during the 1990s in keeping with the shifting demographic profile of the community.

The leading papers with a continuing explicit political refugee editorial line are *Viet Luan* (The Vietnamese Herald) in Sydney and *Nhan Quyen* (The Human Rights Daily) in Melbourne. *Viet Luan* is the main "quality" weekly which has been running continuously since 1983. Established by Nguyen Chanh Si, who was a lawyer in Vietnam before 1975, currently the newspaper is owned jointly by a consortium of local Sydney businesspeople. The typical editorial content balance is one-fifth Vietnamese news, two-fifths Australian news, a community information update and an entertainment, sport and miscellaneous section, while at least half the paper is devoted to advertising. Its influence transcends its 14 000 national circulation. *Nhan Quyen* was established in 1982 by another former lawyer, Long Quan.

The paper with the widest readership, and one that has developed away from the political refugee editorial line, is *Chieu Duong* (The Sunrise Daily). Established in 1980, and based in Cabramatta, it went daily in 1986 and remains the only daily Vietnamese newspaper in Australia. *Chieu Duong* was set up by Nhat Giang, who had established newspapers in San Jose and in France as well. It is run by Nhat Giang's son, Nhi Giang, in the late 1990s a member of the New South Wales Ethnic Affairs Commission. It has a weekday circulation of 15 000, with the Saturday edition going to 18–19 000. Editorially as well as in format, *Chieu Duong* is tabloid, minimising political content and emphasising human-interest, society and entertainment news. Other papers include *Chuong Saigon* (Saigon Bell), which was first published in 1979 and ran to 1993 as mostly a weekly magazine, though for a time it was a biweekly.

The broadest public sites of ideological monitoring are indeed these newspapers. The papers have historically been closely aligned with the Vietnamese Community Organisation, the peak national lobby for the community, which vows constant vigilance against the Vietnam government and its attempts to compromise the integrity of the anti-Communist refugee stance. Attempts by members of the community to have this stance softened — in the interests of either a principled recognition of a changed environment since Doi Moi (Renovation) policies from the late 1980s, or the pragmatics of the advantages of being able to do business or facilitate family reunions — are met with harsh rebuke (see Thomas, 1996: 143). The exception to this is *Chieu Duong*, which largely avoids these issues of community division, instead facilitating a community identity around shopping, social scandal and entertainment.

A typical example of newspaper heritage maintenance at the time of writing was a campaign against SBS-TV adding Hanoi TV News to its *WorldWatch* news schedule — programming discussed in Chapter 2. *Viet Luan*'s edition of 19 February 1999 (pp. 30, 50) editorialises vehemently against such a proposed move, saying that the community has "patiently put up with the screening by SBS of poorly produced, poorly sub-titled Vietnamese programs from Hanoi that often carry naked propaganda messages". But proposing to add a daily news bulletin is seen as "go[ing] too far", and the community is asked to mobilise around a petition.

Some of the importance, as well as the ambivalence, accorded the press is expressed in this comment from a young woman who, though her parents had been forced to leave in 1978 because of the communists' nationalisation of their business, was not wedded to maintaining a reflex anti-communism stance:

> Read Asian newspaper just once a week to keep in touch ... not very true ... too far away now and they don't know now ... yes I agree with them Communists bad before, really nasty ... but now the way they run the country is far better because they can look after themselves. The Vietnamese papers don't know any more that's why I don't read that part [overseas politics] ... I just read the community part ... a lot of news I can't understand in Australian paper ... 50–50 I understand that so I read the Asian paper to understand better the politics and economy story ... mostly read about what happen in Australia ... like budget ... I don't understand in Australian paper.

Mandy Thomas (1996: 145) compares mainstream and community newspaper discourse about the Vietnamese:

> The Vietnamese press, while attempting to secure for its readership a sense of control and empowerment, is often overtly political, as well as being a promoter of immutable and uniform images of Vietnamese people in exile. While the mainstream press images the Vietnamese as ... intrusive and destructive within Australian spaces, the Vietnamese press is often making a plea to its readers to turn their focus of attention beyond Australia, to the past in Vietnam, and to a new and different future in that country.

"The New York of the East": Hong Kong Attractions

The structure of diasporic distribution of Chinese language video (film and television), and also some of the close intersections of Chinese media and its consumption by Indochinese in Australia, have been covered in Chapter 2. Coming at this intersection from the side of the Vietnamese communities, it is clear that, along with Vietnamese diasporic music video, the audiovisual product that is the site for most intense engagement is Hong Kong film and television. Compared with Hong Kong audiovisual influences, cultural anthropologist Mandy Thomas argues, Euro-American cultural influences are "almost insignificant" in Vietnamese-Australian households (personal email communication, 12 December 1996).

It is these two bodies of entertainment product that are drawn on as a series of (popular) cultural debates are played out in the overseas communities. Very lively cultural work — around the three axes of maintenance, adaptation/negotiation and hybridity; and perceptions of popular culture as frivolous and lowbrow on the one hand and affirmative and empowering on the other — is in play in Vietnamese engagement with both these sets of screen media. The tendency is for older, less educated people, and those with less English-language cultural capital, to embrace Vietnamese diasporic video and performance, particularly in their heritage maintenance role, and in their cultural negotiation role in terms of the middle-of-the-road production that forms the large majority of its output. Members of this same grouping are also consumers of Hong Kong television series, but not film. Vietnamese diasporic video is also strongly embraced by well-educated young adults as a form of contemporary cultural assertion — they are those members of the diaspora who most distinctively have created a fan culture around the product.

Young Vietnamese — particularly teenagers and boys, and to a lesser extent those who may have less education — embrace Hong Kong film on video as compatible with their particular youth culture. This may be influenced by the need to carve out cultural space away from the Vietnamese family unit and also because consuming Hong Kong product doesn't require Vietnamese language skills (even if there are Vietnamese subtitles). This is a major form of cultural *negotiation* rather than hybridity — it creates space for a distinctive youth culture that is neither (traditional) Vietnamese nor Anglo and attracts, as Hong Kong action film does more generally (Wilson and Yue, 1996), dismissive rejection by mainland Chinese as well and can be used to mark out a space of rebellion from the expectations of cultural consumption for Vietnamese youth. Vietnamese diasporic music video can be eschewed by these same young men and boys as too embarrassingly middle-brow and "ultra-Vietnamese", but also by many urbane professionals for exactly the same reason! The third position, that of assertive hybridity, is exclusively played out around Vietnamese diasporic music video and a small group of New Wave performers and their followings.

Most specialist East Asian video stores in Australia, whatever else they carry, stock Hong Kong television product from either of the main international suppliers, TVB or ATV — typically game shows, variety shows, and series and serials. Hong Kong action films also feature prominently. By volume of titles rented, television series are more popular amongst Vietnamese than feature films. There are a very small number of video titles sometimes available from Saigon television (through a small distribution company, Saigon Video), and some Taiwan movies are available subtitled in Vietnamese, but Vietnamese people prefer to watch TV shows or movies made in Hong Kong with Chinese actors and contemporary story lines. They tend to shun Vietnamese television on video due to poor production quality, outdated story lines and communist subtext. They feel anything that comes out of Vietnam will be, in the words of various informants, "vetted by the government" and therefore "contaminated with communist ideology" — or at the very least of inferior quality. No one who dismissed Vietnamese product for these reasons also regarded the Hong Kong product as being ideologically motivated. In this, they seem to share the general industry perception: "Born out of a competitive market with cultural *laissez-faire*, the serials are fast paced, melodramatic, apolitical and entertaining." (Chan, 1996: 141)

These Vietnamese and Taiwanese videos do find a small niche market among older men and women who have been unable to learn English or adapt as well as Vietnamese in their forties or younger. These people have memories of Vietnam that predate the 1970s, and they tend to seek out Vietnamese folk tales or operas or Taiwanese television dramas which are set in a rural or village life, generally in a mythical past. They may even view Vietnamese television available through Saigon Video, just in order to see Vietnamese sets and actors. It is a phenomenon found by Naficy (1993: 42–43) among the Iranian exiles:

> B movies and videos freeze fetishized images of Iran in the prerevolutionary periods, rekindling viewers' nostalgic memories of their homeland and helping them to *relive* their experience of viewing films in Iran ... they are viewed as souvenirs of an inaccessible homeland, irretrievable memories of childhood, a former prosperous lifestyle, and a centred sense of self.

Younger Vietnamese tend to be dismissive of this nostalgia for an unrecoverable or purely mythic past, and most Vietnamese families are more interested in Hong Kong long-form episodic drama as their soap opera fare of choice. Hong Kong, both the "imagined nation" and the media product, has been embraced — of course, not just by Vietnamese — as "the New York of the East", an Archimedean space equidistant between West and East (for discussion of the absorption of Western influence into Hong Kong broadcast television, see Lee, 1991), an Eastern image of modernity between a denigrated/ irrecoverable homeland and a Western setting in which they find themselves as an "Asian minority". This material is consumed because it provides settings where Asian faces and values predominate. Certainly Vietnamese speak of Hong Kong as being culturally "other" to them, and this is usually spoken of in the context of being frequently perceived as socially inferior within Asian pecking orders — an experience ambivalently created or reinforced by many refugee Vietnamese spending their first long months or even years of "freedom" in Lantau, the huge refugee camp on Hong Kong territory.

But the appeal lies in the fact that they are not as "othered" in Hong Kong media as the white Western culture that they find themselves living in. Punning on geographical, as well as cultural, proximity, Thuy, a well-educated community worker and educator, said: "It's close *enough* to Vietnam." Interlocutors often claimed to like these videos simply because they didn't have to struggle with language (for many, their Chinese language skills were adequate, together with irregular subtitling into English or Vietnamese). Clearly, though, the representation of Asians as hegemonic can be read as of equal appeal, particularly within Anglo host cultures where Asian peoples are still the subject of ongoing racist exclusion and attack. In viewing Asian videos, they are at least not being written out of existence, as is their experience in viewing Australian television.

Apart from these generic characteristics, there have been a number of Vietnamese characters, storylines and personnel in Hong Kong cinema and television. Producer and director Tsui Hark is Vietnamese, and has spoken of his thematic preoccupations being influenced by his status as a refugee and of the parallels between Vietnam under communism and the incorporation of Hong Kong into China — an allegorical but also political gesture regularly raised by Vietnamese fans of Hong Kong cinema and television. There are hero figures in features that are depicted as Vietnamese in origin, such as Mark in the cult films *A Better Tomorrow 1, 2* and *3*. Narratives about the plight of refugees are featured in, for example, Ann Hui's *The Story of Woo-Viet* and *Boat People*, and there are films with characters based on the Ah-Chan persona, a refugee from Vietnam who is reunited with or adopted by Hong Kong relatives.

The most popular Hong Kong video material amongst Vietnamese falls into two distinct interest areas. One is in action adventure/ martial arts; the other in family melodrama. Knowledge and interest in the first is found predominantly amongst boys and young men whose pleasure mainly derives from the representation of superhuman skills in martial arts. This aspect of Chinese tradition, like so much of it also very much part of Vietnamese culture due to millennia of Chinese cultural influence over and in Vietnam, is "owned" as their own culture through this sense of shared heritage, but also by being transformed into a contemporary generic "Asian" context.

The genre is characterised by stylised hyper-violence and by melodramatic, unequivocally heroic male characters. One Vietnamese male teenager interviewed suggested that these hero figures act very much as role models and fantasies about fathers who are now absent due to war or exile, or who have been rendered socially and professionally marginal, and therefore marginal in the family, within the host culture. And their textual violence was often sharply defended in sociological and psychological terms of the Vietnamese community having experienced social violence beyond that of the general Anglo population. Social violence, as well as textual violence, is often offered as a political allegory of anti-communism by young Vietnamese in trouble with the law (Smith and Tarallo, 1995; Thomas, 1996: 144).

The ambivalence of storylines such as that in the popular Hong Kong feature *The Bodyguard from Beijing*, where numerous references are made to the looming reunification of China and Hong Kong, can be read allegorically by Vietnamese as parallelling their quixotic opposition to communism while it inevitably continues in power in the homeland. Communist military discipline is pitted against Hong Kong's *laissez-faire* Western consumerism and jokes are made at the expense of the Chinese police working for the British force. However, the Beijing bodyguard, in reprises of the Kevin Costner vehicle *Bodyguard* or *Someone to Watch Over Me*, triumphs in the end and achieves a kind of *rapprochement* between mainland and island.

Several of our interlocutors mentioned the burden of being the "perfect citizen" in the host country. (As Ghassan Hage argues in *White Nation*, the discourse of "worry" about the legitimacy, adaptability or disruptiveness of "Third World-looking" migrants is so pervasive that "If there is a single important, subjective feeling behind this book, it is that I, and many people like me, are sick of 'worried' White Australians" (Hage, 1998: 10).) They have experienced the effects of concerted media campaigns "worrying" about the community and their knock-on effects at street and community level, such as the killing of John Newman in Cabramatta (see Thomas, 1996: Ch. 6; Loo, 1994). "The entire Vietnamese community wears the brunt of this witchhunt," said one respondent. Hong Kong cartoon-like hyper-violence allows a fantasmic space for boys and young men outside the often-crushing internal expectations of the Confucian family and the external expectations of a watching and worrying world.

More popular as family entertainment are Hong Kong television serials and series from TVB and ATV. These are limited-episode series requiring the viewer to rent episodes in order and screen them either over several consecutive nights or over, say, a month two or three nights a week. Each video typically has three episodes dubbed on to it. Both the form of this video rental and its content (television programming rather than feature films) are quite distinct from the typical patterns of mainstream rental, indicating that there is significant substitution of the broadcast television schedule by a video-constructed diet that provides a sense of the reliability and "dailiness" derived typically from a such a schedule.

European Australians normally rent movies on video once or twice a week; rental of television series or any other long-form release is very marginal. Video rental figures for 1996 provided by the Video Industry Distributors Association suggest 62 per cent of Australia's VCR homes rent at least once a month with a minority of much younger "videoheads" renting up to six titles a week. However, the Asian video store proprietors and desk workers interviewed for this study confirmed that a characteristic of immigrant communities was high use of video. Several said it was not abnormal for customers to rent up to ten or more video cassettes a week, at least half of which contain three episodes per tape of a mid-run TVB or ATV series.

In a series of interviews and participant observations of family and individual rental and viewing of Hong Kong long-form fiction drama over recent years, shows like *Before Dawn, Kindred Spirits, Nothing to Declare, Plain Love* and *It Runs in the Family* — family melodramas from TVB or ATV, some subtitled in Vietnamese — were often mentioned as favourites. *It Runs in the Family* is a comic melodrama of a family separated by circumstance, and their attempts to reunite. The comedy is based on the fact that the twin brothers who were separated at a very young age actually live in the same household with the mother, their true relationship only perceived by the viewer. The mother and one brother continue to search for the other brother/son, even though he is already living with them as a boarder. An intruder answers an advertisement seeking the missing brother/son. The viewer's frustration is amplified by this false brother's claim to the family. The father is absent.

Participants spoke consistently of enjoying/identifying with the similarities between such a classic melodramatic narrative structure and their experiences of displacement and family fracturing. Looking back, the tragedies inherent in the often totally arbitrary nature of success or failure to keep families together during escape and relocation can be distanced through comic melodrama. Even the stock melodramatic trope of the false/assumed identity was woven in as memorable in terms of the need to dissemble or hide one's own or loved ones' identity under communism and/or in attempting to escape from it.

Almost without exception, participants spoke of the importance of familial ties and the difficulty of maintaining them in a host country that threatens established hierarchies and traditions. Marie Gillespie, in her discussions of television soaps, and particularly the use of *Neighbours* within the Punjabi community in Southall, emphasises the:

therapeutic effects of the mildly cathartic narrative resolutions to be found in soaps. Although many parents feel that their values are undermined by soaps like *Neighbours*, they can exploit the situation to reinforce traditional norms and values, or to renegotiate them with their children. Similarly, their children may affirm, or challenge, parental values around the TV set ... In using and interpreting soaps, young people are constantly comparing and contrasting their own social worlds with those on screen. (Gillespie 1993: 31)

Like Gillespie's teenage Punjabis, who creatively "misread" the household structures of the fictional universe of *Neighbours* as being like their own extended families in order to use the soap opera as a platform for working through issues of control and authority, so the stock melodramatic device of mistaken/misplaced identity in a family seeking reunification is "usefully" misread as a diaspora metaphor.

Vietnamese Diasporic Video

The live variety shows, and music video productions based on and arising from them, produced by Vietnamese-owned and operated companies based in Southern California and exported to all overseas communities, are the only media form unique to the diaspora as audiovisual media made by and for the diaspora. This media form is unlike the Croatian and Macedonian diasporic video analysed by Kolar-Panov (1997), which comprised amateur video letters. Nor is it of the same dimensions as that studied by Gillespie (1993), which was India-sourced video fiction or mainstream broadcast product. It certainly bears many similarities to the commercial and variety-based cultural production of Iranian television in Los Angles studied by Naficy, not least because Vietnamese variety show and music video production is also centred in the Los Angeles conurbation. The Vietnamese grouped there are not as numerous or rich as Naficy's Iranians and so have not developed the extent of the business infrastructure to support the range and depth of media activity recounted in *The Making of Exile Cultures*. The business infrastructure of Vietnamese audiovisual production is structured around a small number of small businesses operating on low margins. It is, as Kolar Panov (1997: 31) dubs ethnic minority video circuits as they are perceived from outside, a "shadow system", operating in parallel to the majoritarian system, with few industry linkages and very little crossover of performer or audience.

To be exilic means not — or, at least, not "officially" — being able to draw on the contemporary cultural production of the home country. Indeed, it means actively denying its existence in a dialectical process of mutual disauthentification (Carruthers, 1999). The Vietnam government proposes that the *Viet Kieu* (the appellation for Vietnamese overseas which carries a pejorative connotation) are fatally Westernised, whereas the diasporic population propose that the homeland population has been de-ethnicised through, ironically, the wholesale adoption of an alien (Western) ideology of Marxism-Leninism.

The widely dispersed geography and the demography of a small series of communities frame the conditions for "global narrowcasting" — that is, ethnically specific cultural production for widely dispersed population fragments centripetally organised around an officially excluded homeland. This makes the media — and the media use — of the Vietnamese diaspora significantly different from media consumption in the Chinese, Indian or Thai diasporas, which revolve around large production centres in the "home" countries.

These conditions also determine the nature of the production companies (Thụy Nga, ASIA/Dem Saigon, Mey/Hollywood Nights, Khanh Ha, Diem Xua and others). These are small businesses running at low margins and constantly undercut by copying of their video product outside the United States (particularly in Vietnam itself), where their ability to police copyright is restricted by not having the time or resources to follow up breaches. They have clustered around the only Vietnamese population base which offers critical mass and is geographically adjacent to the world-leading entertainment–communications–information (ECI) complex in Southern California. There is evidence of internal migration within the diaspora from the rest of the United States, Canada and France to Southern California to take advantage of the largest overseas Vietnamese population concentration and the world's major ECI complex.

Conditions of Production

Thuy Nga Productions is by far the largest and most successful company. It organises major live shows in the United States and franchises an appearance schedule for its high-profile performers at shows around the global diaspora, and has produced more than 60 two-hour videotapes since the early 1980s (see Appendix 3.1), as well as a constant flow of CDs, audiocassettes and karaoke discs. President and owner of Thuy Nga, To Van Lai, was a university psychology professor before establishing Thuy Nga in 1969. Named after his wife, Thuy Nga was set up as a recording and production label which actuated To's stance as a cultural intellectual bringing traditional folk and contemporary Vietnamese music traditions into contact with popular American and French music.

To Van Lai escaped with his family to Paris at the fall of Saigon, and continued to produce audiocassettes and to branch out into music video, CDs and karaoke output. The initial venture into music video was precipitated by To approaching a French TV executive in 1983 for assistance with making "a cultural exchange between the French and the Vietnamese". According to To (1996), "the title of Paris By Night was chosen because during the day people worked hard with very little time, but in the evening they have more time for themselves. For anyone who has lived in France, there is nothing more beautiful than being in Paris at night; therefore the title Paris By Night was established." Since then, at least two music videos have been produced each year (with current production at four annually).

A short history of the company was presented in 1998 on its fifteenth anniversary video (Thuy Nga Productions (hereafter TNP) 63, *Paris By Night* (hereafter PBN) 46 — see Appendix 3.1). The early Paris By Night productions evoked pre-1975 Saigon through its revival of cabaret music and entertainment from previously well-established Vietnamese performers, such as Elvis Phuong, Jo Marcel and Khanh Ly. Due to the rising costs of production, more public demand for live concert performances in the United States and Canada, the demand for regularisation of music video production protocols, and the fact that the majority of Vietnamese performers were living in the United States, To moved Thuy Nga Productions to Orange County in the late 1980s. The first Paris By Night video produced in 1983 was recorded in Paris and cost about US$19 000. It consisted of eleven performances with local Vietnamese in Paris. In comparison, in the late 1990s, Thuy Nga releases at least four videos a year, consisting usually of 24 performances from a range of international Vietnamese performers, a stage and technical crew of approximately 300 people, often recording in front of packed audiences. Production costs per video have moved to US$500 000.

Paris By Night had the challenging task of breaking into the well-established demand for Chinese-language video in the United States, which "monopolised" the overseas Vietnamese market through the 1980s. Mostly Hong Kong product of the sort previously discussed, heavy consumption of multi-tape series television — indeed, according to To, the Vietnamese audience's "addiction" to these series — had a deleterious effect on their working lives and their lifestyles. Within the wider issues of dealing with the new country, the contribution of "addiction" to Chinese videos worsened the community's social dilemmas. To Van Lai's attempt to provide an alternative to the Chinese language material began to work after 1986 when the release of its first special documentary edition, *Gia Biet Saigon* (Farewell Saigon), which is discussed below.

The revenue and profit generated from the live performances and shows helps to fund the production of music videos, CDs and karaoke discs. To Van Lai claims sales figures per video of approximately 40 000 and up to 80 000 for "specials" in the United States, but also states that overseas sales are not a significant or stable revenue source due to illegal dubbing of tapes. Income from overseas sales is a "bonus": every country has its own laws on copyright and it would cost him more money to hire overseas lawyers to prevent piracy than to pursue the issue (To, 1996). Recent prices in US dollars are videos $25, CDs $15 and karaoke discs $85, with concert tickets ranging from $75 to $200. On these prices, Thuy Nga can count on about US$1 million in video sales in the United States alone, with costs of production for a single music video up to US$500 000.

Thuy Nga attempts to stay close to its audience by including a questionnaire in every purchased new release in the United States which requests information on favourite songs, who should perform them, and assessments of previous releases. Indicators of Thuy Nga's success include the fact that mainstream advertisers are starting to place promotions in the videos and performers are prepared to work for free because of the worldwide recognition they receive. There are agents in the main population centres representing Thuy Nga Productions who franchise both the live shows' organisation and the sales of video and other product from single master tapes sent from Southern California.

Apart from the artists, the regular Thuy Nga show comperes, Nguyen Ngoc Ngan and Nguyen Cao Ky Duyen, are both notable figures in the diaspora in their own right. Ngoc Ngan is a well-known political writer and novelist. After spending three years in re-education camps from 1975 to 1978, he escaped to Malaysia by boat in 1979, and in that year completed his first novel while in the Malaysian refugee camp, *Nhung Nguoi Dan Ba Con O Lai* (The Women Left Behind). His first published work was *The Will of Heaven* (about his own personal journey as a refugee), written in English and published in New York in 1980. In 1992, Ngoc Ngan began his career as an MC for Thuy Nga. Nguyen Cao Ky Duyen's father was former Republic Vice-President and Air Force Commander Nguyen Cao Ky. Her family fled the country in the 1970s while Ky Duyen was an infant.

The other most popular company committed to high production values is ASIA Productions (Dem Saigon/Saigon Nights) (see Appendix 3.1). It was established in the United States in the early 1980s. In contrast to Thuy Nga, ASIA is not a family business, but is owned by shareholders and run by a manager. ASIA reaches out beyond the established community performers, focusing more than Thuy Nga on promoting new talent in the United States and Canada. Through an annual "star search" competition, Truc Ho, ASIA's music director, scouts for talent, offering contracts to perform live shows, video taping and CD recordings for the company. It also encourages its audience to take part in the "quest for stardom" by testing talent using its karaoke recordings, and then sending in tapes of the performances. Shortlisted singers are given the opportunity to perform in front of a live audience to get feedback on their performance. Like all other production companies, the main revenue and profit derives from the ticket sales of live shows and the domestic sale of CDs, videos and karaoke discs.

Other companies are not so popular, mainly because their productions are basic taping of live shows and do not enjoy the production values of the larger companies. MEY Productions (Hollywood Nights) is based in Westminster (as are all these companies) and established itself in the early 1990s with a series of "Hollywood Nights" videos conspicuously patterned on the successful Paris By Night formula. Mey's emphasis is less on stand-alone music videos as the company also focuses on producing *Van Nghe Vietnam* (Vietnamese Entertainment), a regular program on the local community-access television station. These smaller concerns must look further afield for their talent, as Thuy Nga and ASIA tend to sign the well-known, popular performers.

Khanh Ha Productions is a family-controlled business. The father, Lu Lien, a popular composer and singer from the famous singing trio AVT, is of the same generation as composer Pham Duy, who just happens to be an in-law (Lu Lien's son, singer Tuan Ngoc, is married to singer Thai Thao, who is the daughter of Pham Duy). Khanh Ha and her siblings (Tuan Ngoc, Anh Tu, Luu Bich, Lan Anh, Thuy Anh and Bich Chieu) and other performers are a close-knit group performing live regularly in their family-owned night club, recording CDs and producing occasional music videos.

Conditions of Consumption

From data supplied by the production companies and distributors, the rates of sale and rental derived from samples of video store retailers, and the scale of attendances at regular live variety performances, it can be surmised — in the absence of large-scale tracking surveys for which the industry does not have resources — that most overseas Vietnamese households may own or rent some of this music video material, and a significant proportion have developed comprehensive home libraries. Its popularity is extraordinary, cutting across differences of ethnicity, age, gender, recency of arrival, refugee or immigrant status and home region. It is also widely available in pirated form in Vietnam itself, as the economic and cultural "thaw" that has proceeded since Doi Moi policies of greater openness has resulted in extensive penetration of the homeland by this most international of Vietnamese expression. (Carruthers (1999) points to data from 1996 which estimates that 85–90 per cent of stock in Saigon's unlicensed video stores was foreign.) As the only popular culture produced by and specifically for the Vietnamese diaspora, there is a deep investment in these texts by and within the overseas communities — an investment by no means homogeneous but uniformly strong. The social text which surrounds — indeed, engulfs — these productions is intense, multi-layered and makes its address across differences of generation, gender, ethnicity, class and education levels, and recency of arrival. "Audiovisual images become so important for young Vietnamese as a point of reference, as a tool for validation and as a vehicle towards self identity." (Trang Nguyen, 1997)

The central point linking business operations, the textual dynamics of the music videos and media use within the communities is that what we have called the three cultural positions or stances in the communities, and the musical styles which give expression to them, have to be accommodated somehow within the same productions because of the marginal size of the audience base. From the point of view of business logic, each style cannot exist without the others. Thus the organisational structure of the shows and the videos, at the level both of the individual show/video and at the level of whole company outputs — particularly those of Thuy Nga and ASIA — reflects the heterogeneity required to maximise audience within a strictly narrowcast range. This is a programming philosophy congruent with broadcasting to a globally spread, narrowcast demographic.

This also underscores why "the variety show form has been a mainstay of overseas Vietnamese anti-communist culture from the mid-seventies onwards" (Carruthers, 1999). In any given live show or video production, the musical styles might range from pre-colonial traditionalism to French colonial-era high modernist classicism, from crooners adapting Vietnamese folksongs to the Sinatra era through to bilingual cover versions of Grease or Madonna. Stringing this concatenation of taste cultures together are the comperes, typically well-known political and cultural figures in their own right, who perform a rhetorical unifying function:

> Audience members are constantly recouped via the show's diegesis, and the anchoring role of the comperes and their commentaries, into an overarching conception of shared overseas Vietnamese identity. This is centred on the appeal to … core cultural values, common tradition, linguistic unity and an anti-communist homeland politics. (Carruthers, 1999)

Within this overall political trajectory, however, there are major differences to be managed. The stances evidenced in the video and live material range on a continuum from "pure" heritage maintenance and ideological monitoring, to mainstream cultural negotiation, through to assertive hybridity. Most performers and productions seek to situate themselves within the mainstream of cultural negotiation between Vietnamese and Western traditions. However, at one end of the continuum there are strong attempts to keep both the original folkloric music traditions alive and also the integrity of the originary anti-communist stance foundational to the diaspora through very public criticism of any lapse from that stance. At the other end, Vietnamese-American youth culture is exploring the limits of hybrid identities through "New Wave", a radical intermixing of musical styles. We shall consider some textual examples of each style and audience/readership responses to them.

Heritage Maintenance

Heritage maintenance, as we have seen in relation to newspapers, embraces a range of cultural and informational production and is closely connected to the ideological monitoring role of maintaining the salience of the anti-communist stance foundational to the diaspora. Diasporic video is one of the prime sites monitored. This is borne out spectacularly in the *Mother* issue of Paris By Night (PBN 40). Paris by Night 40 was released in 1997 to coincide with Vu Lan, the Season of Filial Piety, a time for special veneration of parents. The video was particularly popular, but popularity turned to condemnation in the diaspora when it was discovered that a small segment of documentary war footage showing planes strafing and killing South Vietnamese civilians was actually of the Republic of South Vietnam (RSA) air forces. Thuy Nga asserted it was the innocent mistake of a young and inexperienced editor; both To Van Lai and compere Nguyen Ngoc Ngan were forced to publish apologies in the main newspapers and calm very angry responses on Websites, in letters to the editor, on radio and in demonstrations outside Thuy Nga's offices. Some even alleged that it was a cynical ploy by the company to establish its good name in Vietnam in advance of a greater entrepreneurial effort in the homeland.

The *Mother* imbroglio has been extensively analysed by Carruthers (1999), who stresses the porosity of communications flows between the diaspora and the homeland, noting that the degree of ideological border-drawing on which the identity and integrity of both the homeland regime and the diasporic community depend is increasingly difficult to sustain under the pressures of globalisation. However, it is appropriate for our themes that we stress that the *Mother* episode illustrates the degree of psychic and ideological investment in the music video corpus and the degree to which it, like all public cultural manifestations, is monitored for deviations from the ideological foundations of the diaspora. The social text of the corpus is subtended by strong community expectations of a proper education for the young in the reasons for cultural maintenance. While much of the dissolution of boundaries between homeland and diaspora proceeds around cultural product, entrepreneurship and travel (it was estimated that about 20 000 Australian Vietnamese visited Vietnam annually in the mid-1990s), there continues to be organised resistance to such dissolution among the overseas populations. Examples include boycotts of restaurants run by government-aligned owners, and the fact that a new shopping complex, known as the "cultural court", in the heart of Westminster on Balsa Avenue that was part-financed by the homeland sources was conspicuously under-patronised — and for a good time virtually boycotted — in the months following its opening in 1996. International attention was drawn in 1999 to the community attacks on a shop owner in the precinct who insisted on flying the official country flag and displaying pictures of Ho Chi Minh.

The main musical expression of heritage maintenance lies in the restoration and preservation of traditional Vietnamese music styles (and the instruments on which they are played). Major cultural figures such as Pham Duy, often titled in American media coverage as the "Woody Guthrie" of Vietnam, have devoted long careers to the maintenance of the received Vietnamese heritage in folk culture. (He wrote a historical treatise, *Musics of Vietnam* (1973); has had several special issue videos dedicated to his corpus; and has recreated as a folk opera the "Iliad of Vietnam", *Truyen Kieu* (The Tale of Kieu).) The purity is maintained through a scholarly attention to the traditions and their transmission to a younger, dispersed generation; the artisanal attention to the playing of traditional Vietnamese musical instruments; but also a preparedness to transmit this heritage by contemporary technologies such as CD and the Internet. Into this category should also be placed a considerable amount of traditional folk balladry and a residual element of traditional Vietnamese opera on the tapes. This form of "pure" heritage maintenance is clearly mainly consumed by the older generation of the educated elite.

A small fraction of the music video corpus is given over to heritage maintenance across the entire tape. These six to eight tapes are constructed quite differently to the rest and are at the other end of the stylistic continuum from the live show formats. They are compilation documentary-style video, and have been produced typically to commemorate historical anniversaries in the overseas communities' lives (examples include TNP 41, *10th Anniversary*; TNP 32, 20 *Nam Nhin La* (Looking Back 20 Years), Asia 7, 1975–95).

An early example of the historical compilation video is Thuy Nga 10 *Gia Biet Saigon* (Farewell Saigon). Made in 1986, this Thuy Nga production has none of the sophisticated production values and choreography of later productions; in fact, it is organised on quite different principles to the variety show format of most of the corpus. The organisational principle is one of popular memory, bearing all the hallmarks of a very specific address to the military, educational, business and government elites of the South Vietnam regime in the period leading to the fall of Saigon.

This principle of organisation makes it a virtually unwatchable tape for all but this specific audience. The great majority of second-generation and recent arrivals who participated in focus groups and interviews asserted that historical compilation material was "for [their] parents" or for those who "had been through the events" being recounted. *Farewell Saigon*, a tape of approximately 90 minutes' duration, comprises historical footage of pre-1975 Saigon (together with some post-1975 footage) with studio-based musical interludes sung by profiled performers of the same or similar generation to the target audience — those performers who successfully transitioned from pre- to post-1975 as part of the diaspora.

The great majority of the elapsed time on the tape is a video essay extolling the strength, social balance and harmony, and dynamism of a well-governed and stable Republic of Vietnam during the Diem and Thieu years. So much can be readily *deduced* from the contents and organisation of the tape. What can be *adduced* from its reception and use within the specific target audience — the original diasporic elites — is both the depth of loss and longing which the tape engenders and, on the other hand, a still-strong politics of disavowal of the regime's complicity in its own downfall and the continued placing of blame on America as a "great and powerful friend" which withdrew its support unilaterally, rendering the defence of the republic impossible. The vertiginous shifts from triumphalism to abjection, from very long static camera angles on impeccably suited parades of military to the hand-held chaos of the end-time of 1975, has strong parallels with the abrupt changes of tempo and testamental nature of the Croatian video analysed by Kolar-Panov (1997: 153).

The footage combines travelogue-style panoramas of market scenes, major downtown buildings, the Presidential Palace, main girls' and boys' schools and a compendium of a religious buildings. The second set of visual materials include a highly structured, syncopated visual hymn to the women of the republic, cut to complement the ballad "Co gai Viet" (The Vietnamese Lady) in a studio setting by three women performers wearing signifiers of North, Centre and South regions of a pre-communist-unified country. The third type is very extensive footage of a military parade that was held on 26 October, the National Day, each year. Voiceover commentary details the different regiments in careful detail and occupies almost half an hour of the tape.

What is readable as flat "propaganda" and inexcusably tedious editing by its non-intended audience is received very differently by its primary audience, the original diasporic elites. For them, *Farewell Saigon* is like a home movie. There are no specific time references to anchor the footage at a particular date apart from its ambience in the later 1960s/early 1970s: it inhabits a modality of popular memory, with very specific anchors of place but not of time. In one family with whom researchers were invited to watch the video, the father had been an RSA fighter pilot and had been interned in a re-education camp for eleven years before being allowed to come to Australia under the family reunion program. *Farewell Saigon* has footage of his military unit which he finds impossible to watch. The mother can point out the school she went to as a girl — the images of a sea of white *ao dai* (traditional dress worn by Vietnamese women) spreading gaily from the gates of the school are images of Confucian educational rectitude and the innocence of youth that are almost equally impossible to watch.

There are also those for whom the politics of this tape are to be foregrounded: "The video brings back emotional memories of how proud and honoured Vietnamese should be with their country and not believe false propaganda and damaging accusations by foreign political analysts and the Vietcong" and "It was produced to remind the Vietnamese and the rest of the world that Vietnam was once an independent nation until it was betrayed in the war by its American allies" are representative of the public construction that can be placed on this material by its intended audience. It is important to note that there is nothing in the tape commentary or visuals that directly attacks the United States — but there is a studied absence of virtually any signifier of what was by the time of the footage an overwhelming American presence in Saigon.

There is also a very direct political sense in which *Farewell Saigon* is like a home movie. Most of the documentary footage used in the video was smuggled out of the country just before the fall of Saigon by the Vietnamese Student Association in Paris. It was then handed over to a senior military figure who gave To Van Lai copyright clearance to use the footage in his assembly for *Gai Biet Saigon*. The footage is a virtual palimpsest of the violence of exile — such media, left behind after the fall of Saigon, would have had prime value in targeting elite members of the fallen regime.

Cultural Negotiation

The auspicers of the inevitable and widespread negotiation between Vietnamese and Western cultural forms are prominently the owners of the small-business music video production houses and the principal well-established performers. Many of these figures were prominent in South Vietnamese cultural production before 1975 and have maintained that position in the ensuing decades. They are educated in the heritage and have maintained the popular memory as they simultaneously auspice inevitable hybridisation of this heritage under the commercial imperative. But this is to continue a well-established historical hybridisation. For the most established, there are direct links back to pre-1975 Saigon, and the continuities of such converged music forms being developed and practised well before 1975 need to be accounted for. The hybridity of Vietnamese music culture has its roots both fundamentally in millennial Chinese–Vietnamese interchange and more latterly with French interchange during the colonial period. In the 1960s, it was the massive influence of

American rock and roll during the war, especially in Saigon, which provided the most recent pre-exile infusion of hybrid elements. Pham Duy's historical treatise *Musics of Vietnam* (1973), even as it is committed to the identification and preservation of the country's folk traditions, shows that the south's major styles of theatrical romanticism in performance, while influenced by French and latterly American traditions, was originally a Chinese influence (1973: 118). As was observed in Chapter 1, Vietnamese area studies could benefit significantly from a greater sense of the mutability and adaptability of its object of study, and this is nowhere clearer than in the area of popular culture. Terry Rambo (1987), arguing this case, shows that even such an exemplary symbol of Vietnamese authenticity, the *ao dai*, is a borrowing from Chinese culture.

Of the cultural positions available to the communities, that which accepts the inevitability of cultural negotiation and adaptation and fashions musical styles around that position seeks to minimise the more liminal postures of heritage maintenance or assertive hybridity. The musical styles are mainstreamed and stable in style, based on established patterns of intermixing Chinese, French and US inputs from before 1975. A major figure, Elvis Phuong — an Elvis cover singer before it became a global industry! — was an established performer in Saigon before 1975 and his career has continued unabated throughout the exile. Other major performers include Luu Bich, Tuan Ngoc and Khanh Ha. Befitting its mainstream status, probably two-thirds of the corpus is of this type, as it is predominantly easy listening or middle-of-the-road "crooner" presentational styles that are the least confronting and of potentially broadest address across audience interests. The style of music renews audience connections to the soft melodic music and sentimental ballads often performed in bars and cabarets of the pre-1975 period. Visually, this style of presentation rarely employs documentary footage characteristic of the first style, nor does it involve the elaborate postmodern-pastiche stage settings and "excessive" costuming of the third style. All the companies aim for this type of predominant content, as it will maximise its target audience. The other two categories occupy together roughly a third of total output.

"Hat Cho Ngay Hom Qua" (Song of Yesterday) (TNP 37, PBN 20, 1993), a "Lien Khuc" (medley) with performers Elvis Phuong,

Duy Quang, Anh Khoa and Tuan Ngoc, is a good example. Performed bilingually, the medley comprises popular Western songs of Elvis Presley and John Lennon, and music from the era of the Vietnam War ("Yesterday, all my troubles seemed so far away, now it looks as though there're here to stay, oh I believe in Yesterday"/ "Yesterday when I was young"/ "And now the time is near and so I face my final curtain"/ "When the night has come and the land is dark and the moon is the only light we'll see, no I won't be afraid, no I won't be afraid, just as long as you stand, stand by me"). The performance draws upon the memories of the mature audience who lived in Saigon throughout the 1950s to 1970s — hence the title: "Hat Cho Ngay Hom Qua" (Sing for Yesterday). That audience's memories of an era of continual war, struggle and devastation are mapped gently on to the "hardships" which are the thematic substance of the original Western songs (lost and unrequited love, etc.) and the massive disjunction is managed in the ambience of nostalgia and tasteful dinner jackets on the set.

Innovation within this style is centred on harmonious both-ways adaptation: Vietnamese interpretation of foreign music or traditional Vietnamese lyrics with the influence of contemporary Western music. New songwriters like Nhat Ngan and Khuc Lan specialise in translating and interpreting Chinese and French songs into Vietnamese New Wave music. Luu Bich is often linked with the latter, performing a wide range of Chinese ballads translated into Vietnamese with one of the most popular song being "Chiec La Mua Dong" (The Leaf of Winter). Composers like Van Phung and Ngo Thuy Mien, for example, are strongly influenced by jazz and rhythm and blues. In "Noi Long" (Feelings) (TNP 56, PBN 39, 1997), Bich Chieu's performance of lyrics which are purely Vietnamese is revamped with a Western influence of jazz and blues. The initial reaction from one focus group of young recently arrived school students watching this was that it was "weird" and "un-Vietnamese". However, during discussion and reflection, they were able to appreciate the new version of the song.

The most productive means of grasping the cultural work audiences are performing with this music is to see it as positively modelling identity transition. The simple lyrics, well known to the point of cliché ("easy listening") in Vietnamese, English or French, provide a reassuring point of recognition for those (mostly the older, more recently arrived) who find themselves displaced in an overseas community where language is the main cultural barrier; while others (mostly the young) are provided with an easier way into understanding their own family's cultural environment. ASIA Productions specialise in this approach. Thanh and Jasmine, well-educated relatives who are dedicated fans of the music, reflected that they were initially attracted to their own heritage by their interest in the re-mixing of traditional folklore music through the music videos of ASIA Productions.

The cultural negotiation position can also be distinguished politically from heritage maintenance insofar as it is prepared to negotiate certain emergent relationships with the homeland — a stance unthinkable within the first category. As Carruthers (1999) points out, the revered composer Trinh Cong Son, who actually lives in Vietnam but enjoys equal popularity both at home and abroad, has had a long collaboration with popular diaspora singer Khanh Ly. Also, diaspora artists are now beginning to test the home market with some live performances, such as at the major Tet celebrations since 1996. Indeed, there is greater reciprocity to this emergent and problematic rapprochement than might at first appear:

> The homeland pirate culture industry has been able to take advantage of lax copyright and censorship laws to enjoy the fruits of overseas Vietnamese media companies' labours without contributing to their revenues, while overseas companies have been able to exploit the first world/third world divide by going to Vietnam to record the voices of local singers, mastering them in studios back in France and the US, and releasing the CDs at a significantly lower price than those produced entirely overseas. (Carruthers, 1999)

"New Wave" Assertive Hybridity

> While the hybrid retains its links to and identification with its origins, it is also shaped and transformed by (and in turn, shapes and transforms) its location in the present.
>
> Belonging at the same time to several "homes", it cannot simply dissolve into a culturally unified form. The complex achievement of the hybrid is a product of [the] obligation to "come to terms with and to make something new of the cultures they inhabit, without simply assimilating to them". The result is a celebration of cultural impurity, a "love-song to our mongrel selves". (Turner, 1994: 124–25, internal quotes Hall, 1993: 362)

The reception for performers who assertively seek to fully appropriate Western rock and pop (in a style that is dubbed "New Wave") can be as intense as the political controversies around incidents such as the *Mother* episode. This "assertive hybridity" is exclusively a phenomenon of youth culture, and centres on its very specific formation at "ground zero" in Southern California. The "excesses" of controversial performers such as Lynda Trang Dai, Nhu Mai, The Magic or Don Ho have some precedent within the context of Californian Vietnamese-American youth culture (as evidenced by the specialist lifestyle magazines for Vietnamese-American young people such as *Viet Now*). However, the economics of live performance and music video production necessitate a much broader audience and thus a context beyond its niche age and style demographic.

New Wave, at its most basic, refers to bilingual — English and Vietnamese — song lyrics. But it is also about playful, political and increasingly ambitious appropriations or pastiches of mostly American rock and pop rendered into Vietnamese — with some examples being "Black Magic Woman", "Hotel California" and "Fernando". But innovative performers like Don Ho have ranged much wider — for example, in *Paris By Night: Las Vegas* (TNP 46 PBN 29 1995), Don Ho's "Caravan of Life" performance was based on a well-known Chinese song, translated into Vietnamese and performed in the setting which highlighted the oppression of the Nepalese.

Lynda Trang Dai is prototypical of this stance, and is a well-established but very controversial figure in Vietnamese music performance. She has established a profile since the mid-1980s modelling herself on Madonna, reprising most of Madonna's personae from the fishnet stockings–crucifix–white trash–material girl to the toned-gym junkie to the feminine-Vogue look. It is entirely possible to see Lynda's confrontational personae as doubly mapped on to the provocations Madonna posed to sexual/musical/religious representations over this period, given that her career has been entirely played out within the Vietnamese community. Her influence can be measured by her pioneering assertive hybridity and by the strength of audience response, which in its extremes is *sui generis* in the Vietnamese music industry. It is not only in sexual Westernisms that this occurs: there is much more stress in this style of music on the dramatic/excessive *surfaces* of performance, costume and reprising contemporary Western rock, pop and rap than on traditional Vietnamese music's emphasis on subtly coded variations of voice and face.

Thanh, the young proprietor of a karaoke coffee shop who is extremely knowledgable about all aspects of the Vietnamese music scene, offered this analysis:

> Linda is the first Vietnamese to do that [fashion a form of extreme hybridity] when she came out. It was a clash of cultures especially with the older generation. They were giving her a bad name. But guys like her performances. Now everyone [that is, Vietnamese performers] just copies Linda while she continues to copy Madonna. Linda was daring to do that because Vietnamese performers at that time were more traditional and very influenced by the Vietnamese culture.

Over time, she has — and very importantly in the Vietnamese community — officially "earned respect" in terms of her longevity and solid track record of performance, and a typical introduction to a Lynda performance by a compere might now be the respectful coding "a Vietnamese women with a Western style of performance", or this saying quoted by one of the MCs linking the performances on Paris by Night 36: "khau za ma tam phat/although the mouth speaks badly, the heart speaks of goodness". Nevertheless, at the level of gossip and rumour in the unofficial culture, a figure like Lynda is the occasion for much boundary-marking.

On the one hand, it is very difficult for the young — particularly those without Vietnamese language skills and/or sufficient background in the formal poetic rhetoric of much of the music embodying the heritage maintenance and cultural negotiation positions — to be able to appreciate them: the Westernised/Americanised posture of a Lynda offers some purchase into Vietnamese culture. For Thanh and Jasmine (Thanh's niece, who works in the grocery store adjacent to Thanh's coffee shop), the single most crucial factor in excluding potential fans of this music video is high-enough levels of language competence. On the other hand, Lynda will often bring out an "ultra-Vietnamese" reaction, with gossip about facelifts, corruption of the language through sloppy lyrics and "inability to sing rather than just perform", and dismissal of her claims to feminist credentials on the basis that "women's rights are a Western issue" — precisely why, for the New Wave youth following, the issue should be foregrounded!

"Cyber Queen" (TNP 49, PBN 32 1995, see Appendix 3.2) is Lynda's reprise of Madonna in her Gaultier cyborg phase. Lynda and her backing singers and dancers are costumed as steely cyborgs, the women sporting conical bras. The English lyrics are consistent with the choreography of the piece, but there is a complete disjunction with the Vietnamese lyrics, which speak in traditional coding of "winds and waterfalls". There is also a disjunctive gesture midway through the song when Lynda unfurls the Republic of Vietnam flag under one arm and the US flag under the other. This nationalistic gesture would be characteristic of a heritage maintenance performance, but is received with some bewilderment as part of this style.

Don Ho is one of the most popular performers for younger Vietnamese. His performances are noted for their elaborate choreography, set design, costuming and innovation, along with sophisticated cover versions of a wide range of exclusively Western songs. "I Just Died in Your Arms" (TNP 53, PBN 36 1996, see Appendix 3.2) was a Western hit song in the late 1980s and, in this instance and compared with "Cyber Queen", there is a close conjunction between the English and Vietnamese "translation" from the English. The Vietnamese lyrics, being a translation and not a lyrical sequence or song in its own right in the language, is, for some, a stronger provocation to Vietnamese lyrical traditions and to traditional models of romance and sexual relations. The song embraces, without reservation, the iconic degeneracy, the female sexual predation, sex and death equivalences, and eviscerated manhood that are at the centre of the European vampire mythologies. And, by and large, the Vietnamese lyrical component is drawn directly into this field of meaning.

There is nothing that compels identification as Vietnamese in either the staging or referencing in the lyrics. The members of one focus group of young school-aged, recently arrived migrants were generally consensual about Don Ho being "American" rather than "Vietnamese" because the mannerisms with which he performs — such as his dress, the Western songs he sings, the way he dances, the fact that there are backup dancers performing with him and, particularly in this performance, the stage design being European Gothic (coffins, chandeliers, the crepuscular smoke, female vampires with extended incisors, black capes and ghostly make up) — are "foreign". Others in the group commented that he is a *lai* — a "half-breed" — as a performer.

In "going too far", the assertive hybridity position provokes criticism and risks losing at least part of its intended audience. A music store owner catering primarily to Vietnamese youth argues that the young listen primarily to Western techno and house music and may regard the more radical performers and styles as in fact assimilationist, as they are "cheap imitations" of dominant Western styles. If they want to "be" Vietnamese in their music tastes, they will turn to the more middle-of-the-road material of cultural negotiation which engages identifiably distinct Vietnamese traditions.

Conclusion

> Each time I view these videos, the feeling I am left with afterwards is one of complete exhilaration or of absolute sadness. There is no in between. It is either one extreme or the other.
>
> Having left Vietnam as a child of seven years of age in 1976, I do not have strong recollection of the physical landscape of Vietnam, of the traditions, the tastes, the smell, the sights, the sounds of this "homeland". Every image that comes on screen builds for me the "reality" of what Vietnam is and was. And it is these images that I collect and refer when I speak of Vietnam. It is not the Vietnam that once existed or the country as it is now that swims in my head. Vietnam becomes for a me a collection of images I have been immersed in through media. (Trang Nguyen, 1997)

The rate of immigration from Vietnam has slowed appreciably over the latter 1990s; the proportion of those who were originally refugees has also diminished appreciably, while the numbers of those visiting Vietnam for business or family purposes has risen. While the official culture of the diaspora continues to remain strongly anti-communist and anti-homeland government, growing numbers, particularly of the young, are forging "Asian-Australian" identities which owe less to the past and more to a globalising present. For a community of somewhat over 200 000 (when a growing number of second-generation Australia-born are taken into account), there is a remarkable diversity both of the population and its economic, social and cultural circumstances. As we noted in Chapter 1, it is arguable that diaspora communities provide examples of cultural formations at their most mutable, with political change both in the homelands and the host countries, inter-generational tension a key given the recency of departures from the homeland, and very sharp socioeconomic differences between the successful and the struggling. The media consumed by overseas Vietnamese people, rather than resolving the conflicts thrown up by such mutability, as a functionalist model of media-social relations would have it, tend rather to "stage" them — to give them voice and manage them in a productive tension. Australian claims to cultural pluralism would be more plausible if the "shadow system" of diasporic video, music and popular culture was to come into a fuller light.

New World promotional pamphlet. The slogan, "Intimacy is to speak your language", inaugurated the New World Television service in Australia in 1994. (Galaxy Media Pty Ltd)

ASIA Productions shopfront, Westminster, California. (Photo courtesy of Tina Nguyen)

* Registered by Australia Post publication number WBF 1436   * Issue No 3520, Saturday 20th February 1999*   * ISSN 0816-7575

NHẬT BÁO
Chiêu dương

Thứ Bảy

● **THE SUNRISE DAILY NEWSPAPER** ●
THE FIRST AND ONLY VIETNAMESE DAILY NEWSPAPER IN AUSTRALIA

P.O. Box 64, Cabramatta NSW 2166   -   Tel: **(02) 9725 6444** - Fax: (02) 9725 6446 - E-mail: chieuduong@auco.net.au

Quản Nhiệm: Nguyễn Lý Nhị Giang   • Giá: $1 Cử kim   Phát hành buổi sáng các ngày: THỨ BA, TƯ, NĂM, SÁU và BẢY • Distributed THROUGHOUT Australia
Year 19th - Năm Thứ Mười Chín   • Perth: $1.50   *Số 3520, Thứ Bảy ngày 20 tháng 2 năm 1999 (Mùng Năm, Tháng Giêng (Dả) Kỷ Mão)

VIETNAM
DẤU TÍCH CHỢ TÌNH

Hillary Clinton có thể sẽ ra tranh cử tại Thượng Viện

Tổng Thống Bill Clinton vẫn còn rắc rối với pháp luật

Quỷ râu xanh rượt bắt cóc thiếu nữ

Tàu chìm tại Mã Lai: 20 người bị tử nạn

Vụ bắt giữ Ocalan có những chuyển biến phức tạp

Nam Vang cầu cạnh các nước để tìm viện trợ

Cướp dữ tấn công cửa tiệm vùng Leichhardt

Do buồn nản, trùm Hanson định giã từ chính nghiệp

CHIẾU DƯƠNG: CƠ QUAN TRUYỀN THÔNG SẮC TỘC XUẤT SẮC NHẤT

Chieu duong. The Sunrise Daily newspaper, the largest-circulation Vietnamese newspaper in Australia. (*Chieu duong*)

Sydney by Night. Poster for one of the regular live shows featuring Vietnamese music stars. (Thuy Nga Productions)

Heritage maintenance. Thuy Nga Video 10, *Gia Biet Saigon* (Farewell Saigon) (1986). (Thuy Nga Productions)

"New Wave" assertive hybridity. Don Ho featured in Thuy Nga 53, Paris by Night, *Ahn Den Mau*. (Thuy Nga Productions)

ASIA Production 11, *Tho va Nhac*
(Poetry and Music)

Wedding photo of a Fiji Indian couple.
Re-Sanskritisation of identity through
posing as a regal couple. (Photo courtesy of Sashi Mahendra Singh)

Cover of *Fiji Times,* Sydney's main newspaper for the Fiji Indian community.

Ramayan Katha. The Indian folk tradition brought from the villages a century ago, reenacted in the new diasporic setting of Sydney. (Photo courtesy of Sashi Mahendra Singh)

Members of the Thai community at the Sunday merit-making ritual at Wat Dhammadharo, a Thai Buddhist temple in Canberra. (Photo courtesy of Chalinee Hirano)

Display of posters and video programs in a Thai video rental store. (Photo courtesy of Chalinee Hirano)

Imported Thai newspapers and magazines, and *Thai-Oz,* the Thai ethnic newspaper. (Photo courtesy of Chalinee Hirano)

Appendix 3.1: The Main Production Companies' Output

Thuy Nga Productions: "Paris by Night" Music Video Series

1986: Video 10 PBN — *Gia Biet Saigon* (Farewell Saigon)
1988: Video 13 PBN — *Giot Nuoc Mat Cho Vietnam* (A Tear Drop for Vietnam)
1990: Video 16 PBN — *Nuoc Non Ngan Dam Ra Di* (The Homeland We Left Behind)
1992: Video 32 PBN 15 — *Mua Xuan Nao Ta Ve* (Which Season Shall I Return?)
1992: Video 33 PBN 16 (Studio)
1992: Video 34 PBN 17 (Studio)
1992: Video 35 PBN 18 (Studio)
1993: Video 36 PBN 19 — *Pham Duy* (Composer/Studio)
1993: Video 37 PBN 20 — *Tuyet Pham* (Studio)
 •Trai Hoi Ngay Xuan/Ai Van, Ai Thanh, Elvis Phuong
 •Lien Khuc Hat Cho Ngay Hom Qua/Elvis Phuong, Tuan Ngoc, Duy Quang, Anh Khoa
1993: Video 38 PBN 21 — *Ngo Thuy Mien* (Composer/Studio)
1993: Video 39 PBN 22 — *Lam Phuong* (Composer/Studio)
1993: Video 40 PBN 23 — *The Gioi Muon Man* (Music Clips)
1994: Video 41 PBN 24 — *10th Anniversary* (Show)
 •Trang Sang Vuon Tre/Ai Van
1994: Video 42 PBN 25 (Studio)
1994: Video 43 PBN 26 — *Dem Hoan Dang* — *Sacree Soiree 1* (Studio)
 •Chi Co Anh Trong Doi/Khanh Ha
 •May Nhip Cau Tre/Ai Van
 •Giang Cau/Elvis Phuong, Quang Binh, Huong Lan, Trang Thanh Lan
1994: Video 44 PBN 27 — *Van Phung* (Composer/Studio)
1994: Video 45 PBN 28 — *Lam Phuong 2* (Composer/Studio)
1995: Video 46 PBN 29 — *Las Vegas* (Show)
1995: Video 47 PBN 30 — *Pham Duy: Tinh Ca* (Love Songs of Pham Duy) (Composer/Studio)
1995: Video 48 PBN 31 (Studio)
1995: Video 49 PBN 32 — *20 Nam Nhin Lai* (Looking Back 20 Years) (Show)
 •Cyber Queen/Lynda T Dai

1995: Video 50 PBN 33 — *Duc Huy* (Composer/Studio)
1996: Video 51 PBN 34 — *Made in Paris* — *Lido de Paris* (Studio)
1996: Video 52 PBN 35 (Studio)
1996: Video 53 PBN 36 — *Houston* (Show)
    •Die In Your Arms/Don Ho
    •Grease Medley/Lynda T. Dai, Tommy Ngo
1996: Video 54 PBN 37 — *Las Vegas 2* (Show)
1996: Video 55 PBN 38 — *Toronto* (Show)
1997: Video 56 PBN 39 — *Anh Den Mau* (Stage Lighting) (Studio)
    •Trai Tim Lam Lo/Luu Bich
    •Noi Long (Fellings)/Bich Chieu
    •China Girl/Tommy Ngo
1997: Video 57 PBN 40 — *Me* (Mother)
1997: Video 58 PBN 41 — *Hoang Thi Tho* (Composer/Studio)
1997: Video 59 PBN 42 — *Giong Nhac Ky Niem* (Songs to
    Remember) (Studio)
1998: Video 60 PBN 43 — *Dan Ba* (Woman) (Studio)
1998: Video 61 PBN 44 — *Tien* (Money) (Studio)
1998: Video 62 PBN 45 — *Vao Ha* (Holiday) (Studio)
1998: Video 63 PBN 46 — *15th Anniversary Celebration*
1999: Video 64 PBN 47 — *Hoang Thi Tho 2*

ASIA Productions: "Dem Saigon" Music Video Series

1993: Dem Saigon
1993: Dem Saigon 2
1994: Dem Saigon 3 — *Hoa Hau Ao Dai Long Beach 17* (Long
    Beach Ao Dai Pageant 17)
1994: Dem Saigon 4
1995: ASIA 5 — *10th Anniversary*
1995: Dem Saigon 6 — *Tac Gia & Tac Pham* (Composers and
    Their Music)
1995: ASIA 7 — *Tinh Ca 75 – 95* (Love Songs 75–95)
1995: ASIA 8
1996: ASIA 9
1996: ASIA 10 — *Goi Nguoi Mot Niem Vui* (Happiness for the
    People)
1996: ASIA 11 — *Tho va Nhac* (Poetry and Music)

1996: ASIA 12 — *Viet Nam Niem Nho* (Memories of Vietnam)
1997: ASIA 13 — *Hoa va Nhac* (Flowers and Music)
1997: ASIA 14 — *Yeu* (Love)
1997: ASIA 15 — *Tinh Ca Anh Bang* (Music of Anh Bang)
1997: ASIA 16 — *Gia Tu 1997* (Farewell 1997)
1998: ASIA 17
1998: ASIA 18 — *Nho Saigon* (Remember Saigon)
1998: ASIA 19 — *Tac Gia & Tac Pham 2* (Composers and Their
      Music 2)
1998: ASIA 20 — *Tinh Ca Mua Thu* (Songs of Autumn)
1998: ASIA 21 — *Chinh Chien* (The Era of Wartime)
1999: ASIA 22 — *Da Vu Quoc Te* (Dances of the World)

Appendix 3.2: Selected Song Lyrics

Performance # 11 — Paris by Night 32

Cyber Queen

Cyber queen in space from a future time and place
She is made of steel and lace
Giving all her heart and soul

"Get your hands off"

Microchip silicon style pumping in her vein
Vixen vis-electrotron bionic brain
Video and TV sound, that's what she's all about
Geek or what funky beat, she steps her feet

She is dimensional, she is so logical
Laser eyes that cut just like a knife
She is phenomenal, master in digital
Metal tears turn heart to stone

Cyber queen in space from a future time and place
She is made of steel lace down to her metallic nails
She's the queen of hearts
Love her till you come apart
She's the spotlight in the dark
Giving all her heart and soul

Em cho anh tinh yeu em trong nhung dem co don minh anh
I give you my love in the lonely nights, only you
Em cho anh tinh yeu em trong nhung dem ai tinh
I give you my love in the passionate nights
Em cho anh tinh yeu em trong nhung dem co don quanh hiu
I give you my love in the forlorn, deserted nights
Em cho anh tinh yeu anh oi, hay xin chut tinh
I give you my love, darling, ask for a little love

Em la mot con gio luon, em la mot anh nang hong
I am a passing wind, I am a rose sunray
Nhin lai anh, voi het dang cay dau buon
Looking back at you, emptying all the bitter sorrow
Em la bai cat trang dai, em la mot khuc suoi tinh
I am a long sandy beach, I am a cascade of love
Nhin lai anh, trong men nong am
Looking back at you in the ferment of love and warmth
Tinh yeu em cho anh, tinh cuong say dau cho mong manh
The love I give you, a mad drunken love although slender and slight
Mot vai giay phut bay qua nhanh
A few moments fly by quickly
Tinh nay se van vuong ngan nam
This love will linger a thousand years
Tinh yeu em cho anh, tinh cuong say dau cho mong manh
The love I give you, a mad drunken love although slender and slight
Mot vai giay phut bay qua nhanh
A few moments fly by quickly
Ngan doi xin nho hoai anh nhe
Remember for a thousand years, love
RAP:
Cyber queen in space of a future time and place
She's the queen of hearts
Love her till you come apart
She's a spotlight in the dark
Giving all her heart

She is dimensional, she is so logical
Laser eyes that cut just like a knife
She is phenomenal, master in digital
Metal tears turn heart to stone

Cyber queen in space from a future time and place
She is made of steel lace down to her metallic nails
She's the queen of hearts
Love her till you come apart
She's the spotlight in the dark
Giving all her heart and soul

Performance # 3 — Paris by Night 36

Chet trong vong tay em
(Excerpts from *I Just Died in Your Arms Tonight*)

. . . .

Em oi vi sao con mong hom nay vo tan
Darling, why is the dream of today broken
Bao ky niem ruc ro nay ve dau
Where do all the radiant memories go?
Nhung thuong yeu dam duoi trong ta sao nay khong con
Why all the passionate love in us exist no more

Nhung cau chuyen cu
The stories of old
Roi mai kia ai nho cho long dau
Who will remember them tomorrow for the heart to ache
Vong tay kia ai dan giac mo thuong dau
That circle of arms weaving a dream of love and pain
Cho ngay thang in sau cuoc song hu hao
For the days and months to imprint a damaged life.

. . . .

Dem thien thu mot vi sao roi lang le
A night in eternity, a star falls silently
Dau cuoc tinh cho anh mot thuo nhung con mong tham thiet
Where is the love that gave me a time with penetrating dreams?
Cho dem thoi xa
For the night to cease to be distant

Cho con tim thoi doi cho
For the heart to stop waiting
Se khong buon ba vi con dau se qua
I will not be sad for the pain will pass
Cuoi chan troi xa
At the end of the distant horizon
Tinh yeu theo con gio bay ai hay
Love follows the blowing wind, who knows
Tinh van nhu ngay vi nhung con say
Love is still as always because of the drunken fits

. . . .

. . . .

4

Bollywood Down Under: Fiji Indian Cultural History and Popular Assertion

Manas Ray

Previously, I used to encourage my children to see documentaries on India. I do no more. These people can't show even Taj Mahal without showing beggars, a few lepers, flies and all that. They can't resist that temptation. Instead, our children should watch Australian documentaries. Things about this land, the trees, insects, snakes, all different kinds of bird. If you have to live here, you must know the land well. Plus, they are growing kids too, you know what I mean? They have their needs, their desires. You must try and understand this. So for entertainment, you have Hindi films. The songs, the dance, the stories, glamour — all those things that they can talk about with their other Indian friends.

My friend, India — like *all* our countries — can only go down and down but Hindi films will prosper. Such is the logic. So don't worry about entertainment. It will always be there, no matter where you live. You may call these films fantasy but it is a better way of knowing, I mean *seeing*, India than these documentaries. (Fiji Indian taxi driver, Brisbane, 1997)

Kay Rasool's film, *Temple on the Hill* (1997), is a short documentary on the banana-growing Punjabi community of Woolgoolga in northern New South Wales. The film is about continuity in the face of change: while the older generation harp on the former, the younger people perform the difficult negotiation between the demands of a traditional, rigid order and the attractions of the liberal, individualised West ("We stick to our culture but the mind travels"). Encased in the performance of Sikh religious rituals, the film stacks up the evident values of Punjabi life for no one to miss: deep attachment to the preachings of the Holy saint, Guru Gavind Singh ("who forms our identity"); allegiance to the family profession (boys return to work in the plantation after completing their university degrees); abiding respect and care for elders; photomarriage ("the parents have to say yes first"); the imported *desi* bride quietly performing the domestic chores ("we wanted a girl who will do all the housework"); assertion of strong familial ties ("my brothers will do anything for me, I will do anything for them"); and so on. Men play billiards or maybe display the new video camera which is "so light" as women milk the cows or look after the children. Breaking this seamless pattern is the girl who felt "more and more uncomfortable with being an Indian" and "just wished I could be an Australian". Glimpses of her preferred Australian life lead to a wholesale change in the visual milieu: swimming in the house pool with her daughter and white husband, the Australian lunch of salad, sausage and roasted meat (in place of *pooris* and hot *bhajis),* her sleek performance as a saleswoman in a department store. The other figure to rupture the settled patriarchal order is the son who takes to Christianity and becomes a passionate evangelist, drawn by the attraction of Christian universalism which he contrasts with the hypocrisy of Sikh religious practice. A Hindi movie of song and dance provides solace to the lonely mother. What is remarkable about the film is that, in around 25 minutes, it manages to encapsulate a whole portfolio of accepted Orientalist "knowledge".

Marie Gillespie's influential *Television, Ethnicity and Cultural Change* (1995) is a comprehensive study of the Punjabi community of west London. A media sociology of Punjabis living in one particular suburb, Southall — and sharing more or less the same history, cultural profile, media habits and class location — the work has been praised widely for its meticulous ethnology and has been influential in the rise of academic interest in the media of diasporic Indian communities (as only befits one of the largest diasporas in the world).

The differences between Gillespie's book and Rashool's film are apparent. The working class suburb of west London, where more than 65 000 migrants (1995: 33) jostle for space, is a far cry from the sprawling green of a remote Australian plantation settlement. In economic terms, too, they are studies in contrast: while the Punjabis of Woolgoolga have it good, the Southall Punjabis continue to struggle. However, in spite of the manifest differences, the picture that emerges of the cultural life in the struggling Punjabi ghetto in London bears real similarities to the time-wrapped, banana-cultivating Punjabis in obscure Woolgoolga. Both constructions draw on an essentialised understanding of an *oriental* community. John Hutnyk (1996) points to this in his review of Gillespie:

> There is not, in this book, any disruption of an ethnographic project that requires particular, not global, essentialized, although hybrid, traditional, although translated, ethnic categories to proceed ... she never leaves go of a notion of culture, which though it changes, is still an unexamined hold-all category doing work for time-honoured anthropological simplicities. (1996: 420–21)

Gillespie's (1995) ethnography produces reasonably predictable results: the parental regime of social control, suspicion and adherence to a homeland culture of unquestioned obedience and religious devotion; the vicious networks of rumour and gossip aimed at constant surveillance of girls' chastity (1995: 25–27, 153–57); young people's preoccupation with style and fashion endorsing Western images; the gendered pattern of viewing (boys prefer science fiction, science programs, documentaries, news and crime series; girls prefer watching pop and quiz programs, cartoons and children's TV and, of course, soaps); girls who (along with the older generation) mostly love Hindi movies while a majority of boys find them not to their taste (1995: 77). What is so specifically Punjabi — or for that matter Indian — about these findings? Gillespie will often throw up more questions than she answers. For instance, if boys are generally condescending about Indian traditions and Hindi films' unrealistic modes, how could the whole family group (boys as well as girls) watch so intently B.R. Chopra's televisual melodrama, *Mahabharata?*

Gillespie asserts that identity as 'not an essence but a positioning', but she rarely makes use of Appadurai's (1990) insight that she quotes programmatically:

> The Hindu diaspora has been exploited by various "interests" both within and outside India to create a complicated network of finances and religious identifications, in which the problem of cultural reproduction for Hindus abroad has become tied to the politics of Hindu fundamentalism at home. (Appadurai, 1990: 302, quoted in Gillespie, 1995: 20)

Instead, what we have is a replay of classic ethnographic persuasion in a new form: she respectfully watches the Dhanis watch the teleserial, *Mahabharata*, as an *authentic* moment of Indian devotion.

Gillespie's book is professedly about the "cultural routes of diaspora" (1995: 6). But what is privileged is her attention to the values "rooted in the subcontinent" (1995: 46), to which the youth are attached even as they try to "maximise their chance of acceptance" in British society (1995: 5). Gillespie's mutual stress on the irreducible difference of migrant cultures and evolving trajectories of assimilation is in a way the crux of contemporary Western multiculturalism: "it 'respects' the Other's identity, conceiving the Other as a self-enclosed 'authentic' community towards which he, the multiculturalist, maintains a distance rendered possible by his privileged universal position" (Zizek, 1997: 44). The extent of the similarities between a painstaking work of academic ethnography and a film *(Temple on the Hill)* made by a young graduate point to the well-established order of knowledge about migrants from which both draw.

For all of her meticulous research into the kinds of audiovisual media watched by the Punjabis in London, Gillespie makes little or no attempt to link diasporic media use with the life of media back in India. I consider this significant, given the intimate relation Indian film and television have had with the politics of Indian nationhood. As a result, Gillespie's readings of film/video as a means of recreating cultural traditions suffer from a degree of aestheticisation. The account that she provides of Hindi films (1995: 78) would be applicable to Bollywood of any decade after the emergence of the "social" as a super-genre (see below, "From the *Ramayan* to Bollywood"). So she misses the potential of post-liberalisation Bollywood from the late 1980s to frame a new diasporic cultural identity for Indian youth. Gillespie (1995) draws on the Habermasian notion of "an enlightened public sphere of communications" (1995: 15), which in her scheme of things fits well with the notion of "postcolonial space" defined as a "pluralistic conception of nationality and perhaps beyond that to its transcendence" (1995: 8). The burden of racism is placed on the nation-state which constructs its internal ethnic "others" — its "racial minorities" (1995: 14). This gives her a reason to ignore the realities of the imbrication of nation-states with the contemporary movements of global capital (both economic and cultural); instead, she places hope on the traffic between "the local and the global that nevertheless transcends the national" (1995: 6). As part of her distrust of the category nation-state, she refuses any consideration of the political background from which Hindi movies emanate and the fact that this cinema is inalienably attached to the politics of the Indian nation-state. Such depoliticised understanding of Indian films inevitably gives them the look of self-enclosed, exotic cultural artefacts whose consumption in the Western world by the Indian diaspora Gillespie makes the centrepiece of her careful ethnography.

Different Diasporic Indias

This chapter examines the process of imagining into existence of a sense of community by Fiji Indians in Australia through the use of Indian-sourced popular media. The sway of Indian filmdom on Indians — *wherever they live* — is widely accepted. The chapter attempts to take a fresh look at this understanding by tracking the history of this twice-displaced community from the days of indenture through the phase of independent subsistence farming in Fiji to their present life in Australia. I seek to explain the significance of Bollywood in the lives of Fiji Indians in terms of the dynamics of colonial and postcolonial histories of this community as it manifests itself in a particular Western cultural setting, namely Australia.

The reason for focusing on the Fiji Indian community is primarily because of its close attachment to Hindi movies. Since the time Hindi movies reached Fiji in the late 1930s (Anon, 1956), they have remained the most important source for the "imagination" of the motherland. Of all the Indian diasporas in Australia, the Fiji Indian community is not only the highest consumer of Hindi videos (going by the estimates provided by various video parlours in Sydney and Brisbane); it is perhaps the only diasporic community in Australia that has been able to rapidly construct a whole cultural environment around Bollywood. Interestingly enough, the cultural trajectory of the Fiji Indians in a way parallels shifts in the history of Bollywood itself — from construction in the early days of indenture of a cultural community based on reminiscences of folk cultural practices that would pave the way to Hindi popular cinema which again in its current, post-liberalisation manifestation would offer the young Fiji Indians a chance to construct their own cultural platform in Australia.

The chapter addresses two theoretical issues central to understanding diasporic media. First, I argue that the different postcolonial diasporas are not "splinters" in a transnational world, ready to rearticulate their identity on the lines of extra-territoriality or nomadism; on the contrary, it is the *historical* subjectivity of a diaspora which holds the key to its cultural life. At one level, there is a need to club the different (postcolonial) diasporas together as those which are not parties to what Partha Chatterjee (1995: 11) calls the "original historical contract" that gave birth to the Western nation-states. At another level, it is also important to recognise the different historical trajectories of these diasporas. Hence the alienation that postcolonial people face in the multicultural West is multilayered; citings of the more visible signs of racism do not register its historical depth. The case of the Fiji Indians will amply demonstrate this. Second, diasporic media needs to be seen in the context of the politics of its production and dissemination. This is particularly so with Bollywood, which from its inception has situated itself in the locus of contending definitions of "Indianness" (Rajadhyaksha and Willeman, 1995: 10).

By no means does this chapter seek to analyse the media use of *the* "Indian" diaspora seen as one monolithic whole. In fact, it is the globality of such a concept that needs be contested and read as a sign of ahistoricity and ethnocentrism that so often underwrites the perception of postcolonial societies. This is not to deny that the different Indian diasporas do deploy their notions of "India" as the broad symbolic horizon for constructing their respective identities. Neither is it to underestimate the crucial role that such pan-"Indianness" (largely derived from Orientalist discourse about India) played in imagining a nation into existence during the course of struggle against colonial rule and continues to do so long after the Raj. It is, however, to highlight the fact that for Indians (both inside India and outside) such "Indianness" — like any other identity concept — is always already fissured. As a matter of *positioning* and not essence, this "Indianness" varies with different communities, is used at times for contradictory purposes, and quite often gives rise to unintended consequences. It may be argued that the different empirical factors like language, region or religion do not by themselves hold the key to cultural difference. It is how communities position themselves in postcolonial space that underpins the cultural lives of different Indian diasporas and sets the course for possible futures.

The different ways that different Indian diasporas frame their identities and cultural lives is remarkable. If the Fiji Indian community is the highest consumer of Hindi films, for the Indian Bengalis, Indian-sourced film and video is not only a private affair; in many cases, it is of little interest and even active disparagement. At one level it may seem that this is a function of class, since the Indian Bengali diaspora in Australia, as elsewhere, is composed of professionals. But class cannot be a major cause, because South Asian diasporas in Australia are more or less of the same class composition, given the history of Australian immigration laws and the entry system it uses to select its migrants.

It is again a case of historicising the question by addressing Bengal's specific encounter with the British regime and the systems of knowledge of post-enlightenment Europe. In its bid to imagine otherwise than the modular Western (Chatterjee, 1993: Ch. 1), cultural nationalism in Bengal had made the *self* the locus of a complex and difficult elaboration from the middle of last century onwards that led to an enormous growth in every department of the Bengali cultural sphere. The basis of the *bradralok* (the educated, Hindu Bengali gentry) was neither trade nor industry, but land. Very early on, Bengal's commerce and industry were dominated by either the colonialists or the traders and capitalists from western India. As a result, the *bradralok* concentrated in education, hoping to achieve through education what was denied through the economy (Chatterjee, 1997: 11). The process was accentuated with the introduction in 1885 of legislation limiting *zamindari* powers. This made the collection of dues more difficult, and rentier incomes began the long process of decline, both in real and absolute terms (Chatterji, 1994: 9).

The project of modernity that the Bengali *bradralok* had framed for itself faced its real challenge after independence with the civic disarray caused by Bengal's stagnant economy and the change in the constellation of political forces. Subaltern classes, empowered by electoral democracy, now staked their claims to enter the political institutions of modernity, originally framed to keep them out. It is from this Bengal that the *bradralok* flees, either to the relatively prosperous parts of India or, if possible, abroad — to the affluent West, taking with them the dream of a nation that they were once so passionate about and the cultural baggage which had expressed that dream.

The Indian Bengali community's relation to their home country is marked by a past which is lost and a present which is a lack. Community members justify their rupture from the motherland by attempting to become "better" Bengalis: revoking a past when Bengal's "today" was India's "tomorrow" is what frames Indian Bengali diasporic cultural life. This has meant framing their cultural lives around the high culture of the past, which has become a fossilised "taste culture". There is a surprising similarity between the menu of Bengali cultural programs in Brisbane or Sydney and that of such places like New York, Toronto or London, where their number is vastly greater. Ironically, the cultural products once deeply rooted in the soil and having organic links to the independence movement and to early post-independence hardship and hope have now come to form an imaginative global geography, lacing together Bengalis in such diverse places as Philadelphia, Boston, London, Dusseldorf, Dubai or Sydney. In a diasporic context, the project of Bengali modernity has been emptied of all political significance, save its impossibility.

If the Indian Bengali community is locked in the past, the twice-displaced Fiji Indian community looks outside, to India, for its cultural sustenance. For the Fiji Indians in Australia, Hindi films mean a whole way of life. Movie theatres that regularly run Hindi films, film music nights, a number of bands that specialise in Hindi film music, nightclubs, design shops offering the latest of Bollywood, film magazines — all of these mean that Bollywood for Fiji Indians is by no means restricted to consuming videos in the seclusion of the home. In this sense, the Fiji Indians of Australia bear a degree of resemblance to Gillespie's Punjabis of Southall. However, the differences between these two communities are crucial. India, properly speaking, is for the Fiji Indians a wholly imagined entity about which they know very little and have experienced even less. The fact that they were drawn mainly from the lower castes has also helped them to largely free themselves as a social group from the shackles of the caste mentality or religious sectarianism in the course of the last hundred years in Fiji. This is in sharp contrast to the mainland Indians and also to the Southall Punjabis.

Migration to Australia from mainland India has mostly been of the professional category. The social composition of India being what it is, this also means that the Indian representation in Australia is largely from the upper castes, many of whom are unwilling to give up their historical memory of unquestioned superiority *vis-à-vis* the lower castes. "Going out" at times also means going back in time. As far as the Fiji Indians are concerned, the romantic construction of India (and Indians) — derived most significantly from the movies — faced in Australia for the first time the rude shock of caste discrimination through their interactions with "compatriot" Indians. This has resulted in a change of focus of cultural antagonism — from the native Fijians, the mainland Indians now constitute the community's "other".

The pervasive dominance of Hindi film culture amongst diasporic Fiji Indians is complicated by the continued presence of folk traditions like *Ramayan katha* (i.e. the recitation and enactment from the Hindu epic, the *Ramayan)*, or *bhajan* (devotional songs) that they had carried with them from the villages of India a century or more back. The *Ramayan*, in its simplified version of Tulsi Das's *Ramcharitmanas*, functioned as a binding force in the fissiparous environment of indenture. It provided a nostalgic identification with motherland and also acted as a vehicle to relativise worldly realities by means of transcendental promises. This chapter shows that, while the rural traditions in their present manifestations are thoroughly imbricated by Hindi filmdom, historically they have provided — in terms of narrative, iconography and emotional and moral ambience — the ideal ground for the overwhelming popularity of Hindi cinema amongst Fiji Indians.

The size of diasporic Indian groupings found in a country like Australia rarely reaches "critical mass". My research shows that the cultural implications of numerical strength of a particular grouping depend on the specificity of its diasporic postcolonial subjectivity. The identity politics of the Fiji Indian community in Australia is more a *post*colonial practice, while that of the Indian Bengali community, their higher professional profile notwithstanding, is distinctly post*colonial*. Being *post*colonial means being beyond or outside nostalgia, while a post*colonial* cultural politics is essentially an act of re-routing one's identity through the past.[1] For the former, the size of the community plays a vital role. Fiji Indians living in Sydney (upper estimates put the figure at about 40 000) have been able to form in the course of the last ten years a whole cultural ecology around Hindi popular filmdom. This has then been transmitted to other cities — for instance, Brisbane, where their presence is much thinner (around 7000). The crucial importance of this process lies in the fact that the second-generation Fiji Indians now have a cultural platform that, though not counter-hegemonic, is markedly different from the host culture. The chapter examines the role "post-Zee" Bollywood (the era since television was substantially deregulated) and the current trend of remixes of earlier songs to new beats play in this form of identity construction. As a contrast to this, the emphasis of the first-generation (post*colonial)* Indian Bengali diaspora on aestheticised cultural forms of the past offers the second generation very little in terms of a home-country popular youth culture with which they can identify.

In an era of the global spread of corporate capital and great demographic shifts, one of the key projects of political modernity is faced with serious crisis: instead of the "nationalisation of the ethnic" that Western nation-states banked their hopes on, we now face the opposite scenario: "the ethnicisation of the nation". The yearning for "roots", as it is called, has become a common phenomenon for both the majoritarian white community and the different diasporas in different ways. As a result, the notion of shared public space is increasingly challenged by a different ordering of space, namely a criss-cross of different primordias tied together by the universal function of the market — what we, in this book, are calling public sphericules. For the Fiji Indians, if it was legislated racial discrimination that compelled them to leave Fiji, in Australia they find themselves in the middle of a new entanglement of different, contesting imaginings of "roots". One of the results of this process is that Bollywood is taking on a new significance in their lives. Historically, the bond between them and India has been one of imagination. With time, as memory of "roots" — the *real* India — was fading away, film took over the responsibility of constructing an empty, many-coloured space through its never-ending web of images, songs, "dialogues" and stars. In the new political context of Australia, this empty space would be shorn of even the pretence of a referent — it is space unto itself, a *pure* space. Bollywood reciprocates this gesture by placing the diasporic *imaginaire* at the very heart of its new aesthetics.

Demography of Fiji Indians in Australia

The Fiji Islands were declared a British colony in 1874 when a group of indigenous "chiefs" signed a Deed of Cession with the British. Five years later, the first Indian indentured labourers arrived in the coolie ships from India, the labour for the sugar plantations and other enterprises that would make the new colony pay without exposing the indigenous population to the harmful consequences of an industrial economy (Kelly, 1991; Jayawardena, 1980). By the end of indenture in 1919, a total of 60 965 Indians had come to Fiji as indentured labourers (see Mishra, 1979; Lal, 1983). They called themselves *girmitiyas* (from the English word "agreement", a reference to the labour contract). The British called them "coolies", as did the indigenous Fijians (the word has an interesting twist, since the word for dog in Fijian language is similar: *kuli)*. The plan had been for the Indians to be "extracted" (in keeping with much of colonial practice, the recruitment of indentured labourers from India was a peculiar combination of legal protocols and fraud — see Lal, 1992) as "a working population and nothing more" (Scarr, 1980: 88, in Kelly, 1991: 181). Once indenture ended — five years per contract, but mostly extended for another five years — many of them did actually return to India, but mostly they stayed on as subsistence farmers. By 1986, the Indian population was in the majority in Fiji (348 704 as against 329 305 ethnic Fijians) (Lal, 1992: 337) and the country's economy was based on Indian management and labour.

The tables were turned in the 1987 coup when the military (manned exclusively by the Fijians) took charge of the country. Fiji became an independent state in 1970 and, until 1987, the Alliance Party held power. In the 1987 elections, the Alliance Party was defeated and the new government was widely perceived as *de facto* Fiji Indian rule. This caused wide-scale racial violence. Later that year, Colonel Sitiveni Ligamamada Rambuka of the Fiji Military Forces led two coups and captured political power. This led to an exodus of Fiji Indians from Fiji. The destinations were primarily Canada, Australia and New Zealand. The exodus has brought about a crucial reversal in Fiji's population ratio: from 51 per cent in 1986, Fiji Indians now constitute around 45 per cent of the population. This, more than any other factor, has cooled down the polity and a new constitution aimed at restoring constitutional rights of the Indians in Fiji is in the process of being enacted.

Australia's Fiji Indian population increased several times between 1987 and 1990. A large majority of the exodus settled in Sydney, which is now one of the major centres outside Fiji, along with Vancouver and Auckland. Immigration of this group has fallen off in the early 1990s, with the overall reduction in intake; however, their numbers still make Fiji Indians the largest Pacific group in the nation excluding the predominantly European-ancestry New Zealanders. Moreover, it seems that there are significant numbers of Fiji-born who are overstayers, so the official Census data probably understate the size of the community. The 1996 Census put Fiji-born population living in Sydney at 21 029 while those in Melbourne numbered 5542 and in Brisbane 4671. The community estimates of Fiji Indians living in Sydney vary between 25 000 and 45 000. Most of the entries to Australia have been via the points system. During those years, there were innumerable applications from asylum-seekers. The Hawke Labor government was, however, reluctant to take the diplomatic risk of souring relations with a neighbouring country and refused to consider the post-coup Fiji Indians as refugees. Instead, the criteria for immigration on the points system and family reunion scheme were relaxed. Also, amnesty was granted in 1989 to those who had come on temporary visas and overstayed. Since the early 1990s, Australian immigration laws for Fiji Indians have been tightened again and now they are treated equally with applicants from other countries. Canada has followed a comparatively relaxed immigration policy both before and after the coup. One of the consequences of the different criteria of immigration followed by these two countries is that the Australian Fiji Indians have a higher presence of professionals compared with their counterparts in Canada.

Fiji Indians' demographic profile in Sydney is described by *The Atlas of the Australian People* (1991 Census, updated 1993):

The recency of arrival of the bulk of the Fiji-born population is reflected in their age structure, which is predominantly concentrated in the young working age groups. Almost three-quarters are aged between 15 and 49 years compared with half of the Australia-born group. It is interesting that women predominate in these groups as well as in the Fiji-born population overall. Only a very small proportion have any difficulty speaking English due to the fact that much of the education in Fiji is in English. The recency of movement has meant that much of it has been subject to selectivity based on education and skills. Hence the population of Fijians with higher education is greater than for the Australia-born (16.4 with 12.7 per cent), although the proportion with other post-school qualifications is slightly less.

The high education profile of the Fiji-born is not fully borne out in their socioeconomic status. Despite having higher proportions than the Australia-born in the highest education categories, they are underrepresented in the managerial/administrative occupation category and substantially overrepresented in blue-collar jobs. On the other hand, they have a similar proportion of workers in the professional/ paraprofessional categories, reflecting the large numbers of nurses and doctors who moved to Australia, especially following the first military coup in Fiji. The proportion of the Fiji-born who own or are purchasing their own home (43.8 per cent) is lower than that for the Australia-born (71.3 per cent), although this may be less a function of their socioeconomic status than the relative recency of their arrival and the youthfulness of their age structure. (*Atlas*, 1993: 52)

Media and Identity Politics

Of all the Indian diasporas in Australia, Fiji Indians have the deepest attachment to Bollywood. In Fiji, Hindi films (and later videos) have traditionally been the primary source of entertainment for Fiji Indians and a prime locus of their cultural life. The process was aided by the Fijian government's reticence about television until recently. Television was viewed as an "economically unviable" apparatus of social pollution. Fiji's emergence as a major tourist destination was one of the reasons why the policy had to be changed (Stewart, 1993). But Hindi film culture has always been of greater significance for diasporic Fiji Indians. The attachment to Hindi films is not restricted to private consumption of Bollywood films and videos, but constitutes a broad cultural ecology. Bollywood provides them with a sense of continuity with the past as well as the possibility of a different (though by no means counter-hegemonic) cultural platform *vis-à-vis* the host white culture.

The folk traditions of *Ramayan katha* and *bhajan* and their relation to Hindi cinema, as an example of the "little" and "great" traditions (local, quotidian practices of cultural Hinduism and Islam on the one hand and the quasi-globalising mass culture of Bollywood on the other),[2] may no longer be overlapping and reinforcing in today's urban Fiji, but in the new diasporic context of Australia the little traditions have regained their role of retaining identity and also function as a moral regime for the second generation.

The role of such media in the identity politics of diasporic Fiji Indians needs to be understood in the context of, first, the changes that Bollywood has undergone since the Indian economy was liberalised in the early 1990s and, second, the tension between the Fiji Indians and mainland Indians in their new diasporic location. Bollywood, in its contemporary manifestation, offers Indian diasporic youth a platform for organising their cultural life which is "acceptable" to the West and at the same time retains a measure of difference. The widely held notion that, for Indians, *no matter where they live,* India largely derives from its movies (Rajadhyaksha and Willeman, 1995: 10) holds a special significance for Fiji Indians for whom India is largely an imagined entity ("mother" but not "home", as a number of my respondents have pointed out). For Fiji Indian youth in Australia, the relation between Bollywood and India is even more an imaginary one. This might suggest that reception takes place in an historical vacuum, but young Fiji Indians, more than any other Indian group in Australia, are keen on appropriating Hindi popular films to fashion a cultural identity that is their own.

Be it in the special meaning that Bollywood has for this community or the reinvigoration of folk traditions inherited from India; be it in their friction with mainland Indians or their bid to re-imagine an entity called "India" (from which they were once "extracted" and to which they do not harbour any illusion of return but nonetheless continually seek recourse to as an imagined nodal point of identity); be it in their relatively Westernised values or in the emphasis placed on tradition — the cultural life of Fiji Indians in their current Western locations is inalienably linked to their genealogy of the last hundred years — the contingent history of the Plantation Raj and after. In what follows, I will not so much embrace celebration of the ontological condition of the diasporic imagination but the formation of the historical subjectivity of a twice-displaced community.

Indenture and Beyond

The caste and cultural heritage of the indentured Indian labourers were varied. The first wave went from Hararibagh and Chotanagpur areas of Madhya Pradesh. Once that area was depleted, the route moved northwards to Bihar — mainly the Chappra, Saharanpur and Gaya districts. But by the time extraction for Fiji began, Bihar had also started drying up, since it was providing labourers for the coal mines of the province, the tea estates of Assam and, principally, for the jute mills and port of Calcutta and the railways. The eastern parts of Uttar Pradesh became the main suppliers of indentured labourers, which constituted about 75 per cent of those who left for Fiji from northern India. This was followed by Bihar (10 per cent), Madhya Pradesh (6 per cent) and Punjab (2 per cent). North Indian representation in Fiji constituted around 300 castes (mostly agrarian, with Brahmin cultivators constituting around 10 per cent) from 200 villages. The Muslim presence was 13 per cent (Lal, 1983). Though, as North Indians, they all spoke Hindi, the dialects varied widely from one region to another. The difference in dialect is particularly important in this case, since the overwhelming majority of those who went to Fiji as indentured labourers were unlettered people. The *lingua franca* that developed amongst Fiji Indians (known as Fiji Hindi) reflects many different dialects, with occasional European and Fijian words. From the standpoint of ethnic identity, the important point is that the Fiji Indian population retained Hindi, which has not always been the case with other indentured diasporas (see Jayawardena, 1980).

South India came into the picture only after 1903. However, even as latecomers, the total number of South Indians going to Fiji between 1904 and 1917 was 14 536, constituting 23.8 per cent of the Indian population when the indenture period was over. The reason for such bulk migration was the different system under which they went —

the *Kangani* system — where the village-head corralled his village people and took them to the colony. In their new destination, the South Indians were moved around and scattered in different plantations and as such they had to adjust to the *lingua franca*. This was a matter of great effort on their part, since the languages of the South emanate from the Dravidian family of languages and are entirely different from Hindi which is part of the Indo-European group of languages.

The indentured labourers were entitled to return to India, but there was the widely held and well-grounded fear that in India they would have faced social ostracisation, since by then many of them had married across caste and regional lines. In the post-indenture period, Indians worked mostly as independent farmers on leased land for different sugar companies owned in Australia and Britain. Their economic condition gradually improved and the hardship of back-breaking routine work also eased. Personal ties with India, even as they dwindled, never ceased entirely. As late as the 1950s, the remittance economy was still — albeit marginally — at work. In terms of a more political and public cultural realm, the traffic from India increased with the rising tide of nationalist movement, with religious missionaries and political leaders visiting Fiji. The news of exploitation of Indian labourers and especially of sexual harassment of Indian women by European males caused major flare-ups in India and provided inspiration to India's independence movement (Kelly, 1991). It has been argued that it was the movement against indenture in Fiji (with the active support of the Indian National Congress) that brought an end to the system worldwide in 1917 (Lal, 1985, 1992).

The Gujaritis first came in large number in the 1920s and 1930s as shopkeepers, moneylenders, artisans, *sonars* (goldsmiths) and in numerous other trades and services. There were occupational as well as residential differentiations. Mostly they lived in urban areas with little social interaction with the rest of the Indian community. While the Gujratis could speak Fiji Hindi, they were careful about retaining their own language and for a long time there was virtually no intermarriage. The extent of separation diminished over time; however, their occupational difference was compounded by cultural difference and a residual sense of superiority because they did not come as indentured labourers.

Unlike mainland India, Fiji was governed by British Common Law with no room for separate laws for different religious communities. Fiji Indians, much like their ethnic Fijian counterparts, were products of a deeply Western background in terms of education, social organisation and legal system. Yet Fijians and Indians were kept separate; every aspect of life — be it work, education, residence, or sport — was racially segregated. As late as 1960, there was little social interaction; each harboured deep prejudices about the other. Sharing of political power since independence in 1970 has predictably brought the two communities closer at a formal level, but this itself contributed new dimensions of complexities to the tradition of segregation and prejudice (Norton, 1990: Chs 6 and 7).

The root cause of indenture lies in the dislocation of village life in India following British conquest and administrative reorganisation (Jayawardena, 1980: 431). Since the poorer section of the rural population were the worst victims of the colonial system, recruitment came almost entirely from them; even the Brahmins amongst them were cultivators. Caste hierarchy broke down considerably in the depots of Calcutta and then in the confinement of the ship which took no less than three months to reach Fiji. It was not possible to maintain the commissarial and other taboos in the new environment. In the plantation economy, they were forced to work in coordinated labour units in close proximity and rewarded not on the basis of social status but on that of individual initiative and endeavour. Even after indenture was over, people did not have the right to choose their place of dwelling. The pattern of the Indian nucleated village simply did not exist.

However, this did not mean that for Fiji Indians the social system of Indian villages, which reinforces compliance with accepted rituals, gave way to the impersonality of a secular order. This could not have happened, given the built-in conditions of inequality of a plantation regime. For the indentured population, re-creating "motherland" in its social, cultural and religious manifestations became part of their wider political struggle.

Jayawardena (1980) observes that the complete proletarianisation of Indians in Guyana meant near total loss of home traditions while the Fiji Indians could maintain cultural traditions because of isolated subsistence farming post-indenture (1980: 436). With time, the population become more scattered and professions diversified. This re-emphasised the need to preserve their culture and religion in order to provide support and solidarity among themselves. Interestingly, very few Fiji Indians embraced Christianity. By the time the Christian missionaries began to take an interest in the Indian community, the Indians had already started to reconstitute out of the fragments of their ancestral culture and fashion a new moral universe. The process was helped by visiting religious figures from India. The Hindu reform movement, Arya Samaj, formed in India late last century, had representation in Fiji as early as 1915 while the more orthodox Sanatani Dharma had numerous *mandalis* (local gatherings) throughout the areas of Indian settlement in Fiji (Lal, 1996).

However, as Indians settled down to post-indenture social and economic order, identity-differentiation occurred. The principal divide was between the North and South Indians. South Indians tried to rediscover their own cultural identity, firstly through another reformist Hindu organisation, Rama Krishna Mission, and then through their own cultural organisation, Sangam, in 1942. Today Sangam is one of the most globalised of cultural fora for South Indian Tamils.

The other divides are of the Hindus and the Muslims and of the Gujratis and the rest of the Indian community. It needs to be emphasised, however, that even though boundaries were maintained cautiously, acrimonies were mostly avoided. The primary reason for this is that, for all these different fragments of the Fiji Indian population, the main sources of cultural threat and political antagonism were the Europeans and the ethnic Fijians. Culturally and morally, what kept providing sustenance to the Fiji Indian community as a whole were the folk traditions of North India, and particularly the ancient epic *Ramayan* (or better, the popular version composed by Tulsi Das in the sixteenth century, *Ramcharitmanas*). This epic — along with other cultural expressions of the *bhakti* movement — not only provided the cultural and moral fodder to the community; in the very process of doing so, it also paved the way for the overwhelming popularity of Hindi popular cinema amongst Fiji Indians.

From the *Ramayan* to Bollywood

The cultural diet of Indians in Fiji right from the beginning of indenture was profusely imbued with elements of the *bhakti* (devotion) movement, the popular social and aesthetic movement that spread across India from the twelfth century onwards (Embree, 1988: Ch. 12). It is through the prism of *bhakti* that they imagined their "motherland" and embraced the popularity of Hindi commercial cinema.

Beyond the narrow sense as a form of worship, *bhakti* set the paradigm for popular creative expression almost singularly from the twelfth to the eighteenth centuries, and later in combination with other currents of thought. The songs were composed in the vernacular, using quotidian metaphors. They advocated struggle against Brahminism and upheld the sacrosanct nature of every human relationship. Mostly a gesture against authoritarian rule, it was spearheaded by the subaltern classes. The movement was a confluence of many traditions and was not a particularly radical movement, at times showing an uncanny ability to suppress other emergent trends. While the transcendent is to be read in the everyday, it is figured in such a way that it has a levelling influence on all social and cultural divides of mundane existence. Tulsi Das's *Ramcharitmanas* formed the centrepiece of *bhakti* tradition and became the unchallenged cultural meta-text of Hinduism. In the course of time, Gandhi was to privilege *Ramcharitmanas* to frame a semiotics of cultural politics against colonial rule, as for different and opposed ends was the Rastriya Sawangsevak Sangha (RSS — the martial arm of the currently ruling Bharatiya Janata Party). Throughout the nationalist movement, the *Ramayan* would function as one of the primary sites of investment for various kinds of rewritings for different cultural and political ends (see Lutgendorf, 1995; Barucha, 1994).

Unlike India (as Chatterjee, 1993 discusses in detail), in indenture Fiji there was no class of gentry to put through a nationalist sieve the various cultural forms that emerged in the encounter with colonial modernity and selectively adopt and combine the reconstituted elements of the supposedly indigenous tradition. In the absence of any philosophical tradition, what prevailed at the beginning were the reminiscences of numerous local cultural traditions of the villages of India. The north Indian village cultural expressions are compact, complex and part of a living tradition. The *girmitiyas* simplified those traditions they remembered — the dances, the songs, the religious rituals, the sports, the games, the riddles. But most of them disappeared with time, since there was no institutional support which could nourish those traditions (Lal, 1992).

The traditions of village India that survived were basically derived from *bhakti* — the devotional songs *(bhajans)* of such composers as Kabir, Mira and Sur Das. But over and above anything else, what inspired their imagination was Tulsi's *Ramcharitmanas*. Very early on, reciting, singing and enactment of the *Ramayan* was revived amongst the Indians of Fiji. This bound together a *cultural* community to brave the chains of bondage in the fissiparous environment of plantation capitalism where everyone was an individual unit of production and daily existence was measured by work hours.

The Fiji Indians never accepted the status of racially and culturally doomed proletariat and went to great lengths to fashion new hybrid diasporic realities. During the indenture period and the early days of post-indenture, both Hindus and Muslims participated in the major ritual festivals like *Holi*, the riotous Hindu ritual of reversals, and the Tazia, the Shi'a Islamic Moharram re-enactment of the martyrdom of Husain and Hassan. Both also participated in *Ram Lilas*, the dramatic re-enactments of the *Ramayan* narrative, which in indenture days was told as a tale of Ram's exile, climaxing with the burning of the giant effigy of Ravan symbolising destruction of evil in the world. In these rituals (which were also to be dynamically appropriated into the Bollywood universe), the Indians found their social identity in relation to gods outside of, and in tension with, their colonial racist and economic definitions as "coolies".

The *Ramayan* was shorn of deeper philosophical meanings. Its primary function was to serve emotional satisfaction and not individual spiritual enlightenment. As mentioned before, the majority of North Indians in Fiji came from the Ayodha region of India, the homeland of the *Ramayan*. The reasons for an overwhelming emotional identification with the epic are directly related to the predicament of an indentured diaspora. The central god character, Ram, was banished for fourteen years. For Fiji Indians, it was for at least five years. Ram's banishment was no fault of his; similarly, it was not the fault of the Indians that they were extracted from their homeland and subjected to inhuman physical labour in this remote island (Lal, 1998). The triumphant ending of all ordeals provided a kind of moral strength to withstand the brutalities of indenture. If

Ram could survive for fourteen years, surely the Fiji Indians could do so for five years. The *Ramayan* thus was used to heal the wounds of indenture and provide a cultural and moral texture in the new settlement. A strong emotional identification to the *Ramayan* and other expressions of the *bhakti* movement — a constrained cultural environment, continued degradation at the hands of the racist white regime, a disdain for the culture of the ethnic Fijians, a less hard-pressed post-indenture life and, finally, a deep-rooted need of a dynamic, discursive site for the imaginative reconstruction of motherland — were all factors which, together, ensured the popularity of Hindi films once they started reaching the shores of Fiji. This was because Hindi film deployed the *Ramayan* extensively, providing the right pragmatics for "continual mythification" of home.

Of cardinal influence on Hindi cinema right from its inception have been the two epics — the *Ramayan* and the *Mahabharata*. Apart from providing moral succour, they were also magnificent sources for narrative tropes and cinematic spectacle. Films based on them initiated from the earliest days of cinema a different mode of spectatorship — devout villagers coming to the cities in their bullock carts to have a *darsan* (devotional sight) of Lord Ram on the screen (Chakravarty, 1993: 35–36). Madhav Prasad (1998) explains the *darsanic* gaze in the following way:

> Contrary to the voyeuristic relation, in the *darsanic* relation the object gives itself to be seen and in so doing, confers a privilege upon the spectator. The object of the *darsanic* gaze is a superior, a divine figure or a king who presents himself as a spectacle of dazzling splendour to his subjects. (1998: 75–76; see also Rajadhyaksha, 1987; Vasudevan, 1993)

Thus a thoroughly Western technology of representation was deployed to generate an altogether different gaze — one that will not be found in the visual codes of Hollywood melodramas but is deeply ingrained in Indian religious modes. With time, Bollywood increased its repertoire of different modes of address but the *darsanic* gaze remained one of the most important moments in its relations with spectators.

Most of the films made during the silent period were mythological and devotional. In the course of time, the predominance of the mythological receded as other genres like the social, historical, comic or fantasy began increasing in popularity. Derné (1995: 195) notes the decline in the number of mythologicals statistically: in 1923, 70 per cent of the films made belonged to this genre; in 1935, it was 22 per cent; and by 1970, it had dropped to 5 per cent. But with the decline of studio production and the rise of independent producers, all these genres gave way to a super-genre called the "social". By the end of the 1960s, this transition was complete. However, it did not mean that all these genres (including the mythological) simply disappeared; rather, they were subsumed within the "social". The genealogy of "the all-inclusive Hindi film", which came to have a variety show look, is contemporaneously called the *masala* film (Prasad, 1998: 48).

Even during the days of the mythologicals, religion was never an offensive presence. Producers were cautious not to annoy the sensibilities of other religions, due to strict censorship regulations. Partly due to the prevailing censorship norms and partly because Hindi films cater to a multi-religious market, religious motifs are seldom absent but subtle (Derne, 1995). A Hindu way of life constitutes the broad environment for moral elaboration while narrative strategies draw very often — even if allusively — from the two epics. Prasad (1998) has shown that, at its most stable, the social genre included a version of the romance narrative, a comedy track, an average of six songs, as well as a range of familiar character types; the *masala* aesthetic served as a handy catch-all, an emotional and cultural "map" of the diversity of Indian spectators.

The epics helped Bollywood to fuse the history of the nation and the history of the family. In the Indian narrative tradition, family history is not strictly demarcated from social history. The most obvious examples are these two epics, which are popularly believed to have a historical basis. In the *Mahabharata*, the battle between the Kauravas and the Pandavas, two branches of the same family, engages vast social, political and cosmic forces, all of which are then sought to be compressed within a single philosophical framework; in the *Ramayan*, Ram's relationship with Sita is largely determined by his obligation to his family and, more importantly, his social *dharma*. Of the two epics, the *Ramayan* is again privileged because of its elaborations of the familial self and the focus on the duties and sufferings of *sati* — the chaste wife. Also to be taken into account is the fact that, in North India, the *Ramayan*'s popularity far exceeds that of the *Mahabharata*. The usual character stereotypes of Hindi films — the suffering but faithful wife (Sita) who is also a loving and somewhat indulgent sister-in-law; the courageous, dutiful and detached husband (Ram); the faithful brother (Lakshman); and the vengeful, evil villain (Ravan) — are mostly drawn from the *Ramayan*. Bollywood would experiment with these role models, bring in other stereotypes (like that of the frolicsome Krishna of the Radha-Krishna *bhakti* motif; or that of *dosti* — the friendship between two adult males which will be posited against heterosexual love for creating emotionally charged moments in the narrative). But never would Bollywood transgress the moral limits of the *Ramayan*.

What this effectively means is an inscription of the epics into the discourse of the nation through Hindi cinema. Partha Chatterjee (1984) has argued that Gandhian ideology led to the political appropriation of the subaltern classes by a bourgeoisie aspiring for hegemony in the new nation-state. Hindi cinema situated itself in this hegemony and aided the historical possibility for the appropriation of the masses into the evolving political structures of the Indian state. This explains its popularity across class lines and ability to reconcile within its narrative scope the contradictory aspects of social order.

Vijay Mishra (1985, 1992) points to the mythic underlying drives structuring the epics, but the role of music and romance is just as important. Music functions to transform the epic narratives by foregrounding a romantic repertoire. Romance is absolutely crucial for Bollywood — it is defined by romance. Here Bollywood draws more from the Radha–Krishna trope (of love, desire and erotica) of *bhakti* than it does from the epics (see below, "Intercommunal Discord and Cultural Assertion"). Bollywood, operating within the moral and social limits of the epics, extends its narrative scope by negotiating with other folk and emerging popular traditions.

Hindi cinema established its traffic to Fiji in the late 1930s. By then the period of indenture was over, the Indian community as independent cultivators had lost the solidarity that characterised life on "the lines" of indenture, and linguistic and religious identities were differentiating. Hindi cinema's primary impact in Fiji was to bond through meta-narratives with which all the different groups of

Fiji Indians could identify. In this cinema, the Fiji Indians found the most lively expression of their yearning for roots and bid to reconstruct an imagined homeland culture in alien surroundings — at once simplified, quotidian and concrete but with a long tradition. And since in Hindi films *nation* is imagined in familial terms, the physical distance between mainland India and Fiji did not interrupt this "work of imagination". Evidently the folk traditions borrowed from the villages of India did not get in the way of Hindi cinema's popularity; to the contrary, by simplifying these traditions in a remote island with very little scope for other kinds of cultural traffic, the folk culture actually prepared the way for the unprecedented popularity of this quasi-globalising mass culture.

As Fiji started urbanising, the local Indian village cultures began to recede in influence, at least in the public cultural spaces of the cities. Once in place, Bollywood created its own public and psychic platform for people to interact. (My numerous respondents have narrated how, as boys or girls, they used to gather around the movie halls long before showtime.) The gossip columns, the 24-hour Hindi radio service, the occasional visits of singers and stars from the then Bombay — all this went into constituting the culture of a community which harboured no illusion of return but, for reasons of identity and cultural makeup, yearned for a romanticised version of India that Bollywood amply provided. The genealogy of unprecedented popularity of the mass cultural tradition of Bollywood in Fiji thus lies in the diasporic rediscovery of "little" traditions that the *girmitiyas* brought with them and preserved for over a century.

The platform that Bollywood provides has much to do with its particular mode of enunciation:

> Repeat viewing is ... a common part of the everyday parlance of film appreciation in Bombay, where people will often tell each other that they have seen a film 10 to 15 times. While it is not always clear that these numerical claims are exactly accurate, they indicate an aesthetic in which repeat viewing is a sign of the committed connoisseur. (Appadurai, 1998)

The typical Bollywood film is not a psychologically integrated unit, but a loose compound of various elements — like action, love, song and dance, dialogue, crime, devotion, special effects and so on. What keeps these disparate elements together is the star system, with its retinue of reviews, magazines, interviews, blow-ups, television shows, ads, publicity materials, gossip columns, enormous billboards dotting the urban landscapes, displaying the stars in larger than life proportions, autobiographies and fan club hagiographies. Rajadhyaksha and Willeman (1995: 10) call this "the distinctive 'insiderism' of a buddy culture of speech and body-language".

Satellite television, with its plethora of programs on Bollywood (mostly, though not exclusively, of song and dance sequences), has made this "insiderism" very much a part of daily living. With the availability of cheap audiocassettes and recorders, the cult of music has spread rapidly — even to the remotest corners of India. The role of music in Bollywood — where almost all the films have at least half a dozen songs by well-known "playback" singers — is absolutely central. These songs have several important features. Written frequently by authors who were Urdu language poets and often migrants to Mumbai from the North, these songs still have roots in certain popular forms of North Indian poetry, notably *ghazal*, which have highly developed and aestheticised verbal forms. Appadurai describes how these songs form a big part of the acoustic ecology of everyday life in cities and small towns. They are a crucial part of the repertoire of street singers who take the place of the "star" duets in the films. All these feed into the social space of the auditorium:

> Anyone who has been to a popular Hindi film knows that a large amount of the leadership in any given audience signals its authority by indicating its command of both songs and script, largely by cheering when a certain "hit" song or song-and-dance sequence is about to begin, by singing along on occasion, and by expressing various bodily signs of pleasure when key songs arrive. This anticipatory pleasure and mnemonic command, which is part of the folk aesthetics of cinema, is closely tied to the collective and interactive nature of film going and cannot be separated from two other elements of popular reception, dialogue and stars. (Appadurai, 1998; see also Srinivas, 1996)

While the very different historical trajectory of indenture and post-indenture paved the way for Bollywood, once in place in Fiji, Bollywood did not need "the particular conditions of the experiment" — that is, similarity to the cultural, economic and political conditions of India. The cult of Bollywood that the Fiji Indians *reproduced* in Fiji is not a case of mimicry, since *repetition* is inscribed in the very mode of being of Bollywood. If Bollywood is made the mainstay of cultural life (which to a very large extent is the case with Fiji Indians), it will of necessity repeat its entire cultural ecology — its "insiderism". This insiderism constructs a sense of mythological nationhood with very tenuous links with the *actual* geography of a nation. Hence living in the realities of Fiji and participating in the life of Bollywood is not a case of split existence, since such a split is postulated on a divide between the real and the imagined, something that Bollywood disavows.

Fiji Indian Cultural Ecology in Australia

Despite the recency of their arrival in Australia, and the structural deficits they face in employment, the Fiji Indians have re-established themselves with a cultural dynamism that is out of all proportion to their numbers and which can be sourced to their embrace of the cultural repertoire proffered by Bollywood. The very strong concentration of the population in Sydney makes it necessary to focus this discussion there.

In Sydney, the professional Fiji Indians are scattered all over the city while those in blue-collar jobs tend to concentrate in one or two regions. In the immediate years after the coup, they concentrated in the Campsie region of Sydney. Latterly, Liverpool — and to some extent Bankstown — are the two suburbs to where a majority of the working-class Fiji Indians have moved. Liverpool, with a number of big Indo-Fijian grocery shops, a couple of garment houses, one movie hall and a night club, is fast emerging as the centre of Indo-Fijian cultural life. In 1998, there were four cinemas that ran Hindi films on weekends in Sydney, with one of them in Fairfield looking at moving to daily screenings. However, the number of movie halls is becoming a less reliable indicator of the popularity of Hindi film culture in its diasporic context since few recent Bollywood blockbusters reach the cinemas outside India due to large-scale pirating.[3]

There are three nightclubs in Sydney catering to Indian film culture. Ashiki started in 1994, followed the next year by the Ambassador Lounge in Fairfield. However, both of these are rented places that operate only on weekends. Their capacity is also restricted to less than 200 people. The first large centre dedicated to Indian entertainment, inaugurated in 1997, is the Bollywood Reception Centre. It is jointly owned by a Punjabi and an Indo-Fijian. It has a capacity of nearly a thousand. These entertainment centres, as well as the Indian garment houses, cater primarily to Fiji Indians. Compared with the mainland Indians, who generally show little interest in Bollywood-centred nightlife, the Pakistanis are relatively more visible. However, even they have a marginal presence. The public life of Bollywood in Sydney — mostly an Fiji Indian affair — is a matter of billing film stars and playback singers, organising film-music nights and beauty contests, with establishments like fashion-shops offering the latest designs from films, production of local music videos, and setting up music schools where young people are trained in film songs.

Beauty contests are organised two or three times a year. Unlike London, where the participants come from the United Kingdom, Western Europe, North America and South Asia, those in Sydney are restricted either to Australia or at best to Australia, New Zealand and Fiji. There are a number of bands specialising in Hindi film music in Sydney, of which two are particularly well known. These are His Master's Orchestra and the Saraswani Orchestra. These bands perform around Australia and also in New Zealand and Fiji. While all the bands are owned and managed by Fiji Indians, there are a number of mainland Indian singers and musicians. However, they identify themselves for professional reasons with the Fiji Indian community. One such singer has brought out several CDs in India. These are mostly popular Hindi movie songs and a couple of *ghazals* (light classical North Indian music that had its roots in the Mughal courts). It is not unknown for well-known artists to have appeared on the popular commercial television network in India, Zee TV.

There are also a few Fiji Indian DJs and a number of karaoke singers. One of the DJs, DJ Akash, has several CDs of Bollywood remixes to his credit. He works in close consultation with DJ Bali Sagu, a second-generation Indo-Britisher, who initiated the trend of remixes of old Bollywood music scores with his album, *Bollywood Flashbacks,* in 1994. Sagu's album was an instant hit and a trendsetter, especially among young diasporic Indians. A Londoner brought up in a black locality, Sagu made creative use of his exposure to Afro-Caribbean and Western rock and pop music to set the Bollywood hit numbers of the past to new kinds of beat. *Bollywood Flashbacks* contains mostly the old numbers of the famous music director, R.D. Burman. Sagu had all the numbers re-sung and remixed to Western rhythms with patches of rap. Sony Entertainment Channel, which brought out the CD, paid for the copyright. The album has been played on the radio stations in Britain and the United States as well as in Australia. In fact, it was the first Hindi CD to hit the charts in the United Kingdom. Since then, a vast number of Bollywood hit songs have been remixed. Mostly HMV brings out these remixed numbers, since until recently it had a near-monopoly over the Indian music market and owned the copyright for these songs. The original voice remains the same, but is put to different music (adding more bass lines, for instance) and a different drum pattern. This offers young Indians dance music which negotiates heritages successfully, and is also widely available on music video. The CDs of DJ Akash remain, however, largely a local affair, with rights limited to the Australasian market.

Sydney has a number of karaoke singers. They sing to pre-recorded Hindi film music. Amongst Sydney Indo-Fijians, it is quite common to employ karaoke singers for small weekend parties. For the singers, this offers exposure and also a source of income. Indian karaoke singers restrict themselves to Bollywood hit numbers and no improvisation is expected.

Several Fiji Indian magazines are published by the Fiji Indian community of Sydney. The majority of these are dedicated largely to Bollywood film culture, like the *Fiji Times*, *Fiji India Sun* and, most recently, *Starblitz*. The *Fiji Times*, with a circulation of 7000 after free distribution and relying on advertising revenue from community businesses, has set a trend: now almost all the Indian magazines are distributed free of cost. Others, like *The Indian Observer* (also run by a Fiji Indian journalist), are more political in orientation, though they too have a regular section dedicated to Bollywood and its cultural expressions in Sydney. Interestingly, the *Fiji Times* is circulated only in Sydney. This is perhaps an indication of the little interest Indian commercial establishments have outside Sydney. (This does not mean that Indian diasporas have no presence in other cities of Australia. What is does indicate is Sydney's disproportionately large concentration of Fiji Indians — the main clientele of Indian commercial houses in Australia.)

Brisbane's Bollywood cultural life, very much like that of Sydney, is mostly a Fijian Indian affair. It has one regular band, Sargam, but relies on Sydney bands for major occasions. There are no nightclubs and no established tradition of karaoke. Public performances, far fewer in number than in Sydney, are hosted in rented auditoriums. Like other Indian communities, for the Fiji Indians the relation to Bollywood is mostly restricted to renting Hindi videos, though as a community they are undoubtedly the highest consumers. (According to different Indian video shops in Brisbane, especially those in the south and southeast parts of the city where most of the community live, about 70 per cent of those who hire videos on a regular basis are Fiji Indians.)

The reason for Brisbane's lack of a public face for Bollywood culture is partly due to the composition of the Indian community with a preponderance of those from the professional class. Primarily, however, it is a question of size. With a population of less than 10 000, the Fiji Indian community does not have the resources to support an ongoing Bollywood cultural economy and, with migration having dwindled to barely a few hundred every year, there is no sign that the Fiji Indian presence in Brisbane will increase substantially. The absence of a public culture of Bollywood impacts on the identity politics of second-generation Fiji Indians. In general, the young Fiji Indians of Brisbane prefer to portray themselves as much less "outgoing" *vis-à-vis* their Sydney counterparts, less experimental about Bollywood ("interested in the professional part of singing and not merely remixes"), less hyped and much more rooted in the *values* of Indian culture. As a young woman active in Brisbane's Fiji Indian cultural world puts it:

> We are more Indians. In the way we mix with people, our morals and culture, the way we dress — in every way, we are truer to our Indian ways. For Sydney, India is a commodity to be bought and sold; for us, India is a way of life.

No matter how Brisbane youth likes to project its difference *vis-à-vis* Sydney, however, Brisbane Fiji Indians do bid to reproduce Sydney's Bollywood culture, albeit with limited success. For instance, Brisbane experimented with a Sydney-style nightclub called "Must Must" (taken from a hit Bollywood score of 1990), but it only lasted four months due to lack of patronage. Very much like Sydney,

Brisbane has a number of Bollywood orchestras. The more prominent of these, Indiana Orchestra, staged around ten programs between 1995 and 1998, mostly with local talent, though they do borrow artists from Sydney on a regular basis. Usually, orchestras from Sydney perform in Brisbane, as they do in other parts of Australia. Of late, however, the relation has been balanced to some extent with the rise of the "Melody Queen of Queensland", Aiysha.

Aiysha's career in Indian music is worthy of some attention. She migrated to Australia when she was only one year old. She grew up in Gatton, where there were no other families of Indian origin. She spoke English at home and had no Hindi until she started watching Hindi film videos brought home by her parents from either Brisbane or Sydney. She was trained in English music at school, where she sang for the school choir. She started taking an interest in Hindi film music, "just as a hobby", around the age of twelve. When she moved to Brisbane a couple of years later, what had been a "hobby" became for her a "passion". She took her first formal training in film music and *ghazals* during a year's visit to Sydney. By the time she was twenty, she brought out her first CD of Hindi film music, the first person from Brisbane to achieve this feat. She has performed with her troupe twice in Sydney, in 1997 and 1998, to packed houses. In the arena of cultural performance, recognition in Sydney is of supreme importance in Australia. It was only after her success in Sydney that Aiysha could bring out her CD of Hindi film songs and ghazals (Aiysha, 1998).

One of the expressions of the overwhelming influence of Bollywood in Sydney is the community's attempts to make video films in Hindi. The process started in 1994 and, to 1998, four such films have been produced and two were in the process of being produced. *Starblitz* calls it "Bollywood Down Under" and has a regular column devoted to it. These are locally financed, low-budget, somewhat experimental Hindi films (on one occasion, the director has tried Fiji Hindi). These films are sold through Indian video shops and on public occasions screened by overhead video projector. Interestingly, these films are usually closer to Hollywood than Bollywood in narrative and moral scheme. One film, *Achanak* (meaning a contingent event), is loosely based on *Basic Instinct*, while another, *Biswas* (Faith), is based on the *Rocky* films. These films are less convoluted in their narrative strategies than the average Bollywood product, with very few songs. The appeal of such films is restricted so far to the younger generation, who have no illusion that the films will travel beyond Australia or in any way infringe on Bollywood's market. Rather, these films are more an expression of the deep involvement with the culture of cinema amongst young Fiji Indians and a desire to capture the new diasporic locale and the specificities of the migrant experience. Another example, *Kayalat* (meaning the desire to be somebody else), narrates the story of a Fiji Indian girl who is trapped in her marriage with a Fiji Indian man. The husband does not try to appreciate the changes in her self-perception that a diasporic situation has brought to her life. Interestingly enough, she does not solve her dilemma by embracing Western culture, but tries to find an identity which is her own. Towards the end of the film, she is found involved with a Fiji Indian man of working-class background. At a deeper level, these films reflect at once the attachment to Bollywood culture and a measure of unease of Fiji Indian youth regarding Bollywood's continued reliance on "traditional Indian mores and morals", notwithstanding the vast changes these have undergone in recent years.

Intercommunal Discord and Cultural Assertion

The ethnic, caste and class differences between mainland Indians and Fiji Indians have given rise to intracommunal tensions and rivalries which are neither new nor restricted only to Australia (see Buchignani, 1980). Many mainland Indians exhibit deeply entrenched casteist attitudes and view the indentured past of the Fiji Indians as a non-negotiable barrier.[4] On the other side, Fiji Indians often characterise mainland Indians with the same kind of negative attributes that they were wont to use for ethnic Fijians. Both realise the need for a united front to deal with Australian racism, but both view each other as an obstacle to better acceptance by the "white nation". Mainland Indians now constitute an *other* for this community, just as the ethnic Fijians did back in Fiji.

What have the implications been for the media and cultural economy from intercommunal discord? There have been acrimonious exchanges across the communities using aligned newspapers as a platform, culminating in inflammatory articles and letters on both sides in the mainland mouthpiece, *Indian Post*, in March and April 1997 and in the Fiji Indian *Fiji Times* in April and May 1997. (A less partisan view was offered in the April and June 1997 issues of another Fiji Indian tabloid published from Sydney, the *Indian Observer*.) *Fiji Times* editor Nick Kumar demanded an apology from the *Indian Post* and virtually threatened that if the editor of the *Indian Post* did not oblige, business establishments that advertised in the *Indian Post* in future would be boycotted by Fiji Indians (Kumar, 1997). This softened the attitude of *Indian Post* considerably and, over some months, a compromise was effected since the main clientele of Indian business in Australia are the Fiji Indians.

However, the rivalry between the two communities continues and often is focused on media and film culture. At the time of the controversy, Sanjay Dello, the editor of the *Indian Post*, argued that while the Fiji Indians are "good Hindus" and "they are the people who spend", their "westernised ways" and "excessive attachment to filmy culture" bring disrepute to the Indian community as a whole (Dello, 1997). However, if sharing of the advertising cake was one of the issues of contention between these two magazines (the April 1997 editorial of the *Fiji Times* argues such: 'Is it a desperate bid by a publisher to regain the readership and advertising base that has been severely eroded by the expanding Fiji India media?'), the *Indian Post* was a clear victor; in terms of circulation, the magazine's gains were considerable (Kumar, 1998). This suggests that the controversy made the *Indian Post* more popular amongst a section of Indian readers.

Such rivalry between the two communities has seen the reassertion of culture and ethnicity by Fiji Indians. This involves a positive mobilisation of indenture history and an emphasis on a Hindu way of life in a Western context that bears similarities to Gillespie's (1995) account of self-construction of identity through the positive assertion of ethnicity (1995: 8–11). The dominant racism of white Australia, the ostracism by mainland Indians, the need of the older generation for a platform to socialise and to reflect (which will also function as a moral regime for younger people) have together fed into a resurgence of religion and revival of folk traditions, neglected in today's urban Fiji.

Jayawardena (1980) notes that, in urban Fiji, European culture is the medium within which members of different ethnic sections interact with one another (1980: 441–42). The impact of Western institutions has been more profound than in India since, unlike mainland Indians, Fiji Indians have been subject to a uniform civil code. However, this uniform civil code in Fiji operates in a power matrix where Fiji Indians were in a distinctly disadvantageous position, initially with regard to the white indenture regime and then *vis-à-vis* ethnic Fijians. The result of a process of "uniformity in the context of inequality" has been that, as a community, Fiji Indians retain their own cultural identity while their public life moves freely in and out of the European, Fijian and Indian cultural spheres. This heritage has contributed to Fiji Indians adapting rapidly to an advanced Western lifestyle in their diasporic contexts.

One of the most creative methods of adaptation is the assertive construction of a cultural community around *Ramayan Katha* and *bhajan mandalis* (small gatherings for devotional songs), which paved the way for Bollywood's popularity. For the last couple of decades, these traditions were mostly on the decline in urban Fiji. Once in Australia, these have regained their popularity as a platform to unite the community and act as a moral regime for young people.

The *Ramayan* narrates the story of the victory of the Aryans over the Dravidians of South India. Understandably, it enjoys little popularity in South India. One of the reasons why the Bharatiya Janata Party (BJP) has not been able to make inroads in the South is its close identification with the cultural tradition of the *Ramayan*. However, in the displaced context of indenture, South Indians as latecomers made *Ram Katha* part of their own cultural tradition. In Sydney, the same tradition continues; in fact, in many cases the initiative and leadership of such occasions come from the South Indians. The situation is made complex by the fact that, along with being patrons of the *Ramayan*, the South Indian Fiji Indians of Sydney have started taking a renewed interest in Sangam, the Tamil cultural organisation that had its origin in Fiji but now operates worldwide from Hawaii.

Such hybridity — at once progressive in its refusal to be bound by millennial caste and regional boundary-marking and traditional in its recovery of deep religious roots — is also evident among the two other important groups of Fiji Indians — the Gujaratis and Muslims. The Gujaratis, as I have mentioned, were always keen on retaining a measure of their ethnic identity due to their different history in Fiji. As primarily a trading community, it is understandable that, of all the communities of Indian origin, they show the most interest in developing transterritorial networks. Consequently, once in Australia, the split between their two identities — namely as Fiji Indian and as member of an ethnic community of a certain professional trait — is enhanced.

The case of Fiji Indian Muslims is similar. In terms of ethnicity, they are part of the Fiji Indian community. But as members of a religious group, life in Australia has meant for them more interaction with Muslims from other parts of the world: both ethnicity and religion are strong but disparate identities for Fiji Indian Muslims. During the indenture period, Muslims had little opportunity for religious and cultural expression of their own; they used to regularly take part in Hindu festivities and folk cultural gatherings. However, with the visit of several Imams from India, attempts were made to reconstitute their identity in religious lines. However, the tradition of attending Hindu celebrations like *bhajan mandalis* and *Ram Katha* never ceased throughout their history in Fiji. As a result of developing new axes of socialisation on religious lines in the new diasporic context, this tradition is much less visible. Mosques now play more significant roles in their lives and there is a marked emphasis on learning Arabic, the language with which Muslims identify globally. The world of Bollywood culture (where their presence is considerable) now provides one of the cultural main links with other members of the Fiji Indian community.

The cultural divide between the Arya Samaj and Sanatani Dharma is taking interesting shape too in the new diasporic location. Traditionally, the Sanatanis were concerned with different rituals of Hindu religion while the Arya Samaj placed more emphasis on education and spiritual enlightenment. The difference was of cultural priorities and rarely one of overt antagonism. In Australia, the two groups have come much closer and they both participate in the same cultural activities. However, since the members of the Arya Samaj are traditionally more educated than the Sanatanis, as a group they belong to a higher class. This has its own cultural ramifications, one of which is that, though Arya Samajis participate in Bollywood-centred cultural activities, their involvement is on a much less active level than that of the Sanatanis.

We need to remember that the domains of the *Ram Katha* cultural traditions and Bollywood are rarely separate. We have noted the impact of the *Ramayan* on Hindi films; *Ram Katha* too borrows episodes from the mass media (Lutgendorf, 1995). Marked by endless digressions and presented in highly colloquial style, *Ram Katha* follows no one particular tradition of the *Ramayan*. Rather, the epic functions as a "cultural meta-text" for individual and collective expression and reflection, where new episodes are often invented, while some others are forgotten.

Significantly enough, in the Hindu religious traditions, devotion and erotica are rarely separate departments of life and one very often evokes the other. This is particularly so with the *bhakti* tradition from which Tulsi Das's *Ramcharitmanas* emanates. In the *bhakti* taxonomy, *shringar* is the highest form of devotion — the erotic bond between the devotee (a woman) and the deity (a man). In one of the forms of *shringar*, the female denies herself, her family, all bonds and social constrictions and pursues the love of Krishna. Radha is the epitome of this love and devotion. The trope of Radha and Krishna puts together social transgression, erotica and devotion. As the supreme expression of desire and pathos, it has for centuries provided inspiration for *bhajans* (i.e. devotional songs). It has also served Bollywood as a source of much of its music, narrative and allegory. This means that cultural and religious assertion of tradition has not been in opposition to Bollywood; in fact, in a Western diasporic context, it provides young Fiji Indians with the cultural capital to really appreciate Bollywood.

The recent media boom in India has contributed to this process in significant ways. Partly as a legacy of the phenomenal success of the television serials, *Ramayan* and *Mahabharata*, and partly as a market response to the rise of Hindu nationalism, there has of late been a flood of mythological and devotional serials available on video in all the major Indian diasporic centres. Producers have responded to demand by importing the latest technology for special effects, resulting in a hi-tech devotional glut: *Mahabharat Katha, Ek Aur Mahabharat, Om Namah Shivay, Jai Ganesha, Daya Sagar* (on

the life of Christ), *Jai Hanuman, Shiv Mahapuram* are a few examples
(Jain, 1997: 70–73).

Linked with this — and perhaps more profound in effect — is the
recent rise of devotional music. Technological reproduction has played
a pivotal role in India from early this century to popularise *bhakti*
music. For instance, the Mira *bhajans* of M.S. Subhalakshmi in the
1940s were a major hit all over India. However, the availability of
cheap audio players and cassettes from around the mid-1980s has
provided a new dimension to this process. Going by industry figures,
the market for pre-recorded Indian cassettes was 505 million units
in 1996, of which the devotional music market was 5 per cent. In
terms of gross number, this represents a steep hike for devotional
music. Front-runner in this trend is the music company called
T-Series which brings out 150 to 200 devotional titles every year at
a relatively cheap price. The logic for privileging devotional music
is its very low production cost (almost one-fifteenth of a pop album)
and relatively longer shelf life. The primary market for this music
is Indian small towns; next on the list are the Indian diasporas.
Along with the expanding market has been a spread of its repertoire
— from the standard *Ramayan* and Bhagabat Gita to Rath Yatra and
Satyanarayan Katha (Chopra and Joshi, 1997: 46–47).

The Fiji Indians, with a long tradition of attachment to *bhajan* and
other devotional songs, have been influenced by this boom in the
devotional music market in India. Coming into contact with mainland
Indians has not only meant digging up casteist and indenture
memories; it has, more positively, opened new possibilities for
creative expressions by exposing the community to the wider world
of Indian music and dance. There are many more Indian dance and
music (especially, classical) schools in Sydney than was the case in
Fiji. The result has been quick to materialise: from receivers of
Indian cultural artefacts, the community has become a producer. In
the field of devotional music, however, this exposure is impacting
the community in a significant way. For more than a century, Fiji
Indians were used to singing the Bhojpuri (from the district in Bihar
called Bhojpur) style of *bhajan* called *tambura bhajan*. Now this is
giving way (at least for a section of the community) to the more
classically-oriented *bhajan* of Anup Jalota, Hari Om Sharan, Anuradha
Paudwal and others through audiocassettes produced in India. The

CDs of some of the *bhajan* singers of the Sydney community are clear proof of this trend. In terms of the dialectics of "great" and "little" traditions, this may be regarded as a case of a "little" tradition being dissolved in the "great" tradition that McKim Marriot calls "universalisation".

Fiji Indian Youth Culture and Post-Zee Bollywood

The most dynamic aspect of Fiji Indian youth culture centres on the use of Bollywood to negotiate a kind of parallel cultural platform to the dominant Western pop culture. This can be understood through grasping the enormous changes that Bollywood itself has undergone in recent years, especially since the advent of Zee TV. Zee programming has branded itself as a halfway house between the Star TV brand and traditional Hindi film, creating a hybrid genre that refers strongly to Western-style music and dance. Such types of dance and music are now also the mainstay of Bollywood, especially of the new genre of "teenage romance" that has come into being in the liberalising India of the 1990s. The Bollywood of tear-jerker melodramatic plots and folksy music with the male and female protagonists dancing in the luxuriant Himalayan foothills or the vast, empty stretches of a beach has not disappeared, but contemporary Bollywood is increasingly driven by contemporary music culture, and in large part by hugely extravagant song-music sequences with ever more tenuous links to the plot.

The satellite television revolution of the 1990s impacted on Bollywood in several ways. On the one hand, it caused huge investment in choreography and spectacle as part of the attempt to bring spectators lost to television back to the auditorium. On the other hand, such song-dance routines not only provide regular fodder for the plethora of song and dance programs on television (in 1997, about 65 programs interspersed over the rapidly expanding multi-channel packages were song-based); because of the popularity of these programs, it is these sequences which determine a movie's fate, both at the box-office and in the exploding music market. There is also the radical transformation in the character of this music. From being mostly a combination of Indian folk music, light classical Indian music and the standard Western popular music, Bollywood now freely mixes rap, Latin American and Black music with traditional Indian music. As part of the same process of the "MTV-isation" of Indian popular entertainment, there has emerged an extra-cinematic realm of Hindi pop-music and pop-stars, like Remo Fernandes, Alisha Chenoy, Sharon Prabhakar, Parvati Khan and "rap" artists like Baba Sehgal. DJ Akash explains the implication of such music for young diasporic Indians in the following terms:

> Ten years back, a young Indian would listen to his music in a very low volume. He would consider his music to be very "tacky" and would have felt awkward to play it publicly in a Western context. The contemporary Bollywood music, by blending Indian melody with Western beats, has changed all this. Today, if you go down the streets of Sydney, very often you will hear Indian music blasting. Young people no longer consider the Bollywood songs to be "curry music". This music no longer sounds strange to the average Westerner.

Arguably *because* of this hybridisation of Bollywood music, it manages to signify something special to the diasporic young Indians. Asked about the continued influence of Bollywood music, a young Fiji Indian performed this analysis:

> Bollywood has got the potential. It has got feeling. When you are happy you have something to sing, in love you sing, when you are sad you sing. You can relate to it. Consider the recent hit, "Dil To Pagaal Hai" (my heart has gone wild). It is about love and affection with which a young person can immediately identify. All those who are in love would buy the CD for their girl friends; they would send requests to the radio channel for the song to be played. We relate to it in two ways: i) visual part — i.e. what the main guy and main girl did in the movie, and ii) the meaning of the lyric. Compared to this, Hollywood music hardly has any message that we can relate to. Take *Men in Black* for instance. We could barely identify with the hit score. The messages of Bollywood with which we are brought up hardly get conveyed to us there. There is nothing of our own in such music.

Fiji Indian young people use a wholly hybridised genre like the remixes to fashion a discourse of authenticity. On the one hand, they will deploy the remixes as part of syncretic metropolitan culture and thus break out of the cartography that views their culture as *ethnic*. On the other hand, they perceive these remixes (for them, an essentially diasporic phenomenon) as part of their attempt to promote Indian popular music by making it contemporary; this they will compare to the Indian nightclub crowd which, according to them, is hooked on unadulterated Western hard rock and heavy metal. A Fiji Indian enthusiast of "Indi-pop" describes her experience in terms that converge as being "Western" and being "Indian": as a Westerner, she prefers Indi-pop to traditional Indian popular music (which for her is "a bit too romantic and at times unacceptably melodramatic"); she is also "far more of an eastern person" *vis-à-vis* her Mumbai counterpart:

> When I went to India, I found that kids are not thrilled with remixes. To be honest, I got the impression that they are quite wary of this kind of experiment; they think that it is corrupting the original music scores. On the other hand, I found night clubs in Bombay [sic.] are more influenced by Hollywood than Bollywood. I was shocked to find many Indian girls dancing to heavy metal and hard rock. This is pretty aggressive by Indian standards. I haven't seen any girl of Indian origin doing that sort of dance in Sydney ... Kids in Bombay go to nightclubs to become western. Here we go to assert our eastern identity. The basic difference lies there.

Apart from remixes of popular scores, *bhangra* as a dance beat serves an important role in the deployment of Indian popular music for the purpose of being "agreeably different" in a Western context. Originated in rural Punjab as a harvest dance, *bhangra*'s potential to provide the right kind of beat for clubbing was first explored by the Punjabis of Southall (Haq, 1997). Fiji Indians were not exposed to *bhangra* in Fiji. But in the last ten years, it has gained great popularity amongst the young Fiji Indians of Australia. In recent years, on every Wednesday night, Sydney community radio 2SER plays *bhangra*-pop. *Bhangra* did not come to Australia from India; rather, it came from London. In fact, it can be argued that the recent popularity of *bhangra*-pop in India with the rise of such stars as Daler Mehendi is very much a case of the diaspora reworking the homeland.

Diasporising Bollywood

Contemporary Bollywood is unabashedly urban and increasingly global in its settings. Less than 5 per cent of films now have rural stories as opposed to 15–20 per cent ten years back (Chopra, 1997: 54–55). Western locales are being juxtaposed with rural and urban India — for example, in *Pardes*, a north Indian village seamlessly gives way to Los Angeles in the middle of the plot; or, in a reverse pattern, the diasporic protagonists of the highly successful *Dilwale Dulhaniya Le Jayenge* travel through the continent to reach the bountiful villages of Punjab of their ancestors where the main action will take place. The urban market now accounts for more than 60 per cent of a film's earnings, compared with 45 per cent ten years ago; the overseas market, too — now a substantial 20–25 per cent — is increasing with every passing year. Many Bollywood films both promote and reflect the diasporic *imaginaire* that has squarely set in for the post-liberalisation new urban middle class. For Thomas Hansen (1996: 603), the cultural significance of globalisation for a postcolonial nation like India lies in the crucial ambivalence between its promises of recognition of nations and cultures, and its simultaneous threat of subversion of political sovereignty and cultural particularity. In these days of a global cultural economy, where more than half of the world's economy revolves around communication and lifestyle industries, the distinction between the cultural-spiritual and the technological-economic is difficult to maintain. And if that is so, it is all the more imperative that differences are imagined all over again.

Bollywood has not only coped with the challenges of globalisation, but taken advantage of the new situation by enlarging its terrain. This it has achieved by creating a spectatorship aware of the specific requirements of the diasporas, as well as those living in India. A globalising world of communication and capital flow, instead of imposing a hegemonic cultural world order, has triggered a politics of space whereby the diasporas of a particular community dispersed worldwide are networked to the homeland culture to such an extent that the traditional divide of outside/inside loses much its analytical purchase. In contemporary Bollywood, it is interesting to see how the inscription of the citizen consumer, its ideal contemporary spectator, has offered spaces for assertion of identity for Bollywood's diasporic clientele *vis-à-vis* the host culture and, in the case of Fiji Indians, with the mainland Indian communities as well.

Perceived as vulgar and prolific, at once strangely irrational and easily masterable, Bollywood until recently managed to generate very little scholarly interest: for Western film academia, it was a matter of regular indifference, while for Indian film criticism, it was a target of unequivocal condemnation. The reasons were: a tendency to stasis at the level of narrative and character development; an emphasis on externality, whether of action or character representation; melodramatic sentimentality; crude or naive plot mechanisms such as coincidence; narrative dispersion through arbitrary performance sequences; and unrestrained and over-emotive acting styles (Vasudevan, 1993: 57). What such shock reactions to this cinema's "lack of realism, restraint and psychological feasibility" conveniently overlook, however, is its enormous innovation in fashioning itself as the most reliable archive of popular hopes and disillusionment, and the ability to locate itself in the locus of influential and contesting definitions of "Indianness".

It can be argued that, following the emergence of the super-genre of the "social" in the 1960s, Bollywood underwent its next major change in the late 1980s–early 1990s, coping with the tides of globalisation. As part of this change, the diasporic Indian (popularly known as the Non-Resident Indian (NRI)) is now very much part of its address. This was necessary not only to embrace Bollywood's diasporic clientele, but also to secure its popularity at home since the one self has to see its reflection in the other for its globalising ideal self-definition. In the new troping of the home and the world, those who are brought up outside India have *India* inside them very much as the *West* is inscribed in the heart of India. This enmeshing of identities has enabled Bollywood to address the moral and cultural alienation that diasporic youth feel with Hindi films made on "standard formula", while it also offers them the difference they want *vis-à-vis* Hollywood.

Earlier Bollywood was not governed by consideration of community "out there"; community was securely at home. Hence representations of abroad could only take the form of the travelogue. For instance, towards the later part of the super-hit *Sangam* (1964), the couple go on an exotic tourist album honeymoon trip to the West. Bollywood in its new incarnation not only very often physically locates itself in the West; the central roles in the narrative too are reserved increasingly for the figure of diasporic youth. Blockbusters such as *Dilwale Dulhaniya Le Jayenge* and *Pardes* are only two examples of a host of such films that include *Lamhe*, *Virasat* and *Aur Pyar Ho Gaya*.

With consumption acquiring a different inscription, recent Bollywood has offered for its diasporic youth clientele a trajectory of "Western-style" glamour, wealth and liberty, but on its own terms. Bollywood manages the ensuing alienation with the mass audience of India by the sheer strength of its vast repertoire, which even now has a large space for films of earlier eras. For the new Bollywood, too, it is not as if though it merely mimics Hollywood. Rather, the semiotics of exchange with Hollywood has in recent years taken an interesting turn. The biggest hit in recent years, *Kuch Kuch Hota Hai* (1998), for instance, completes this India/West circuit by not venturing to go abroad at all; instead, it creates a virtual "West" within the bounds of India. In fact, in terms of *mise-en-scene*, the film has internalised the West into India to the extent that it does not even have to announce that it is the West. Thematically, once the tomboy character of the heroine (played by the mega-star, Kajol) is established, the rest of the narrative concentrates on bringing her femininity to the fore. The framing of the woman as powerless, and above all a wife and a mother, while at the same time allowing her a certain space, a freedom for the pleasure of her subsequent disciplining, has been the general narrative-ethical guideline since the early days of the "social" in the 1950s. *Kuch Kuch Hota Hai* does not alter the terms of what we might call this "Sita" trope, but pushes it to accommodate a decisively urbanised, globalised (basketball-playing, baseball cap-wearing) female prototype; neither is her subsequent realisation of a more feminised, "Indian" self jarring to her earlier posturing. In fact, such realisation will only act to make her a more holistic woman. In a similar vein, the other female protagonist of the film, the Oxford-returned, guitar-strumming girl (played by Rani Mukherjee), who can also quickly switch on to singing Hindu religious hymns — and to whom the hero gets married but who dies at childbirth — is not a "vamp from the West" (as earlier films of similar narrative would almost certainly portray her to be) but a nice, pleasant woman who happens to wear Westernised clothes in a sexualised sense. This, then, would be internalised in the Indian imaginary as not someone who *represents* the West (since "West" is very much in India), but simply as someone who has lived in the West.

Bollywood representation establishes the "Indian" community as a national but global community. To ritually assert — as Bollywood characters often do — that one is part of such an ideal community, it is important that one knows what one is part of. This involves returning to India and seeking sanctions from the original patriarchal order. *Dilwale Dulhaniya Le Jayenge* is a remarkable instance of such reworking of traditional patriarchal moral scheme. The film begins with the memorable montage of the heroine's father (acted by Amresh Puri): as a Punjabi farmer, he is straddling past the mustard fields of Punjab; then through a dissolve, he is seen journeying past Big Ben and Westminster (wearing his Punjabi *ajkan*), and finally feeding grain to the pigeons in the city square of London and remembering ancestral Punjab in a voice deeply laden with nostalgia. In the film, Puri is the epitome of a *darsanic* figure, bestowing sanction within the orbit of his *darshan*. The narrative then moves from the domestic space of the heroine in London to the continent with the couple and finally reaches rural Punjab, where the heroine (acted by Kajol) is supposed to have an arranged marriage with a local boy. Once the couple reaches rural Punjab, the film changes gear and becomes unusually slow. The gaze is fixed on the nitty gritty of the marriage rituals, staged in a static, ornate fashion. The point of view is of the hero, who witnesses the preparations but from a remove. It is important that the occasion is not contested, since the pleasure lies in its staging. The spectatorship at this point is clearly diasporic.

The action takes place at the very end of the film, when the heroine's father throws the hero out of his house and the proposed son-in-law starts beating the hero in a typical vendetta fashion. The hero does nothing to defend himself but significantly, once his father is hit by one of the men of the heroine's father, he plunges into action and manifests aggression to defend his father. It is at this point that heroine's father gives sanction to the hero: defending the father means, by logic of mirroring, defending the future father-in-law — or, in a broader sense, the father principle, the originating source of authority. It is interesting for the elaborate carnival of identity where there is a kind of secret strategy to hold it at bay until one can actualise it on one's own terms, on terms of that freedom that the West has given but which needs to be ratified in the ancestral home. As a form, it has been clearly invented by contemporary Bollywood and has of late been repeatedly deployed as a major device to bring the West and the East to one place. It is also a ploy to reinscribe the narrative space firmly within the *darsanic* orbit and, very much like in old Bollywood, climax comes in the form of defending the *darsanic* object.

Conclusion

London dekha, Paris dekha, aur dekha Japan
Michael dekha, Elvis dekha, Doosara nahin Hindustan
Eh duniya hai dulhan, dulhan ke maathey ki bindia
I love my India

(Seen London, seen Paris, and also Japan
Seen Michael, seen Elvis, no place like Hindustan [India]
The world is my bride, my bride has *bindia* [dot] on her forehead
I love my India.)

The "cheepy" celebration of motherland by a diasporic character on return to India in the film *Pardes* provided the Bollywood superstars, Shah Rukh Khan and Juhi Chawla, a perfect note on which to conclude their dance and music shows during their tour of Australia and New Zealand in 1998. Such celebration of India is by no means new to Bollywood. In fact, the legendary Raj Kapur stole the hearts of millions more than four decades back with a similar song (in *Shree 420*, 1955): *"Mera joota hai Japani/Ye patloon Englistani/Sar pe lal topi Roosi/Phir bhi dil hai Hindustani"* (My shoes are *"Japani"/* This pantaloon *"Englistani"/* The red cap on head *"Roosi"* [Russian]/ Yet the heart is *"Hindustani"*).

In spite of their apparent thematic similarity, the two songs register radically different points of view. For Raj Kapur, the aim is to realise a cosmopolitan Indian self in the very soils of India (in keeping with the reigning Nehruvian ideals of that time). The song in *Pardes* is clearly a song of the Indian diaspora, of reconstructing "India" outside India. That the song would hit the pop charts in India almost instantaneously on its release testifies to the globalisation of "India" across these four decades.

Speaking of the hybrid nature of Bollywood, the influential cultural critic Ashis Nandy argues:

> Mass culture and popular do not fully overlap. Elements of mass culture, disembodied from their global context, can become popular (e.g. denims and cold drinks). But that by itself means little; for these elements have to be processed through the local popular culture which provides, exactly for that purpose, an indigenously forged cultural sieve. The Indian cinema not only does this processing on behalf of a vulnerable section of the Indian population, it also has an in-built plurality that tends to subvert mass culture even when seemingly adapting to it passively. This has another implication. If Indian popular cinema has to be seen as a struggle against the massified, it must also be seen as a battle over categories — between those that represent the global and the fully marketized, in tune with India's now almost fully institutionalized official ideology of the state, and those who by default represent the culturally self-confident but low-brow multiculturalism in which the country has invested an important part of its genius during the last hundred years or so, both as a means of survival in our times and as a technology of self-creation with an extended range of options. (Nandy, 1998, quoted in Das, 1998: 7)

My previous analysis tries to show how Bollywood in its contemporary manifestation promotes more than ever the category of "the global and the fully marketised" but manages to stop short of allowing it an over-determining role *vis-à-vis* what Nandy calls "the culturally self-confident but low-brow multi-culturalism" of Indian cinema. Bollywood's ability to negotiate Hollywood on its own terms has been widely discussed: Rajadhyaksha (1998: 173) persuasively demonstrates the error of viewing Bollywood as "insufficiently Hollywood" and advocates a space for this cinema in its own right within the terrain of film theory. Richard Dyer (1986) has argued that Hollywood associates the factor of glamour with aristocratic privilege and regularly pits it against the "openness" of

Western liberal democracy where talent and perseverance are always duly rewarded. As a contrast to this, the world that Bollywood constitutes is one of "heteropia" (Foucault, 1986: 24) where the *real* world outside the auditorium is simultaneously represented, simplified, inflated, contested and inverted. Very often, the basic narrative line is repeated as if the same language game is played time and again; along with it is repeated (as I have discussed in the section entitled "From *Ramayan* to Bollywood") the whole cultural ecology of Bollywood.

The viewing subject of Bollywood is not so much the individual of Western film theory but primarily a member of a "narrative community". Indian political theorist Sudipta Kaviraj elaborates the concept of narrative community in the context of postcolonial democracy in the following way:

> The telling of a story brings into immediate play some strong conventions invoking a narrative community … To some extent, all such communities, from the stable to the emergent, use narrative as a technique of staying together, redrawing their boundaries or reinforcing them. (Kaviraj, 1992: 33)

The source of Bollywood's phenomenal success as a commercial medium seems to lie in its ability to bring within its narrative fold the diverse narrative communities not only of South Asian origin but even wider — of large parts of the so-called Third World. In other words, inscribed in its address is the postcolonial predicament of an audience which, in the case of the Fiji Indians, has been twice displaced.

I have sought to show how negotiation with the "culture of motherland" became for the Fiji Indian community part of a much broader question of negotiation with (post)indenture definition of the self. Needless to mention, this negotiation could not remain the same from the early days of "extraction" and the physically arduous schedule of indenture through a post-indenture life of subsistence agriculture, diversification of occupation, and differentiation of the community to entry into a Western context of late modern times with the option of "multiplicity of forms of life and conscious adoption of lifestyles" (Dean, 1996: 213). The situation has been made more complex by the recent changes in the Western landscape of the "social". Here I go by the definition of the social provided by Nicholas Rose: a large abstract terrain of collective experience, the sum of bonds and relations between individuals and events within a more or less bounded territory governed by its own laws. Rose argues that, ever since global capital attained prominence, the *social* in the West has been undergoing a transmutation in favour of the *community* — not one but a series of communities with different aims and constituencies but nonetheless basically constituted of self-monitoring, self-governing subjects (Rose, 1996). The norms of such particularised communities of the contemporary West can have grafted on to them the religio-civilisational norms of the "narrative community" in ways that support the notion of public "sphericules" as advanced in Chapter 1. Hence, for Fiji Indians, the move from post-indenture Fiji to advanced, capitalist, Christian/secular Australia is primarily a move between different regimes of ethical comportment: a stable ethnic identity being attracted to new forms of association and intimacy along with a sense of imagined nationhood kept alive by continuously transforming and reconstructing its constitutive myths. Bollywood, as it caters to the changing market patterns of home and abroad, serves this dual purpose extraordinarily well.

Compare the Fiji Indians with Hamid Naficy's Iranians in *The Making of Exile Cultures* (1993). The Fiji Indians who came to Australia just before or after the coup are not an exilic group, even though they were dislodged from their country. This is because of their attitude to Fiji ("home but not mother") and the fact that they harbour no hope or determining desire to return, either to Fiji or to India. Hence they made no investment in the kind of exile media that Naficy's Iranians did to form their cultural identity. Rather, they have invested their energies in the *continuation* of cultural practices they were engaged with in Fiji which, as I have shown, contain within them dynamic hybridising tendencies easily sufficient to withstand the community's displacement into a Western culture. Unlike Naficy's (1993) instance, where the hermeticism of exilic television is forced to negotiate with American mainstream media after a point of time, Bollywood's own momentum will take this platform ahead. The tension of the young Fiji Indians is the tension between Bollywood's representation of change and real-life experiences. This is reflected — though in a very minor way — in the remarkable films that they make, which I have discussed earlier. Hence, by all accounts, life for Fiji Indians in their new diasporic location is not a cultivation of indeterminacy — a "slipzone" of indeterminacy and shifting positionalities (Bhabha, 1994).

The literature of transnationality has seldom shown interest in investigating the different histories of postcolonial dynamics "back home" as they manifest in the "new imaginings and politics of community". Rather, its main concern is to write diaspora as an enigmatic excess and privilege the aleatory nature of diasporic temporalities: the *true* people are the liminal people. It may be argued that what Bhabha does is to route the experience of the South Asian intellectual-in-exile through the discourse of black counter-hegemonic culture. This intellectual-in-exile syndrome, however, occupies only a minor part in the South Asian diaspora, which is made of either professionals or the working class who have left their homeland in search of a better living. This is not to say that they escape the problem of "othering" in the West, nor it is to suggest that they would like to give up their own identities and become "assimilated" in the dominant cultural order without a trace of difference. Rather, it is to bring home the point that the discourse of liminality offers little help to understand the South Asian diaspora's ability to *recreate* its cultures in diverse locations.

This chapter has privileged the *Ramayan* and folk traditions of India as well as Bollywood as some of the most significant discourses that have framed the cultural life of Fiji Indians and continue to do so. The attempt has been to investigate the historical formation of a cultural community and not to posit any singular determination. A detailed account of how socialisation has been constructed around these cultural artefacts — the historical forms they took, the rationalities they deployed, the various registers, practices and institutions through which they were disseminated — is beyond the scope of this chapter, but could form part of a thorough historical anthropology. Finally, the continuing significance of popular cultural formations in quickening diasporic life is brought into sharp relief in this examination of a small but vibrant community.

Notes

1   Keya Ganguli has used a similar set of terms (*post*colonial and post*colonial*), though the meanings I attribute to them are not the same. For Ganguli, *post*colonial refers to the "'extraction' of ... people from an ex-colonial territory to what might be called a neo-colonial one" while postcolonial refers to the much broader process of "the exploitative dynamic central to the production of colonial subjectivity" (Ganguly, 1992: 28).

2   The terms "great" and "little" traditions were introduced and elaborated in the 1950s by Chicago anthropologist Robert Redfield (1956). McKim Marriott (1955) further expanded their scope by applying them to the north Indian village tradition where he saw a two-way process: i) local practices being promoted over a period of time to the Sanskrit canon (universalisation); and ii) ideas and practices contained in canonical texts being adopted locally (parochialisation). I have adapted and somewhat skewed the concepts to update them for a media context.

3   Piracy of Indian popular movies is a cultural technology in its own right. From semi-professional telecine to making video copies in the theatres with hand-held cameras, almost all possible means of pirating are evident. A good percentage of rental films in Indian video parlours in Australia (which are mostly spice shops) are pirated copies — their price is around one-fifth of the legal ones. The quality of such tapes is usually extremely poor. They are rented out very cheaply (in Sydney, there are shops that rent out cassettes for as little as 50 cents a week) and mostly the popularity of a video does not depend on its reproduction quality. There have been attempts to rent better quality videos at a higher price. The experiment did not work. A remark common amongst Indian video parlour owners is that, though Australia has very strict piracy laws, it is seldom that any effort is made to implement them with 'ethnic' videos. Also, since piracy is a civil — and not a criminal — offence in Australia, the video-rights owner or someone deputed by them needs to be personally present in court. Given the size of the Australasia market, Bollywood has not so far taken such an initiative.

Many video parlour owners make the point that the same customer who shows a great deal of alertness about quality of "English" videos, is much more tolerant when it comes to Hindi videos. In the curt words of an owner, "They do not watch Bollywood, they consume. It is a daily ritual." DVDs of Bollywood superhits (both the old and recent ones) are reaching the Australian market and the catalogue is increasing rapidly. The clientele, however, comprises not so much the avid consumers of Hindi films but is restricted to the professional middle class which takes a more "cultivated" interest in Hindi films.

4   The attempt to reassert such values as part of Hindutva — the cultural and political ideology especially of recently reframed Hindu nationalism — in a diasporic setting is indeed ironic. It has been argued that Hindutva for diasporic Indians is on the increase, with the rise of Hindu nationalism in India since the mid-1980s. But there is a significant difference between diasporic practice of Hindutva and the politics of the currently ruling Hindu nationalist Bharatiya Janata Party (BJP). In its attempt to imagine the nation in terms of Hindutva, BJP has inadvertently put the ideology of the upper castes under the greatest challenge that they have ever experienced from inside — namely, the political need to expand their ranks and thus give up their claim to monolithic superiority. Diasporic Hindutva, generally, suffers from no such "crisis" or obligations. In this way, BJP is realising its idealised self outside its actual political terrain.

5

Mi Arai Mai Mai Mai?
Thai–Australian Video Ways

Glen Lewis and Chalinee Hirano

"Mi arai mai mai mai" (Is there anything new?) is the first question often asked by Thai expatriates living in Australia when they visit their local Thai video rental store. The purpose of this chapter is to explore how two Thai expatriate communities in Sydney and Canberra use the media to fulfil their needs for cultural continuity. It will consider whether their mainstream media use facilitates their cultural relocation within Australian society, and how they interpret the cultural text of the Thai videos they watch so eagerly. These rented Thai videos are viewed as cultural objects, conveying meanings which are reinterpreted by individuals as their readings of the videos and the mainstream media intersect with their everyday life experience.

Australia has one of the highest levels of VCR ownership in the world. Also, as in other expatriate communities — such as Cambodian refugees in the United States (Smith, 1994) or Punjabis in London (Gillespie, 1995) — Thai expatriates and students mainly rely on the inexpensive rental of free-to-air TV programs copied in Bangkok that are flown to Australia, usually within a week of their broadcast. This phenomenon has attracted some comment and movement in Thailand itself, as in an August 1996 *Bangkok Post* feature on the "Video Link Home". Yet, although these programs are invariably pirated, Thai TV stations and producers have made no serious objection to the widespread use of their material by Thais in Australia or the United States.

The media channel that is the main agency of cultural retransmission for the Thai diasporas in Australia is clearly Thai-language rented videos. Although Kolar-Panov's (1997) research on expatriate Croatians in Western Australia found that the use of specially recorded family video newsletters was a feature of that community's media use, we found no evidence that the Australian Thai community uses video in that way. Rather, the rented videos are primarily used for two reasons. The first is for keeping up to date with news and current affairs. These are mainly from Channel 7, the top-rating Thai news channel. Second, they are used for entertainment and cultural transmission between the generations. Thai game shows and variety programs, as well as drama series (*lakorn*), were mostly favoured by our respondents.

The methodology of this study combined ethnographic audience analysis and social survey research into the studies of media consumption of Thai audiences. As Ang (1996: 136–37) suggests, qualitative reception analysis needs to be placed in a broad theoretical framework, one that encompasses the understanding of both structural and historical factors and the place of media in society. Accordingly, this study conducted its inquiry on three levels between October 1996 and May 1998. The first looked at the video industry, its history and the availability and distribution of Thai videos. In-depth interviews with the owners of seven selected stores were conducted. Most of them were cooperative, with the exception of some who suspected an attempt to inquire into video piracy.

The second level studied media consumption among the Thai-Australian community. A survey form about Asian-Australian diasporic media use was designed for interviews with adult members of the household. This asked about their television viewing habits and preferences, with particular attention to Thai-related materials and video viewing. It also asked about their use of radio, newspaper, computers and films. Additional questions were about their birthplace, citizenship and cultural identity, as well as socio-economic status indicators, such as household income, occupation and education. A sample was selected from the Thais living in Sydney and in Canberra. There were approximately 5500 Thailand-born immigrants in Sydney and fewer than 1000 in Canberra in 1997. Our study conducted a two-hour long interview with twelve households in Sydney and eight in Canberra. Except for two Laotians, almost all the respondents were born in Thailand.

The final level concerned the textual analyses of Thai programs. These were conducted to understand how particular Thai popular programs, such as variety shows and drama series, are interpreted in a diasporic setting. First, an audience-based textual analysis was made of a 22-minute selection of programs, including a variety show (*Jan Kra Prib*/Blinking Moon), news from Channel 7, an historical drama series (*Rattanakosin*/Bangkok Dynasty) and five commercials. This was done by showing excerpts from those programs accompanied by questions to the ten selected survey respondents (five each in Sydney and Canberra) after the two-hour interview. Second, a further textual analysis was conducted of two popular talk and variety shows — *The Twilight Show* from Channel 3 and *Si-Tum Square* (Ten O'clock Square) on Channel 7 — and two drama series from Channel 3 — *Jintapatee* and *Por-Krua-Hua-Pah* (The Chef) — by showing fifteen-minute excerpts of each to two additional focus groups in Sydney and Canberra. These programs were selected on the basis of their popularity and their ready availability in the video rental stores.

Our study has assumed that the degree of difference in video consumption and reception patterns among the Thai ethnic audience will depend on the extent to which a person is incorporated into the mainstream culture. The basic factors influencing this are their length of residence in Australia, their English language ability, their educational level and their age. Accordingly, Thais aged between 27 and 65, who had not been in Australia more than five years and had little English language ability, were selected for the Sydney focus group. The Canberra participants comprised those who could be considered second-generation migrants: teenagers between fifteen and twenty years of age who had grown up in Australia and were fluent in English. These demographic choices were made partly out of the constraints of availability, but also to highlight the possible role of generational difference in program reception.

Thai–Australian Connections

The Thai community presence in Australia is not a numerically strong one in comparison to other much larger Asian groups, such as the Chinese or the Vietnamese. In 1996 there were about 17 500 Thai-born residents in Australia, with an additional 5500 born in Australia who had at least one parent born in Thailand (Coughlan, 1996: 51).

Although research studies of Thai expatriates in Australia are scarce, it would seem that one distinctive feature of their experience has been the predominance of women as immigrants.

Thai immigration to Australia began in the early 1970s, following the formal abolition of the "White Australia" policy by the Whitlam government in 1973. Most of these Thais gained entry as students or visitors, and later became permanent residents. Like the Thai women who migrated to the United States after the Vietnam War, the second stage of Thai emigration consisted of Thai wives of Australian nationals; this phase commenced in the late 1970s. During the 1970s and 1980s, there were many mail-order bride advertisements in Australia. Most of these were for Filipinas; however, a small proportion were also for Thai women. So the third main stage of Thai emigration to Australia in the 1980s and 1990s included the immediate family members of Thai wives and fiancees who had been sponsored under the family reunion category. Sixty per cent of Thai residents in Australia arrived under this category (Studdert, 1996: 2).

The greater international movement of Thai people in the late 1980s was the result of Thailand's remarkable economic growth. Thailand had its own version of the Asian economic miracle through the 1980s, during which time it had one of the highest economic growth rates in the world (Pasuk and Baker, 1996). Because its centrality to the trade routes of mainland Southeast Asia and its history of never being colonised, Thailand is an important regional state — not only in economic terms, but strategically and politically. The spread of democratisation in East Asia since the 1980s has included Thailand. After the Black May crisis of 1992, the Thai polity has become more civilianised. Although corruption is still rife during Thai elections (McCargo and Callahan, 1995), the Chuan government since November 1997 has had a leader who is the first civilian to become an elected prime minister. Chuan Leekpai's own political track record is a model of integrity, though his previous ministry was brought down in 1995 because of its involvement in land scandals in the South, the party's power base.

Thailand traditionally has been one of the most outward-looking Southeast Asian states. Because it was never directly colonised, as most other Asian nations were, it has retained a very clear sense of its national and cultural identity (Reynolds, 1991). Also, the Thai capacity for cultural syncretism is comparable with Japan's in its ability to incorporate overseas influences while retaining its own core cultural values and fostering what Barme (1993) has called "nationally-imagined nationalism". Since the 1930s, this has been expressed in the slogan "My nation, Buddhism, and the King" (Barme, 1993). The image of King Bhumibol is broadcast daily on TV and radio at 8.00 a.m. and 6.00 p.m., with news of the royal family featuring nightly for ten to fifteen minutes at the end of each 45-minute evening news bulletin. Thai film audiences also still stand to attention for the national anthem at the start of each movie session.

The Thai media play a central role in this process of symbolic nation-building, both domestically and through a high level of engagement with the media and video use by Thai expatriates. In California, for instance, where there are an estimated 350 000 Thais, they have their own program slot on a Los Angeles cable television channel, while a 24-hour satellite radio channel is broadcast from Thailand to the US West Coast. Some cable broadcasts to Thais in Europe from England were made in 1996–97 by the Sahaviriya group, though this has now shut down (*Thai Tourism Journal*, 1996: 28). In 1998, Army TV Channel 5 commenced 24-hour broadcasting via the THAICOM-3 satellite to expatriates in Eastern and Western Australia, as well as to the United States and Europe. This new audience is limited to elite subscribers due to the high subscription fee of $1500 in Australia.

Thai–Australian trading and cultural links so far, however, remain quite limited. Thailand's image in Australia is positively seen mainly as a tourist destination, while it is often negatively stereotyped by the international media as a global centre of prostitution, political corruption and AIDS. Thai culture in Australia mostly is physically visible in the large number of Thai restaurants. Conversely, Thai knowledge of Australia is limited, though it has become an increasingly popular destination for students and tourists. Closer links have been established more recently. The current Australian Deputy Prime Minister, Tim Fischer, has had a particularly close association with Thailand. The introduction of Thai language classes in several secondary and tertiary institutions has also helped make Thai culture more accessible to Australians (Coughlan, 1996: 50). Moreover, because of the growing affluence of the Thais, the number of Thai tourists and students coming to Australia has jumped sharply in recent years. Whereas there were 19 600 tourist arrivals in 1990, in 1994 there were 66 900, and there were 8844 Thai students in 1996 (ABS, 1995–96: 35). It should be pointed out that both tourist and student numbers have declined sharply since the economic crisis beginning in mid-1997; however, the field research for this study was completed before that time.

In media terms, the ABC-TV show *Bananas in Pyjamas* has become extremely popular in Thailand, where in 1998 it was being screened weekly by Channel 7 on Tuesday nights between 8.20 p.m. and 8.30 p.m. (peak viewing time is 6.00–9.00 p.m.). The characters also have been successfully merchandised in Bangkok's huge mega-malls with B1 and B2 even appearing on kids' T-shirts promoting the "Amazing Thailand" tourism campaign. The cross-cultural appeal of the show builds on its suitability to be dubbed in Thai — as with other puppet, masked and animated programs for children, including the Japanese cartoons also popular on Thai TV. There is practically no English-language programming on Thai broadcast television. Two Australian daily news programs, *Sunrise* and *Australia Television News*, however, are available on Thai Pay TV, as are the ABC's *Foreign Correspondent* and *World at Noon*. Australia Television, originally the ABC's and now Seven's regional channel, has been available via satellite since 1993, while News' Star-TV service is available both by satellite and through the cable provider, UBC.

At some stages of the Pauline Hanson immigration debate in Australia, some leading Thai media figures, such as the editor of the *Bangkok Post*, Pichai Chuensuksawadi, criticised Australian attitudes to Asians (Lewis, 1997). Yet this probably goes against the long-term trend of Thai perceptions, as there is more coverage — and generally positive coverage — of Australia in the Thai media now than there was five years ago. Educational exchanges, as well as increased Thai tourism, have been the main sources of this change. An Australian Studies Centre, for example, was established in 1996 at Kasetsart University — one of Thailand's premier universities in agricultural education (both countries are major primary producers) — with links to Griffith University. Some of the Thai elite also have been Australian-educated, such as the Crown Prince who studied at Duntroon, and Dr Meechai Viravaidya, a Melbourne University alumni who currently heads Thailand's Telstra, the TOT. The Australian government also contributed A$1 billion to the IMF rescue package for Thailand in mid-1997.

However, the Thai community in Australia is a collection of individuals scattered across all states and territories, unlike the Vietnamese in Sydney's Cabramatta, or the Chinese in Ashfield, Chatswood and Chinatown. This is perhaps due to the nature of their migration, which has been mostly on marriage grounds. The common physical place that the Thai communities can gather and share their stories of past and present Thailand is the *Wat*, or the Thai Buddhist temple. The *Wat* provides Thai migrants with a cultural space where the shared pull of symbols helps to create a sense of belonging, in the same way that ethnic clubs do for other migrants (Kolar-Panov, 1997: 76).

The Thai community in Australia is an homogeneous Buddhist group. There is little evidence of a Thai Muslim subculture in Australia, though there are some two million Patani-Thai Muslims in Southern Thailand. The *Wat* gives these Thai-Australians a space in which their members can share their spiritual beliefs, participate in regular merit-making rituals, speak their own language and build social networks of friendship and support. The Buddhist monks who reside in the temples carry out their duties, providing spiritual guidance for the Thais. Due to the limited support and counselling services provided for new settlers, these monks sometimes act as migrant counsellors, especially to Thai women who are married to Australians, giving advice on how to cope with lives in the new land (Chotimont, 1997).

The majority of Thai immigrants to Australia are women who migrated in the 1980s through marriage. While some of these have strong educational backgrounds and full-time jobs, and are well integrated into society, the majority are not qualified for the Australian workforce. Most stay home and are relatively isolated from non-Thai Australian society. Language and educational background are major obstacles preventing these Thai brides from assimilating themselves into the host society. The mainstream media provide little to help in terms of their settlement and English language education (Bednall, 1993). As a result, these media are not heavily used by these Thai brides. For those who work full-time outside the home, "*Mai mee wae la*" (No time) was often the answer when they were asked why they didn't watch TV, or why they didn't listen to the radio or read the newspaper.

What does it mean to be Thai-Australian in contemporary Australia? Questions of media use need to come back to this starting point. A simple answer to this might lie in the way the Thai migrants live their lives, eat their food, worship their King, visit Thai restaurants or decorate their houses. The Thai elements embedded in these activities are crucial in the process of self-identification of being Thai *(ekkalak Thai)*. Most of the houses we visited were decorated with Thai ornaments, with Buddha statues set carefully in one corner as a shrine surrounded by plastic garlands and daily food offerings. Some had piles of Thai newspapers and magazines in one corner of the living room, and the television in another, covered with beautiful traditional handmade silk, often from *Isarn* (Northeast Thailand), and topped with some Thai wooden dolls in classical dance costumes. This remaking of the domestic environment — the coding with souvenirs, handicrafts and objects from the homeland — enhances the collective diasporic experience (Nacify, 1993: 106). The reconstitution of the television set encourages the viewer's glance to switch between the monitor and the objects as part of the process of cultural (re)identification.

Before considering Thai video use in detail, the next section will analyse the expatriate use of Thai-language radio and print media, as well as the mainstream Australian media.

Thai Community Use of Broadcast TV, Radio and the Press

Mainstream Media

The Thai media presence in Australia is small, reflecting the size of the expatriate community. There is a Sydney Thai-language fortnightly paper, *Thai-Oz*, that acts mainly as a social and community channel for Thais in New South Wales and the Australian Capital Territory (ACT). The paper also provides summaries of leading domestic Australian political issues that may impact on the Thai community. For example, in December 1996, one article carefully listed the wide range of English-language (and Chinese-language, as Sino-Thais play a central cultural and business role in Thai society) coverage of the controversial rise to national influence of Pauline Hanson (*Thai-Oz*, 28 November–11 December 1996: 28). Otherwise, SBS radio broadcasts two hour-long programs per week in Thai (Tuesday 9–10.00 p.m. and Saturday 8–9.00 a.m.), which do not appear to be widely listened to. One attempt by a Sydney FM station to establish a volunteer Thai service from a North Sydney location in 1996 failed through lack of support.

There were a wide range of television programs regularly watched by our respondents in Sydney and Canberra. For example, popular entertainment programs among the Canberra residents were game shows, such as *Sale of the Century* and *Wheel of Fortune*. They prefer watching these to soaps because, according to one Canberra resident: "I've been here seventeen years, the plots [of the soaps] are all the same, *Neighbours* is still *Neighbours*." Matters of taste may be the source of dislike here. Although in both Australian and Thai family dramas, family conflict is part of the essential plot, Australian television families are perceived to be far more permissive than Thais. Furthermore, Australian TV dramas rarely reflect the cultural diversity and aspects of multiculturalism of the society in which these Thai migrants are living. Most of the dramas are full of blue-eyed, white-Anglo casts, with the exception of some that have recently added a few ethnic characters. Australian television, in general, is nationalist and populist, due to its assumption of a majority ideological perspective (Jakubowicz, 1994). This assumption is, generally speaking, shared by pay TV providers.

Similarly, the Australian cinema has little interest in catering for the needs of an extremely marginal Thai audience. There has been only one Thai movie screened publicly in Australian cinemas so far. *Khon-Lieng-Chang* (The Elephant Keeper, 1990) was shown in Sydney (Potts Point) and in Canberra (Electric Shadows) in 1991. Not surprisingly, all of the respondents in this study wanted to see more Thai movies screened in Australia. One Thai who was a regular Chinese filmgoer even said: "I watch Chinese movies just for fun. It's quick, Chinese style, but it's not Thai." Respondents also stated their disappointment that Thai movies had been less frequently screened on SBS in comparison to Chinese or European movies. When asked if they had seen Thai programs or films on SBS, each respondent could name only one or two films.

There have been no more than four Thai movies broadcast on SBS over the last five years. Most of them are considered old, though they were award-winning films. These included *Butterfly and Flower* (Pee-Suar-Lae-Dok Mai) (1983) and *The Path of the Brave Man* (Wi-Thee-Klon-Kla) (1987). Critical comments were made by several respondents regarding the intentions of SBS in screening *The Path of the Brave Man*, as its story revolves around the lives of a primitive mountain tribe. They felt that this kind of movie would create a wrong image of Thais among Australians. All of the respondents wanted to see more Thai movies on SBS, but they desired new, good quality ones. They also wished to see news from Thailand broadcast in the morning on SBS in a similar way to the programming of other Asian news at that time.

Australian ethnic radio programs seemed to play an insignificant role in helping Thai migrants either in settlement or in cultural identification. There was low awareness among the respondents about the availability of Thai radio programs in Australia. The Thai-language radio programs on SBS are broadcast twice a week in Sydney on FM 97.7 and once a week in Canberra on FM 105.5. A Sydney volunteer-based radio program, *Thai Smile Radio*, used to broadcast every Sunday afternoon on FM 98.5. However, the program was cancelled in January 1997 because it failed to attract sponsors.

Seven Thai respondents living in Sydney sometimes listened to SBS radio. Only one respondent in Canberra listened to SBS Thai radio programs every week. Some respondents suggested that the SBS radio programs could be improved by including information concerning the welfare of new arrivals and changes in government policies which might affect Thais living here. However, all of the respondents expressed the same concerns about the language used by the DJ. One, for example, said that the program was "too boring. The DJ can't speak Thai properly. Not much is talked about how the Thais living here are doing." This requirement for the correct use of the Thai language on radio not only indicates their patriotism, but also their desire to affirm their diasporic identity. They consider that more attention to the proper use of their native language on radio would give such programs greater credibility with the local Thai audiences.

Thai News as Bad News

Our study showed that watching news on Australian commercial TV channels, particularly Channels 7 and 9, was more popular among the respondents than either the ABC News or *World News* on SBS. Although they all agreed that news stories on commercial channels covered few important events in Thailand, or about Thais living here, they still preferred to watch the news on the commercial channels because of its local content. One respondent, for example, said: "I just want to know if anything has happened in the neighbourhood." Several complaints about the content of news programs on ABC and SBS were also voiced — for example: "World News on SBS rarely covers Thailand; it tends to focus on Eastern and Southern Europe" and: "I watch the late night news on ABC. There is little news from Thailand. They focus more on Singapore, Indonesia and Malaysia."

Not only did most of the respondents feel that they got inadequate information about Thailand and about Thais living here from Australian television; they also believed that the image of Thailand portrayed in the Australia media was often negative. One respondent claimed news reports on commercial stations about Thailand were bad and exaggerated. Programs such as *Witness, 60 Minutes* and *A Current Affair* often sensationalised Thai stories, emphasising traffic problems, drugs, AIDS and prostitution as major problems in Thailand. Here commercial ratings factors are likely a major influence on the selection of stories by those programs. As Loo argues (1994: 36), journalists tend to stereotype by assimilating their descriptions of events into terms familiar to the dominant audience.

The treatment of Thailand in Australian-made media such as *Bangkok Hilton*, a 1989 mini-series about the imprisonment of Australians for drug-running in Thailand starring Nicole Kidman, reinforced media stereotypes that our subjects disliked. Some even said that they felt too humiliated and bashful to walk on the street or go to work the next day after the screening of such programs because they were afraid to answer any questions from their colleagues. They wanted to see more unbiased reports about their country, as well as more nature programs and personal success stories.

Newspapers and the Internet: More News Channels

There was only one respondent who did not read a newspaper of any kind. When asked about *Thai-Oz*, a fortnightly paper published in Cabramatta with a circulation of some 6800 and distributed mainly in New South Wales and the ACT, eleven of the twelve respondents in Sydney confirmed reading it. All the Canberra respondents, with the exception of the two Laotians, read *Thai-Oz*. The main content of *Thai-Oz* includes headline news from Sydney's major papers, such as the *Sydney Morning Herald*, and news from leading Thai papers, such as *Thai-Rath*, *Daily News* and *Matichon*. Most respondents said that they read *Thai-Oz* to get information and news about Thailand and news that concerned Thais living here, such as changes in immigration policy. One respondent, for example, clarified his motives in reading *Thai-Oz:* "Most of us like to keep up to date with the main issues, to see movements in Thai politics and change in Thailand."

Limited English was cited as another reason that the Thais turned to the ethnic press, as it helped them in terms of their settlement and facilitated the adaptation process to Australian ways. One Sydney respondent admitted: "The new articles in the Australian newspapers are too long and my English is not good." Other comments regarding *Thai-Oz* were: "It helped me understand the Australian news better, such as issues regarding Mrs Pauline Hanson" and "I also read the news about Pauline Hanson in *Thai-Oz*, which made me understand the issue better." However, *Thai-Oz* was often criticised by the respondents for using the Thai language incorrectly, and they suggested a need for improvement. One Thai language university lecturer said: "This newspaper is also read by Australians who are learning Thai. They even make references from it. We've to get it right."

All respondents wanted to see more Thai-language newspapers. Other than *Thai-Oz*, 50 per cent of respondents (ten out of twenty) regularly read imported newspapers, such *as Thai-Rath*, *Daily News* and *Matichon*, which arrived only two days after their publication date. These were read to find out about changes in Thai politics and the economy. Some papers also have a gossip column about the Thais in Australia. Bangkok's large-circulation *Daily News* runs a column every Wednesday (*Duang stamp kham kob fa*/Stamp from across the sky), written by a Thai expatriate in Australia under the pen-name of "Jarupan Praisaeng". Moreover, imported women's magazines such as *Koo Sang Koo Som* (Destined Couples), *Di-Chan* (female pronoun for I), *Sakulthai* (Thai Heritage) and *Matichon Sudsapda* (Public Opinion Weekly/ Politics) were widely read. A respondent commented that the purpose of reading Thai magazines was to read the entertainment news, to see if there were new drama series on air in Thailand. She would then calculate the time it would take the tape of the first episode to arrive in Australia, and sometimes ring the store to book the tape in advance.

Use of newer media to stay in touch with Thailand was quite limited. Sixty per cent of households in this survey had computers, yet only 25 per cent had access to the Internet. Computers were mainly used for professional work and for study purposes. Two of the respondents in Sydney had computers at home, but never touched them. Only three respondents used the Internet to keep in touch with their friends or relatives at home by email. This was because: "Not many people in Thailand have access to email or the Internet." In fact, commercial Net services in Thailand only began recently, in March 1995 (Thaweesak, 1998). There were only two respondents who regularly read Thai English-language newspapers available on the Net, such as *The Nation* and *Bangkok Post*. Another respondent said that she often caught up with upcoming episodes of her favourite drama series on the TV station's Website.

Ethnic Videos and Thai Urban Culture

Recent studies which apply ethnographic approaches to ethnic video audiences, such as Gillespie's (1995) and Kolar-Panov's (1997) studies, have noted the significance of this medium in maintaining cultural identification among diasporic groups. These videos, they argue, create a cultural space in which the present of the viewer is interrupted while their past is renewed. In this way, their cultural identities are reinvented and renegotiated (Kolar-Panov, 1997: 209). The diasporic audiences allow their past to talk to them through watching the visual images of their shared cultural symbols, and by listening to the shared stories and myths of their homeland culture, as presented in the videos. As Stuart Hall states:

> The past continues to speak to us but it no longer addresses us as a simple factual past, since our relation to it, like the child's relation to the mother, is always already after the break. It is always constructed through memory, fantasy, narrative and myth. (1990: 226)

Memories of the past, which are constructed through symbols, stories and myth, act as a catalyst fuelling the need for belonging or, in Kolar-Panov's terms, the need for continuity (1997: 210). Diasporas have a desire to catch up on what they have missed by leaving their homelands. This need for continuity is a necessity, not nostalgia, for it helps them understand themselves — who they are, where they came from, their sense of their everyday lives — and at the same time negotiate the host culture. These needs of the expatriate Thais in Australia can at least partially be met by the ready availability of Thai videos: "I watch the news from Channel 7 every week. It's about three hours long. Sometimes after I finish watching, I thought I was sitting and watching in my home in Thailand." (Sydney respondent, April 1997)

This respondent, a woman who had migrated to Australia three years previously, seeks to re-liminalise her experience of an in-between space, in which her present and her past are connected. For Thai migrants, their homeland is a country in the middle of an economic transformation, riddled with constant political and social changes. Many people left the country at a time when the economic boom was giving rise to a new urban culture, replacing the older notion that Thai culture was distinctively royal and rural (Pasuk and Baker, 1996: 115). The backbone of the nation was changing from the rural farmers to urban businessmen and white-collar workers in the early 1980s. Since then, a new urban culture has been developed by this new middle class, including those who enjoy their new wealth and also enjoy letting others know about it. Part of Thai psychology, as Mulder (1992) explains, is the display and sharing of wealth, not only as an act of personal pride, but as a way of collectively sharing the wealth around, or making merit *(tambun)*.

This new urban culture of conspicuous consumption is directly represented in many Thai TV programs. At least until the mid-1997 crash, they were filled with locally made popular dramas telling stories of being rich, or becoming rich with good spirits *(jai dee)*. Pasuk and Baker (1996: 123) identify three main types of these popular TV dramas: historical series; family melodramas; and dramas about the changing role of women. Some dealt with the increasing role of women at work, which contrasted with the traditional role of Thai women as home-carers. Television game shows provided a chance for ordinary people to get rich quickly. Popular talk and variety shows had well-known businessmen as their quests, telling their stories of success. Music videos and programs were also flooded with images of *luk-krueng* (half-Thai, half-foreign) singers, who were once social outcasts, but more recently have been successful through their distinctive looks, as well as by developing new styles of pop songs about growing up in a modern, commercialised Bangkok. They see themselves as guiding the older generations to understand the new world (Jiraporn, 1996). These *luk-krueng* increasingly appear in films, TV dramas and advertisements, and are the media emblems of a new, urban youth culture in a globalised Thailand (Lewis, 1998b).

Moving from a country with a deeply rooted traditional culture undergoing rapid change to one which is more politically secure, but with a less-established cultural identity, can pose a major challenge for Thai immigrants. On the one hand, they need to adapt and adjust to an Anglo-dominated Australian society, which is still debating the meaning of multiculturalism (e.g. Birch, 1997). On the other, they retain their desire for cultural continuity by catching up with the rapid changes and the new developments in their original homeland. Studies of Thai immigrants to the United States, where national cultural identity is more clearly defined than in Australia, also show that Thai expatriates there still retain strong religious and moral ties with their homeland's culture (Pressman, 1993).

Thai Video Stores: A Product or a Community Service?

The practice of Thai ethnic video distribution in Australia has developed from informally watching videos at home socially to the commercial provision of tapes since the early 1980s. Families and friends of Thai expatriates recorded Thai popular programs for their loved ones overseas to keep them up to date with home news and entertainment. The first wave of Thai video rental stores in Australia started around the same time as a revival of popular local dramas based on traditional stories was taking place in Thailand. These replaced the American films and TV dramas that had become popular program content during the Vietnam War years. Several expatriates who were running grocery stores saw renting Thai TV programs as a potentially profitable sideline, so they asked their relatives to record popular programs and send them over for renting out to their customers. This practice continues today, although now several dubbing studios have been hired to do the job instead.

The Thai video stores studied in New South Wales and the ACT began business around 1990. Of five stores in Sydney, three are owned by Thais, one by a Laotian and another by a Chinese-Vietnamese. The two Canberra stores are owned by Laotians. Laotians and Thais have a number of strong similarities in their languages and culture and, in Laos itself, Thai television is widely watched. In Sydney, all five shops in the survey were completely devoted to the video rental business, with small corners selling sideline products, including Thai magazines, newspapers, popular music cassettes, CDs and homemade snacks. The Canberra shops, on the other hand, were originally grocery stores and started renting videos only to "draw customers into the shop. Profits from selling groceries and food ingredients are much higher than renting videos." (Southlands, 24 December 1996). The most frequent borrowers are Thai women, yet borrowers cover a wide social range, from housewives to labourers and business people temporarily working in Australia, students and Laotians, Cambodians and Chinese-Vietnamese (with a higher proportion of these in Sydney). A small number of Australians are also regular customers. Some rent Thai boxing videos. Others are interested to learn the language by watching Thai news and documentaries.

All stores have a wide range of programs. About 50 per cent are drama series, while 30 per cent are game and variety shows. The remainder are comedies, news, sports, beauty contests, music videos, Hong Kong-Chinese drama series dubbed in Thai (notably the Taiwanese TVB program, *Paw Boon Jeen* (Judge Pao), which is a special Thai favorite), and popular American films dubbed in Thai. The most popular shows are historical drama series from Channels 3 and 7, such as *Rattanakosin* (Bangkok Dynasty) from Channel 7, which tells the story of the early nineteenth-century life of the royal court, and family dramas such as *Koe-Sawad Had-Sawan* (Paradise Island), which deals with the theme of love and romance and about being rich without losing your soul. There are also dramas dealing with the changing role of women in Thai society, such as *Jintapatee*, as well as game shows such as *Ching Roi Ching Larn* (Take a Hundred or a Million) and variety shows such as *Si Tum Square* (10 O'clock Square) from Channel 7 and Channel 3's *Twilight Show*.

Mi Arai Mai Mai Mai? (Is There Anything New?)

This is the question most often put by customers when visiting the stores. To satisfy their desire for keeping up to date with news, fashion, dramas and other changes in Thailand, all programs are recent. They are only a week behind the date they are televised in Thailand. The master tapes are illegally dubbed in several studios in Thailand — which all stores refused to identify — then sent by air twice weekly to stores in Sydney, which also act as Australia-wide distributors. Each master tape is very expensive. Several shop owners in Cabramatta try to reduce this high cost by sharing the master tape. However, profits can still be made, owing to the low cost of video reproduction. When new tapes arrive, between ten and twenty copies are made of each program, depending on demand, while tapes are often reused many times. Despite complaints of poor-quality tapes from customers, store owners keep using old tapes due to low rental costs, low profit margins and delays in getting the tapes returned.

So the master tapes are stored for only two or three months, then reused, with the exception of one store in Sydney which keeps master tapes of every drama series since 1990. This business has about 100 000 tapes in storage. Rental fees are very low, ranging from A$1.50 to $3.00, with no specified borrowing period. Although the rule is intended for overnight rental, most of the tapes are passed between relatives and friends before being returned to the store, as no fine is imposed. In Sydney, the average number of tapes borrowed each week is about 1000–1500 tapes per shop, while about 500 are passed between relatives and friends before being returned. A frequent comment by the store owners was: "Video renting is not highly profitable. It's more of a community service, but once I have committed, I have to continue." Although Thai video renting is more of a community service than a profitable business, it seems certain to continue to provide an alternative TV diet for Thai expatriates.

The only likely obstacle to this is if TV program producers, the main channels and video rental companies in Thailand decide to actively prosecute the copying of their products for overseas distribution. Both the Thai television and video rental markets in Thailand are fiercely competitive, especially given recent declines in advertising revenues. So far, however, the only instance of the enforcement of bans of the use of Thai TV overseas has been in relation to Cambodia, where there was widespread pirating of Thai TV programs, especially those of Channel 3, by Cambodian television operators. Thailand itself still has a high rate of piracy of intellectual property, such as in computer software and also textbooks, despite increasing US pressure to enforce international copyright laws. Yet it is unlikely in the near future that any restriction on the outflow of Thai TV programs overseas will be undertaken. If this did happen, it would probably affect the larger North American Thai video market more than Australia's.

Thai Community Video Use and Cultural Representation

Thai Videos as Alternative Community Television

The Anglocentric narrowness of mainstream Australian television, together with its reliance on certain stereotypes about Thailand, has probably been a factor in encouraging the Thai communities to rely on rented videos as their alternative television. The relatively low rental costs, the availability of programs and the absence of commercials are a combination of incentives for watching Thai videos. One Sydney respondent explained:

> Every program is available here. I have more time to watch variety programs and drama series than when I was in Thailand. In Thailand, each channel always had its best shows on air on the same day and same time, so we had to choose what to watch. Here, we rent tapes, so we can watch everything we want to and there are no commercials.

Households	English-language videos	Thai videos
Sydney (12)	68	220
Canberra (8)	46	110

Figure 5.1: English-language videos and Thai videos watched last month

Although the survey results showed that gender was an important factor in determining watching frequency, it was less significant when considering program preferences. Education and job status, on the other hand, were quite crucial in the selection of video programs watched, as well as the amount of videos hired. However, the purposes of watching videos among the respondents were strikingly similar — that is, to get information about any changes in Thailand, and to act as a source of entertainment. Overall, there were three distinctive aspects of the alternative television used by Thai diasporic audiences: to be a breaking-news channel; to provide escapism for expatriate Thai brides; and to act as a generational go-between between older and younger Thais.

Video as an Alternative News Channel

Expatriate communities normally have a strong desire to know the latest news from their own countries. In Nacify's (1993) study of the Iranian diaspora in the United States, for example, he argues there was a constant drive, or an "epistephillic desire", for information among the Iranians about recent changes in their homelands (1993: 107). This seems true also for Thais in present-day Australia. The rented Thai videos are used as a means of gratifying this desire for current information, and in this way they serve as an alternative news channel, supplementary to the little that can be gathered from the mainstream Australian media. In order to keep up with the most recent events in Thailand, the Thai-Australian audiences watch Thai

TV news, especially from Channel 7, as well as current talk and variety shows, on a regular basis. One Sydney respondent said: "I watch because I try to keep up with what's going on in Thailand." Another similarly voiced the reason: "I need to know about the changes, otherwise I will be out of date *(cheoy)* when I return home to programs in Thailand."

Some of the results of the textual analyses of the programs clarify the extent to which Thai rented videos serve as an alternative community news channel. Respondents were shown a short passage from Channel 7 news on 6 December 1996, about the then-recent Thai election in which Chavalit Yonchaiyudh had been successful. This bulletin is the top-rating news program in Thailand, and each evening, as it begins, there is a preview of the main items, spoken dramatically against a background soundtrack of rattling drums. The respondents were asked: "Do you always follow what's going on in Thailand, particularly the election?" The majority said they did by watching news from Channel 7 on video and by reading Thai newspapers.

Two Sydney respondents noted correctly that, in this particular bulletin, one of the two women newsreaders (Sansanee Nakpong) had been an unsuccessful election candidate. One also knew that Sansanee had represented the Buddhist reform Palang Dhamma Party then headed by Thaksin Shinawatra. Thaksin is one of the better-known Thai politicians and had briefly been Foreign Minister under the first Chuan government. His Shinawatra company had launched the first THAICOM communication satellite in 1993 (Lewis, 1996). He was also the only politician independently and favourably mentioned by one of the respondents.

"Hard" news about Thai politics and business, however, was not the only or primary type of news that the expatriate Thais surveyed wanted. They were just as interested in getting the latest "soft" news about fashions, personalities, scandals and show-biz gossip. For instance, the respondents were also shown an excerpt from *Jan Kra Prib* (The Blinking Moon), a Channel 7 variety show that was celebrating its seventh anniversary in December 1996. They were simply asked: "Did you watch this in Thailand?" The majority acknowledged that they did, then most of their discussion centred around the preferences of the viewers for individual singers in the program. They discussed whether they remembered each one and which of the seven singers and the two MCs they liked best.

Two comments were notable here. First, two of the ten respondents noted approvingly that it was unusual to see a pregnant Thai MC (Poosacha Tonawanick). Second, one of the same two noted disapprovingly that Sukanya Migail, the least traditional looking women singer among the performers and a *luk-krueng* (half-Thai, half-Filipina), was rumoured to have "dark past" *(adeet tee-mued)*, meaning that she may once have been a prostitute — something not uncommon among professional women entertainers in Thailand. It was notable that the Thai respondents were very well informed about the personal lives of popular Thai TV stars. Especially in Bangkok, there is an extensive subculture centred around television soaps and *luk-thoong* (Thai rural music) video clips that links up with a suburban and provincial café, bar and restaurant entertainment circuit, where the same stars can be seen performing live.

It was evident in the survey, too, that Thai sensationalised current affairs programs such as *Cheod* (Close Call), and *Tam-La-Ha-Kwam-Jing* (Search for the Truth) were seen as popular sources for information concerning the increase in crime which has grown in parallel with the booming Thai economy. These shows, modelled on American "reality docu-dramas" are exactly the opposite to the rural, historical romances that were also popular with the respondents. Reports about violent crime, fraud and briberies in these programs, however, did not discourage the expatriate Thais from visiting their homelands. One respondent stated the necessity of knowing what was happening in Thailand, even though she expressed no desire to return to live there.

Finally, a bracket of five Thai commercials was shown. The respondents were asked what they thought of current Thai TV ads and how they compared with Australian commercials. There was a consensus here that the standard of recent Thai ads had greatly improved, although a few respondents saw no significant difference. In making a comparison with Australian ads, two commented on the stronger Thai preference for indirect sales appeals, while one also correctly pointed out that direct product comparisons were not permitted on Thai TV (Chalinee, 1994). One positive comment on a patent medicine ad *(Tamjai)* was that it was qualifying its pitch by the use of a warning that medical advice should be sought if the medicine did not work. Consumption of various substances in the guise of medicine, especially vitamin drinks, remains relatively common in Thailand. Lastly, another respondent stated that Australian ads paid more attention to health and environmental issues.

Video as a Site of Escapism for Thai Brides

As has been discussed, Thai brides make up a large proportion of Thai-Australian families in the wider population. The salience of female marriage as a factor in the Thai presence in Australia, and the media preferences of Thai women married to Australian men, touches on one of the more widely debated issues in feminist media studies — the extent to which the viewing of soap operas and light entertainment TV shows should be seen as a culturally inferior activity, or whether it should be reinterpreted more positively as an example of the way that women use media to negotiate personal identity issues (Ang, 1996). It seems more likely that the average Thai bride married to an Australian man uses the media, and especially rented Thai videos, as a site for re-liminalising, dramatising and personalising their often significantly constrained social space.

Eight out of twelve Sydney respondents and six out of eight Canberra respondents regularly watched Thai drama series. Most importantly, all of these were women. One respondent regularly watched 75–80 Thai videos per month. For Thai expatriates whose language skills are not good, Thai videos were identified as a reliable and undemanding source of entertainment. Most popular Thai dramas are straightforwardly melodramatic, often using the ingredients of love, goodness and riches. One respondent explained why she preferred watching Thai dramas to Australian: "The plots of Australian soaps are hard to relate to. They often revolve around country life and complicated relationships. Thai plots are easy. The good ones defeat the bad ones and they all have happy endings."

A primary focus of Australian drama was perceived often to deal with family conflicts, in which right or wrong is not easily determined. Plots of Thai teledramas, on the contrary, centre on romance and personal success. Most of them are predictable and indefinitely iterable. The difference between Thai serial dramas is more about setting and the performers rather than the plot. Popular Thai dramas during the years of the economic boom (from about 1988 to 1996) competed for ratings by featuring many grandiose houses, luxurious cars and romantic, foreign settings. One 1994 series was shot in Sydney, with the dialogue taking place entirely in Thai between the all-Thai cast.

Yet this common fictional model of romance between Thais overseas, or sometimes Thais and *farangs* (Westerners), in exotic, faraway places rarely fits the more prosaic realities. The majority of Thai women who were married to Australian citizens arrived here with minimum English proficiency (Sansanee, 1997). Their expectations of fulfilling their dreams of living a better life were often hampered by language problems and sometimes by a dramatic clash of cultures. For example, Thai brides who have language difficulties and difficult migration experiences tend to seek to establish a social network with other Thai women through meetings at temple or household visits.

However, the notion of friendship visits in Thailand and Australia is different. While unannounced visits are common in Thai society, the respondents felt that social visits in Australia had to be prearranged, and the purpose of the visit properly explained. Frequent disruption of household activities by visiting Thai friends of the Thai wives was perceived unacceptable by their Australian husbands. Lacking an alternative support network, Thai wives have few to communicate their emotional problems to (Sansanee, 1997). The use of video drama series is captured in comments such as: "A video is a perfect escape, and it helps me get through the day." The speaker came from a deprived background with grade four education, and met her Australian husband and moved to Australia when she was seventeen. Now she has been here for three years, yet has barely improved her English language ability. While watching a Thai drama series together, she told the researcher that she dreamt of having romantic love, and a successful and luxurious life like those women in the dramas. She knew she could not have it, yet she hoped that one day when her son — who is a *luk-krueng* — grows up and returns to Thailand he would become famous. Then she could have a better life. For this Thai bride, videos offered her space to move beyond the constraints of everyday life and explore other situations and identities, profferring her some means to constitute herself in acts of becoming.

Most of the women respondents also agreed when asked if they liked watching historical dramas. In the first survey meeting, as well as showing Thai news and ads, an excerpt from an historical drama series, *Bangkok Dynasty*, was also viewed. The only exception was one young mother who said she preferred teenage programs. Reasons given for liking the Thai historical dramas were mostly nostalgic — for example, "They reminded me of my country home." Another viewer said that she wanted her children to know about Thai history. Several of the respondents also commented that they recognised particular actors, while some also commented on the good looks and popularity of the *luk-krueng* stars. Several more popular 1996 Thai TV rural drama series were mentioned, such as *Mon Rak Luk Thoong* (The Magic of the Country) and *Rak Kham Khlong* (Love Over the Canal).

As most of the respondents were from Bangkok, this raises the question as to why these rural dramas appeared to be so popular. In comparative terms, there are some Australian parallels, such as the international popularity in the 1980s of *A Country Practice*, still showing on ATV in Thailand. This is perhaps due to the style of narrative discourse used in these rural dramas, where the country is constructed as a place where there is a cooperative community, where notions of individuality are absent, and life is more tranquil. This is contrasted with fast-paced urban lives, where people are too individualistic and there is too much crime. Thailand is actually less urbanised than Vietnam, yet the primate city role of Bangkok, with its eight million people, dominates Thai media culture (Lewis, 1998b). The daily problems of living in Bangkok — *rot-tit* (traffic jams), *mollapit* (pollution) and crime (especially violent crime directed against Thai women) — make rural TV romances appealing.

Thai–Australian Media Use and Cultural Identification

Video and Cultural Identification

However, the most popular programs among the Thai diasporic audiences were variety shows, such as *Si-Tum Square* (10 O'clock Square) from Channel 7 and *The Twilight Show* from Channel 3. Both programs are broadcast weekly and have had high ratings for many years. The content of the two shows is quite similar in that they feature interviews with famous people, live music and comedy acts *(talok)*. However, the characters of the MC in each program are very different. Witawat Soontornwinatre *of Si-Tum Square* is very outspoken, abrasive and straightforward, whereas Traipop of the *Twilight Show* is more quietly spoken, subtle and tactful. The different image and characters of these two hosts had a great impact on our respondents program preferences. While watching an excerpt from *Si-Tum Square*, one commented: "The program is getting worse. It has no quality at all, especially the host. He has gone absurd", whereas the same person said: "*The Twilight Show* is very informative. Traipop has a good character and is very polite."

This preference underlines a long-standing Thai cultural value that a successful person has to be competent and have substance, yet most important of all, they should have a soft and polite appearance, and style of presentation (Suntaree, 1991: 146). The Thais in Australia still maintain their preference for a polite and subtle TV show host over an aggressive and blunt one — a manner which, by contrast, is usually more acceptable to Australian viewers. This expectation by the audience of a certain style of media presentation familiar to them is described by Nacify (1993: 111) as "ritual courtesy". The expectation of a familiar type of ritual courtesy among the Thai ethnic audiences reflects their collective subjectivity, which they share with the audience in their homelands. Partly because of criticism of the confrontational personality of the *Si-Tum Square* host, Witawat, the program was ordered off the air in Thailand in March 1997, despite its high ratings. Witawat's mistake, however, may have been more one of substance than style. It was reported that his comments had been critical of a senior government member at a time when the besieged Chavalit ministry was growing impatient with media attacks (Matichon Sudsupda, 14 March 1997: 14).

Videos of drama series — historical drama series in particular — also stirred the patriotic feelings of the Thai respondents. The story of these series is often based on the moral leading role of the "great ladies" of the royal court *(chao wang)* in the old days. Although these series have been remade many times, they still gain high ratings due to the use of well-known traditional and mythological stories and their popular stars. Many comments made by respondents while watching an excerpt from *Rattanakosin* (Bangkok Dynasty) reflected a strong sense of Thai patriotism. One Canberra lady, for example, said: "I feel proud of our traditions, and our ancestors. I also want my children to see the way of life in the old days of Thailand." Another respondent said: "I like historical drama more than contemporary ones, because the latter are exaggerating. It makes me wonder if the Thai society now is really like that." Not surprisingly, this comment was made by a female respondent who had left the country prior to the rapid changes in the Thai society in the last two decades.

Her particular views on modernity as a possible threat to tradition were strikingly similar to those of the elderly Southall Indians in television research conducted by Gillespie (1995) in London. They viewed modern Hindi movies as challenging traditional values — thus they were regarded by their descendants as having retreated into a cultural conservatism and traditionalism: "they are more Indian than Indians" (Gillespie, 1995: 80). In a similar vein, these Thai migrants still retain their perceptions of Thai society as it was at the time when they left the country, and some are now unwilling to accept subsequent changes. They, too, can be considered "more Thai than the Thais themselves", where to be seen as "un-Thai" is to risk being socially undesirable (Kasian, 1995).

Video Program Preferences and Generational Change

In contrast to the Thai migrants who arrived in Australia earlier, those who came more recently are more used to transitions and more willing to accept changes back home. However, they still try to make sense of those changes, give them new meanings and connect them with their own personal experience. Generational as well as cultural change is a factor here. The media preferences of younger Thais in Australia may be quite different from those of their parents.

Media use — especially Thai rental video use, which is more favoured by older Thais, housebound Thai wives or Thai student sojourners than the younger generation of Thai-Australians — is an important part of inter-generational communication. Young Thais and their parents may share core values, yet also may have different leisure tastes and living standards. An analysis of comments by focus group participants in both Sydney and Canberra after viewing excerpts from two drama series, *Jintapatee* and *Por-Krua-Hua-Pah* (The Chef), reflects some of these differences. The Sydney group was older and less well educated, while the Canberra group was younger and better educated.

The first excerpt shown was from *Jintapatee*, the name of the leading female character, a young woman in her mid- to late twenties. This drama examined women's changing roles in the 1990s in a contemporary Thailand caught between the rise of a technocratic class and powerful, but corrupt, politicians. The show suggested that education, not just beauty or a rich husband, had become a necessity for modern, urban Thai women. A related theme was the extensive use of technology by the leading character, Jintapatee, a journalist who, with the help of technology of the postmodern world, could expose a corrupt politician and his underworld. PCs, laptops and digital cameras became just as important features of this melodrama as its love scenes.

Although *Jintapatee* broke the generic conventions of Thai melodrama, which rely on predictable black and white characterisations, traditional sex roles and happy endings, it received a generally warm welcome from the respondents. Comments were: "It is a very modern story. It used a lot of technologies, very stimulating"; "It's quite a change in Thai modern drama"; "Good. I hate the story that only talks about love, hate and money"; "I prefer dramas like *Jintapatee*. It reflects what is going on in our country." And from a 45-year-old mother: "I think it's unusual but it makes me want to be able to use a computer. When I went back to Thailand, my nieces and nephews asked me if I could use the Internet. I felt embarrassed because I don't know even how to use a computer. I feel like taking a computer course here."

Jintapatee not only introduced technology into the television world of Thai women; it also defied tradition by the heroine becoming the family breadwinner and choosing her own career. Responses from the youth group after viewing the excerpt show how these second-generation Thai migrants deal differently with conventional ideas about women. They are constructing identities that are perhaps more complex, transnational and cosmopolitan than those of their parents. For example, a 15-year-old girl who participated in the Canberra focus group commented that Jintapatee could be an appropriate young woman's role model, as she represented a new generation with high levels of education and a secure and respectable job, and she was socially independent. However, when asked whether she had any particular character in Australian television that she could take as her role model, she answered that she could not identify any, but definitely did not see herself as someone like Allison in *Melrose Place* — "too bitchy", she said.

In contrast to *Jintapatee, Por-Krua-Hua-Pah,* or The Chef, has a more traditionally melodramatic theme. The story is based on a famous novel about a rich man searching for true love by disguising himself as a poor but skilful chef. Since the story has been frequently remade as a TV drama, extra features are added to the main theme each time. In this episode, the vulgarity of the new rich becomes the new comic ingredient. The narrative reflects certain behavioural patterns of typical urban rich Thais, where their money, power, connections, and lack of morality and refinement are used to satirise the worst features of the new society. Some observations among the Thai viewers were that, in present-day Thai society, there are too many "new rich or *setthee mai*" — which refers to the commoners who become rich as a result of the economic boom — while there were too few "old aristocrats" *(phoo-dee kao)* — those noble families who had traditional virtues and competence. The new rich are too vulgar.

All of the participants in the first group — the new settlers — shared the view that the division of classes in Thai society had changed from the royal and the rural to the rich and the poor in the city since the economic boom. One said: "If you have money you can be or can do anything in Thailand." He also referred to a recent scandal revolving around a previous Thai prime minister, Banharn Silpa-archa, who had been accused of buying his Masters degree. The younger group of second-generation migrants, on the contrary, had no interest in class division. Rather, their comments centred around the urban "Bangkok" culture shown in the drama corresponding to their individual experience in their own youth culture.

While girls in the teenage focus groups preferred *Jintapatee*'s social values, the Thai-Australian boys like *The Chef* better. They preferred the simpler — even slapstick — comic style of the actors in that show. *The Chef* was also more traditional, as it featured *katoey* (lady-boys) in a variety of comic parts as well as more conventional women's roles. This suggests that the very different images of women on Thai TV are indicative of social change of contemporary Thai life, although Western-style feminism has gained little ground. An increasing number of self-assertive women are now widely seen in game shows and news, where — especially on ITV — they have been chosen to be newscasters because of their journalism training as well as their looks. So far, however, the independence of Thai women has found only a limited place in Thai TV dramas. A drama like *Jintapatee* has defied earlier conventions by providing new female role models. However, most popular Thai teledramas are still produced by veteran male directors from famous novels written decades ago.

Conclusion

Unlike many of the other Asian communities which have migrated to Australia through the 1980s and 1990s, the Thais have come from a relatively successful and peaceful society. Perhaps this is why there are so few of them. The exception here is some of the Thai-Laotians who were previously refugees in Thailand. Nevertheless, Thai society has changed at a breakneck pace in those two decades. The economy was transformed while Thai politics continued to endure military coups and endemic corruption as well as moving towards political democratisation. Thailand at the end of the 1990s is radically different from what it was in 1980. It is vastly more wealthy, yet the gaps have grown larger between the rich and the poor (Mydans, 1997).

Thai migrants to Australia have come from a country in the middle of an economic transformation, with an unstable polity, to a society that is politically more secure, but struggling to maintain its living standards. This, at least, was true until the mid-1997 economic crash

(Lewis, 1998a). These rapid changes must have presented Thais with potentially paradoxical life experiences. Their use of the media, especially rented videos, to stay in touch with their cultural heritage seems to have centred around an interest in how Thai television was representing the great changes that had taken place — for instance, the new position of younger women in Thai society and the rise of a technocratic class (the theme of *Jintapatee)*, or the arrogance and vulgarity of the new rich (the *setthee-mai* in *The Chef).*

The recency of Thai immigration makes it difficult to be certain about the directions of likely generational change. The older Thais who came before the peak of the economic boom in 1996 may find the new wave of Thai media culture centred on young consumer audiences much less to their taste than do their children. Normal generational change is certainly taking place, with younger Thais as likely to watch *The Footy Show* or *Melrose Place* as they are Thai soaps. Yet there may be a real gap developing in the life experience of those Thais who remember a pre-1980s Thailand that was very different from the materialistic society of the 1990s. On the other hand, the savage reversal of fortune Thailand underwent after mid-1997 might reframe the portrayal of Thailand that the expatriate Thais watched in these videos as a baroque museum piece. Such opulent images may have helped to prolong the psychology of the bubble economy and unrealistically inflated Thai expectations about the future.

The two small Thai community networks in Canberra and Sydney evinced no major differences in media use. The Sydney video rental business is much larger and more commercialised, which is natural considering the larger Sydney market. Socially, the Canberra Thai community is much less representative of Thai society, given the presence in Canberra of the Embassy, the National Thai Studies Centre at the Australian National University, and the tendency for many Canberra Thais to work in public-sector jobs. This contrasted with more socially diverse and mostly private-sector backgrounds of the majority of our Sydney respondents. Their media use, however, was basically the same.

Moreover, the media preferences of the Thai-Australians largely reflected popular viewing tastes in Thailand. The most watched video news program, from Bangkok's Channel 7, also rates first in Thailand.

Similarly, the entertainment programs both groups watched on Bangkok Channels 7 and 3 were from the most popular domestic channels. What was not watched by our respondents also corresponds largely to domestic viewing behaviour. For example, neither programs from Bangkok Channel 11 (started in 1987 as an educational channel), nor from the new news channel ITV, were watched. Few respondents were aware of the availability especially of ITV programs. Since mid-1996, ITV has established a reputation for critical TV news reporting. This contrasts with the largely pro-government news Bangkok's main four channels (3, 5, 7 and 9) usually present.

Perhaps the feature that most clearly distinguished the media use of Thai-Australians compared with their cousins at home, however, was their emphasis on the need for media programs to use the Thai language properly and correctly. This was a concern for both Sydney and Canberra groups. That comment was made in relation to the perceived shortcomings of SBS-radio's Thai programs, as well as about the use of written Thai in the Sydney paper *Thai-Oz*. The point also figured recurrently in our subjects' discussion about the Thai TV programs, whether it was a source of concern — as in negative responses to Witawat's blunt speech style on *Si-Tum Square* — or of amusement — as in the speech differences between the satirised *"setthee mai"* characters of *The Chef*. In both of these, the need for careful attention to the Thai language was our respondents' common theme.

This emphasis on the proper use of the Thai language is reflected at another level in domestic Thai society: namely, in the government's broadcasting policy. This follows a well-established rule for national broadcasting to rely almost exclusively on the use of the standard Central Thai speech style, with the exception of programs concerning the Thai Hill Tribes (Hamilton, 1991: 1993). The Office of the National Culture Commission, which interprets cultural policy to include the preservation and propagation of Thai culture, emphasises correct language use as a *sine qua non* of Thai identity. However, in the far-away Australian setting, our subjects' emphasis on the use of proper Thai in the media seems to be an attempt at a more personal identification with the geographically distant, yet emotionally still close, sources of Thai culture available in the various media in Australia.

This is different from the state-focused strategic and nationalist aims of Thai broadcasting policy. What seems more important to Thais in Australia is that the preservation of the good name of Thai society should not be impugned, either by stereotypical Western media reporting of Thailand as a sex tourists' paradise, or by the incorrect or improper use of the Thai language in local ethnic media. Because of the excessive international media attention to Thailand's sex trade and AIDS problems, Australians may not realise how strict conventional Thai moral codes are, or the degree of moral censorship in the Thai media. Currently, TV ads that are seen to have improper nuances are being put off air — a Mitsubishi ad for air-conditioners was banned for wordplay suggesting how airline pilots usually slept with their air hostesses (Krungthep Thurakij, 24 February 1999).

Thai cultural identity among Australian expatriates remains very strong. There is no marked difference between competing versions of what it means to be Thai, as there is for the overseas Chinese. The testimony about how the meaning of that identity is being renegotiated in Australia was a recurrent theme in our respondents' stories. All expressed a strong sense of belonging towards Thailand. One who identified himself as a Thai and who had lived in Australia for nineteen years described his feeling towards Australia thus: "I'm just a part of the Australian nation. I happen to live here and I'm a taxpayer." At one stage, the researcher was asked by another Thai lady who had been living here for nine years: "What does it mean to be an Australian? I live here because my husband is here. It is a necessity. I still feel that Australia is not my home, or my country. My country [Thailand], no matter how messy it is, is still my country." Many Australians might say the same.

Select Bibliography

Aiysha (1998), Interview with Manas Ray, Brisbane, May.

Alongkorn P. (1996), The Video Link Home, *Bangkok Post*, 28 August, http://www.bangkokpost.net.

Anderson, Benedict (1991), *Imagined Communities*, London: Verso.

Ang, I. (1996), *Living Room Wars: Rethinking Media Audiences for a Postmodern World*, London: Routledge.

—— (1992), "On Not Speaking Chinese: Diasporic Identification and Postmodern Identity", paper presented at Trajectories: A Symposium for Internationalist Cultural Studies, 5–19 July, Taipei: National Tsing Hua University.

—— (1993), "To Be or Not to Be Chinese: Diaspora, Culture and Postmodern Ethnicity", *Southeast Asian Journal of Social Science* vol. 21, no. 1, pp. 1–17.

—— (1996), *Living Room Wars: Rethinking Media Audiences for a Postmodern World,* London and New York: Routledge.

Anon (1956), *Indian Talkie: 1936–56*, Bombay: Film Federation of India.

Appadurai, Arjun (1990a), "Disjunction and Difference in the Global Cultural Economy", *Public Culture* vol. 2, no. 2, pp. 1–24; also published in Mike Featherstone (ed.), *Global Culture: Nationalism, Globalization and Modernity*, London: Sage, pp. 295–310.

—— (1998), "The Politics of Repetition: Notes on the Reception of Indian Hit Films", *Workshop on Media and Mediation in the Politics of Culture*, Centre for Studies in Social Sciences, International Globalization Network, Calcutta, March, pp. 4–7.

Askew, M. (1998), "Thai Women Sex Workers and Western Men in the 'Pleasure Space' of Bangkok", in J. Forshee and C. Fink (eds), *Converging Interests: Traders, Travellers, and Tourists in Southeast Asia,* Berkeley: Center for Southeast Asian Studies.

Atiya A. (1998), "For Richer, For Poorer", *Bangkok Post,* 22 June, http://www.bangkokpost.net.

Atlas of the Australian People — 1991 Census (National Overview) (1993), Graeme Hugo (University of Adelaide) and Chris Maher (Monash University) (eds), Canberra: Australian Government Publishing Service.

Atlas of the Australian People — 1991 Census (Queensland) (1993), Graeme Hugo and Chris Maher (eds), Canberra: Australian Government Publishing Service.

Atlas of the Australian People — 1991 Census. (1993), "National Overview", Canberra: Australian Government Publishing Service.

Australian Bureau of Statistics (1996), *Migration 1995–96,* Canberra: Australian Bureau of Statistics, Cat. No. 3412.0.

Barme, S. (1993), *Luang Wichit Wathakan and the Creation of Thai Identity,* Singapore: Institute of Southeast Asian Studies.

Barucha, Rustam (1994), *A Question of Faith,* Delhi: Oxford University Press.

Bednall, David (1993), "What the Media Has Contributed to Ethnic Communities in Australia", *Migration Action,* vol. 15, no. 3, pp. 7–10.

Bednall, David H.B. (1988), "Television Use by Melbourne's Greek Community", *Media Information Australia,* no. 47 (February), pp. 44–49.

Bell, Philip (1993), *Multicultural Australia in the Media,* Canberra: Office of Multicultural Affairs.

Bell, Phillip, Heilpern, Sandra, McKenzie, M. and Vipond, J. (1991), *Different Agenda: Economic and Social Aspects of the Ethnic Press in Australia,* Working Papers on Multiculturalism no. 8, Centre for Multicultural Strides, University of Wollongong for Office of Multicultural Affairs

Bennett, David (ed.) (1998), *Multicultural States: Rethinking Difference and Identity*, London and New York: Routledge..

Bhabha, Homi (1985), "Signs Taken for Wonders: Questions of Ambivalence and Authority under a Tree Outside Delhi, May 1817", *Critical Inquiry* no. 12 (Autumn).

—— (1994), *The Location of Culture*, London and New York: Routledge.

—— (1996), "Unpacking My Library ... Again", in Iain Chambers and Lidia Curti (eds), *The Postcolonial Question: Common Skies, Divided Horizons*, London & New York: Routledge, pp. 199–211.

Birch, D. (1997), "Tricky Task to Redefine and Re-orient The Lucky Country", *Straits Times,* November 9, http://web3.asia1.com.sg/archive/st/0/pages/stfea8.html

Bogle, Deborah (1996), "Consumers Slow their Rush to Worldwide Web", *The Weekend Australian*, 14–15 September, p. 9.

Buchignani, Norman (1980), "The Social and Self-identities of Fijian Indians in Vancouver", *Urban Anthropology* vol. 9, no. 1.

Carruthers, Ashley (1999), "National Identity, Diasporic Anxiety and Music Video Culture in Vietnam", in Yao Souchou (ed.), *House of Glass: Culture, Representation and the State in Southeast Asia*, Institute of Southeast Asian Studies (ISEAS), Singapore.

Castles, Stephen, Kalantzis, Mary and Cope, Bill (1994), *Access to Excellence: A Review of Issues Affecting Arts and Arts from Non-English Speaking Backgrounds*, Canberra: Office of Multicultural Affairs, Department of Prime Minister and Cabinet.

Chakravarty, Sumita S. (1993), *National Identity in Indian Popular Cinema: 1947–1987*, Austin: University of Texas Press.

Chalinee A. (1994), An Analysis of Marketing Communications Development and Practices in Thailand from 1987 to 1991, MA (Com) Thesis, University of Canberra.

Chambers, Iain (1996), *Migrancy, Culture, Identity*, London and New York: Routledge.

Chan, Joseph Man (1996), "Television in Greater China: Structure, Exports and Market Formation", in John Sinclair, Elizabeth Jacka and Stuart Cunningham (eds), *New Patterns in Global Television: Peripheral Vision,* Oxford and New York: Oxford University Press, pp. 126–60.

Chatterjee, Partha (1984), "Gandhi and the Critique of Civil Society", in Ranajit Guha (ed.), *Subaltern Studies III,* London: Oxford University Press.

—— (1993), *Nation and Its Fragments: Colonial and Postcolonial Histories,* Princeton: Princeton University Press.

—— (1995), "Religious Minorities and the Secular State — Reflections on an Indian Impasse", *Public Culture,* vol. 8, no. 1, pp. 11–39.

—— (1997), *The Present History of West Bengal: Essay in Political Criticism,* Delhi: Oxford University Press.

Chatterji, Joya (1994), *Bengal Divided: Hindu Communalism and Partition, 1932–1947,* Cambridge: Cambridge University Press.

Chen, Kuan-Hsing (1996), "The Formation of a Diasporic Intellectual: An Interview with Stuart Hall", in David Morley and Kuan-Hsing Chen (eds), *Stuart Hall: Critical Dialogues in Cultural Studies,* London and New York: Routledge, pp. 484–503.

—— (1998), "Introduction: The Decolonization Question", in Kuan-Hsing Chen (ed.), *Trajectories: Inter-Asia Cultural Studies,* London and New York: Routledge, pp. 1–53.

Chen, Xiaomei (1995), *Occidentalism: A Theory of Counter-Discourse in Post-Mao China,* New York and Oxford: Oxford University Press.

Chopra, Anupama (1997), "Bye-bye Bharat", *India Today,* 1 December, pp. 54–55.

Chopra, Anupama and Joshi, Namrata (1997), "Singing a Divine Tune", *India Today,* 29 December, pp. 46–47.

Chotimont Y. (1997), "Disillusioned Down Under Fed Up with Thailand", *Bangkok Post,* 8 August, http://www.bangkokpost.net.

Chow, Rey (1991), *Woman and Chinese Modernity,* Bloomington: Indiana University Press.

—— (1993), *Writing Diaspora: Tactics of Intervention in Contemporary Cultural Studies*, Bloomington: Indiana University Press.

Clifford, James (1992), "Traveling Cultures", in Lawrence Grossberg, Carey Nelson and Paula Treichler (eds), *Cultural Studies,* London and New York: Routledge, pp. 96–116.

—— 1994, "Diasporas", *Cultural Anthropology*, vol. 9, no. 3, pp. 302–38.

—— (1997), *Routes: Travel and Translation in the Late Twentieth Century*, Cambridge, Mass: Harvard University Press.

Collins, Richard (1990), *Television: Policy and Culture*, London: Unwin Hyman.

—— (1994), "Trading in Culture: The Role of Language", *Canadian Journal of Communication*, no. 19, pp. 377–99.

Coughlan, J. (1996), "The Changing Characteristics of Thailand-Born Immigrants to Australia Since the Early 1980s", Conference Paper, 6th International Conference of Thai Studies, 14–17 October, Chiang Mai, Thailand.

Coughlan, James E. and McNamara, Deborah J. (eds) (1997), *Asians in Australia: Patterns of Migration and Settlement*, South Melbourne: Macmillan.

Coupe, Bronwyn and Jakubowicz, Andrew with Randall, Lois (1993), *Nextdoor Neighbours: A Report for the Office of Multicultural Affairs on Ethnic Group Discussions of the Australian Media*, Canberra: Office of Multicultural Affairs, Department of the Prime Minister and Cabinet, Commonwealth of Australia.

Cunningham, Stuart and Jacka, Elizabeth (1996), *Australian Television and International Mediascapes,* Melbourne: Cambridge University Press.

Cunningham, Stuart and Miller, Toby (1994), *Contemporary Australian Television*, Kensington: University of New South Wales Press.

Das, Arvind N. (1998), "Reels of Indian Reality", *Biblio: A Review of Books*, New Delhi, September–October, p. 7.

Dean, Michelle (1996), "Foucault, Government and the Enfolding of Authority", in Andrew Barry, Thomas Osborne and Nikolas Rose (eds), *Foucault and Political Reason: Liberalism, Neo-liberalism and Rationalities of Government,* Chicago: University of Chicago Press.

Delafenetre David G. (1997), "Interculturalism, Multiracialism and Transculturalism: Australian and Canadian Experiences in the 1990s", *Nationalism & Ethnic Politics*, vol. 3, no. 1.

Dello, Sanjay (1997), Interview with Manas Ray, Sydney, May.

Department of Immigration and Multicultural Affairs (1997), *Population Flows: Immigration Aspects*, Canberra.

Derné, Steve (1995), "Market Forces at Work: Religious Themes in Commercial Hindi Films", in Lawrence Babb and Susan Wadley (eds), *Media and the Transformation of Religion in South Asia*, Philadelphia: University of Pennsylvania Press.

DITARD (Department of Industry, Technology and Regional Development) (1994), *Media Developments in Asia and Implications for Australia: A Discussion Paper*, Audiovisual Task Force, DITARD, March.

Dyer, Richard (1986), *Stars*, London: British Film Institute.

Edols, Barbara (Manager of Program Purchasing, SBS) (1995), Interview with Jo Chichester, June.

Embree, Ainslie (ed.) (1988), *Sources of Indian Tradition 1*, Harmondsworth: Penguin.

Esman, Milton (1986), "The Chinese Diaspora in Southeast Asia", in Gabriel Sheffer (ed.), *Modern Diasporas and International Politics*, London and Sydney: Croom Helm, pp. 130–63.

Featherstone, Mike (1990), "Global Culture: An Introduction", in *Global Culture: Nationalism, Globalization and Modernity*, London: Sage, pp. 1–14.

Foucault, Michel (1986), "Of Other Spaces", *Diacritics* vol. 16, no. 1, pp. 22–27.

Gandhi, Leela (1998), *Postcolonial Theory: A Critical Introduction*, Sydney: Allen & Unwin.

Ganguly, Keya (1992), "Migrant Identities: Personal Memory and the Construction of Selfhood", *Cultural Studies*, vol. 6, no. 1, pp. 27–50.

García Canclini, Néstor (1995), *Hybrid Cultures: Strategies for Entering and Leaving Modernity*, Minneapolis: University of Minnesota Press.

Giddens, Anthony (1979), *Central Problems in Social Theory*, London: Macmillan.

Gillespie, Marie (1993), "Soap Viewing, Gossip and Rumour Amongst Punjabi Youth in Southall", in P. Drummond, R. Paterson and J. Willis (eds), *National Identity and Europe: The Television Revolution*, London: British Film Institute, pp. 25–42.

—— (1995), *Television, Ethnicity and Cultural Change*, London & New York: Routledge.

Gilmore, S. (1993), "Minorities and Distributional Equity at the National Endowment for the Arts", *Journal of Arts Management and Law*, vol. 23, no. 2, pp. 137–73.

Gilroy, Paul (1993), *The Black Atlantic: Modernity and Double Consciousness*, Cambridge, Mass and London: Harvard University Press/Verso.

Gitlin, T. (1998), "Public Sphere or Public Sphericules?" in T. Liebes and J. Curran (eds), *Media, Ritual and Identity*, London: Routledge, pp. 175–202.

Gunew, Sneja (1993), *Framing Marginality: Multicultural Literary Studies*, Melbourne: Melbourne University Press.

Gupta, Akhil and Ferguson, James (1997), "Culture, Power, Place: Ethnography at the End of an Era", in Akhil Gupta and James Ferguson (eds), *Culture, Power, Place: Explorations in Critical Anthropology*, Durham and London: Duke University Press, pp. 1–29.

Habermas, Jurgen (1974), "The Public Sphere", *New German Critique*, vol. 1, no. 3, pp. 49–55.

Hage, Ghassan (1998), *White Nation: Fantasies of White supremacy in a Multicultural Society*, Annandale/ West Wickham: Pluto Press/ Comerford and Miller Publishers.

Hall, Stuart (1990), "Cultural Identity and Diaspora", in Jonathan Rutherford (ed.), *Identity, Community, Culture, Difference*, London: Lawrence & Wishart, pp. 222–37.

—— (1993), "Culture, Community, Nation", *Cultural Studies* vol. 7, no. 3, pp. 349–63.

—— (1995), "New Cultures For Old", in D. Massey and P. Jess (eds), *A Place in the World: Places, Culture and Globalization,* Oxford: Oxford University Press, pp. 47–48.

Hamilton, A. (1993), "Video Crackdown: Censorship and Cultural Consequences in Thailand", *Public Culture*, vol. 5, no. 3, pp. 515–31.

____ (1991) "Mass Media and National Identity in Thailand", in C. Reynolds (ed.), *National Identity and Its Defenders,* Bangkok: Silkworm Books, pp. 341–81.

Hanley, Pam (1995), "Spectrum Research", *Spectrum: The Quarterly Magazine of the Independent Television Commission*, Summer, p. 17.

Hannerz, Ulf (1990), "Cosmopolitans and Locals in World Culture", in Mike Featherstone (ed.), *Global Culture: Nationalism, Globalisation and Modernity*, London: Sage, pp. 237–51.

—— (1996), *Transnational Connections: Culture, People, Places*, London and New York: Routledge.

Hansen, Thomas (1996), "Globalisation and Nationalist Imaginations", *Economic and Political Weekly*, no. XXXI, 9 March, p. 603.

Haq, Rupa (1997), "Asian Kool? *Bhangra* and Beyond", in Sanjay Sharma and John Hutnyk (eds), *Dis-Orienting Rhythms: The Politics of the New South Asian Dance Music*, London: Zed Books.

Hartley, John (1992), *Tele-ology: Studies in Television*, London: Routledge.

—— (1999a), *Uses of Television,* London: Routledge.

—— (1999b), "What is Journalism? The View From Under a Stubbie Cap", *Media International Australia incorporating Culture and Policy*, no. 90 (February), pp. 15–34.

Hartley, John and McKee, Alan (2000), *The Indigenous Public Sphere*, Oxford: Oxford University Press.

Harvey, David (1989), *The Condition of Postmodernity*, Oxford: Basil Blackwell.

Hawkins, Gay (1996a), "Chinese Television in Australia: Narrowcasting, Difference and Diaspora", paper presented at the XX Biennial Conference of the International Association for Mass Communication Research, Sydney, August.

—— (1996b), "SBS: Minority Television", *Culture and Policy*, vol. 7, no. 1, pp. 45–63.

Helweg, Arthur (1986), "The Indian Diaspora: Influence on International Relations", in Gabriel Sheffer (ed.), *Modern Diasporas and International Politics*, London & Sydney: Croom Helm, pp. 103–29.

"Hong Kong Films Conquer the World" (1997), *Asian Business Review*, March, pp. 20–22.

Husband, Charles (1992), *Minorities, Mobility and Communication in Europe*, Bradford: Race Relations Research Unit Research and Policy Papers series.

—— (1994), *"Race" and Nation: The British Experience*, Bentley, WA: Paradigm Books/Curtin University of Technology.

—— (1998a), "Differentiated Citizenship and the Multi-ethnic Public Sphere", *The Journal of International Communication*, vol. 5, nos 1&2, pp. 134–48.

—— (1998b), "Globalisation, Media Infrastructures and Identities in a Diasporic Community", paper presented to International

Association for Media and Communication Research (IAMCR) Conference, Glasgow.

Hutnyk, John (1996), "Media, Research, Politics, Culture", *Critique of Anthropology*, vol. 16, no. 4, pp. 417–28.

Jain, Madhu (1997), "The God Factory", *India Today*, 31 May, pp. 70–73.

Jakubowicz, Andrew (ed.) (1994), *Racism, Ethnicity and the Media*, Sydney: Allen & Unwin.

Jamieson, Neil (1987), "Relata, Relationships, and Context: A Perspective on Borrowed Elements in Vietnamese Culture", in Truong Buu Lam (ed.), *Borrowings and Adaptations in Vietnamese Culture*, South East Asia Paper No. 25, Centre for South East Asian Studies, School of Hawaiian, Asian and Pacific Studies, University of Hawaii at Manoa, pp. 124–40.

Jamrozik, A., Boland, C. and Urquhart, R. (1995), *Social Change and Cultural Transformation in Australia*, Melbourne: Cambridge University Press.

Jayawardena, Chandra (1980), "Culture and Ethnicity in Guyana and Fiji", *Man* no. 26.

Jiraporn W. (1996), "Once Outcasts, Mixed-Blood Thais Ascend to Pop Stardom as Hip Icons", *Los Angeles Times*, 23 June, p. 6.

Kalantzis, Mary and Cope, Bill (1997), *Productive Diversity: A New Australian Model for Work and Management*, Sydney: Pluto Press.

Kam-sung Sai Far Farth Plod Si-Tum Square Sia Wi-thee Kwan (Sudden Order to Off-Air Si-Tum Square), *Matichon Sudsupda* (Public Opinion Weekly), vol. 17, no. 865, p. 14

Kaplan, Caren (1996), *Questions of Travel*, Durham, NC: Duke University Press.

Karim, Karim (1998), "From Ethnic Media to Global Media: Transnational Communication Networks among Diasporic Communities", paper presented to the XXI Biennial Conference of the International Association for Media and Communication Research, Glasgow, July.

Kasian T. (1995), *The Post-Modernisation of "Thai-ness"*, paper presented to the ISEAS Conference on National Identity in Southeast Asia, Singapore, October.

Kaviraj, Sudipta (1992), "The Imaginary Institution of India", in Partha Chatterjee and Gyanendra Pandey (eds), *Subaltern Studies VII: Writings on South Asian History and Society*, Delhi: Oxford University Press.

Kee, Pookong (1995), "The New Nanyang: Contemporary Chinese Populations in Australia", in Chan Jin Hui, Bun Kwok and Soon Beng Chew (eds), *Cross Borders: Asian Transmigration*, Singapore: Prentice Hall, pp. 290–316.

—— (1997), "The Growth and Diversification of Australia's Chinese Community", in Julia Hsia Chang, Pooking Kee and James Chang (eds), *Chinese Cultures in the Diaspora: Emerging Global Perspectives on the Centre and Periphery*, Taipei: National Endowment for Culture and the Arts, pp. 139–53.

Kee, Pookong and Huck, Arthur (1991), "Immigrant, Second and Third Generation Chinese in Australia: A Profile Drawn from the 1986 Census", *Asian Studies Review*, vol. 14, no. 3, pp. 43–71.

Kee, Pookong, Shu, Jing, Dang, Trevor and Khoo, Siew-Ean (1994), "People Movements Between Australia and Asian-Pacific Nations: Trends, Issues and Prospects", in Pookong Kee (ed.), *Asia-Pacific Migration to Australia*, Manila: APMJ, Scalabrini Migration Center.

Kelly, John Dunham (1991), *A Politics of Virtue: Hinduism, Sexuality, and Countercolonial Discourse in Fiji*, Chicago: University of Chicago Press.

Kissane, Karen (1988), "Ethnic Press Alive and Well", *Time Australia*, 14 March, p. 32.

Kolar-Panov, Dana (1997), *Video, War and the Diasporic Imagination*, London: Routledge.

Kotkin, Joel (1992), *Tribes: How Race, Religion, and Identity Determine Success in the New Global Economy*, New York: Random House.

Kumar, Nick (1997), Interview with Manas Ray, Sydney (May).

—— (1998), Interview with Manas Ray, Sydney (May).

Lal, Brij (1983), *Girmitiyas: The Origins of the Fiji Indians*, Journal of Pacific History monograph, Canberra: Australian National University.

—— (1985), "Kunti's Cry: Indentured Women on Fiji Plantations", *Indian Economic and Social History Review*, no. 22.

—— (1992), Broken *Waves: A History of the Fiji Islands in the Twentieth Century*, Pacific Islands Monograph Series no. 11, Centre for Pacific Islands Studies, School of Hawaiian, Asian and Pacific Studies, University of Hawaii, Honolulu: University of Hawaii Press.

—— (1996), "The Odyssey of Indenture: Fragmentation and Reconstitution in the Indian Diaspora", *Diaspora*, vol. 5, no. 2.

—— (1998), Interviews with Manas Ray, Canberra, May.

Langdale, John (1997), "East Asian Broadcasting Industries: Global, Regional, and National Perspectives", *Economic Geography*, vol. 73, no. 3, pp. 305–21.

Lash, Scott and Urry, John (1994), *Economies of Signs and Space*, London: Sage.

Lawe Davies, Chris (1997), Multicultural Broadcasting in Australia: Policies, Institutions and Programming, 1975–1995, PhD thesis, University of Queensland.

Lee, Paul S.N. (1991), "The Absorption and Indigenization of Foreign Media Cultures: Hong Kong as a Cultural Meeting Point of East and West", *The 15th Hong Kong International Film Festival Retrospective: Hong Kong Cinema in the Eighties*, Hong Kong: Urban Council Press, pp. 78–84.

Lent, John (1990), *The Asian Film Industry*, London: Christopher Helm.

Lewis, G. (1996), "Communications Internationalisation and Regionalisation in Thailand", *Journal of International Communication*, vol. 3, no. 2, pp. 7–18.

—— (1997), "The Media and the Pauline Hanson Debate: Cheap Talk or Free Speech?", *Australian Journal of Communication*, vol. 24, no. 1, pp. 9–23.

—— (1998a), "The Markets and the Media — Southeast Asia's New Nationalism", *The Asia-Pacific Magazine* nos 9/10, pp. 34–39.

—— (1998b), "Capital of Desire: Bangkok as a Regional Media Metropolis", *Social Semiotics*, vol. 8, no. 2, pp. 239–54.

Loo, Eric (1994a), "Riding on Platitudes and Prejudice: Media Coverage of John Newman and Vietnamese", *Media International Australia*, no. 74 (November), pp. 73–77.

—— (1994b), "The Burdekin Report Versus State of Nation: Journalism in the Market Place", *BIPR Bulletin*, October, pp. 35–40.

Lovelock, Peter and Schoenfeld, Susan (1995), "The Broadcast Media Markets in Asia, in John Ure (ed.), *Telecommunications in Asia: Policy, Planning and Development*, Hong Kong: Hong Kong University Press, pp. 147–91.

Lutgendorf, Philip (1995), "All in the (Raghu) Family: A Video Epic in Cultural Context", in Lawrence Babb and Susan Wadley (eds), *Media and the Transformation of Religion in South Asia*, Pennsylvania: University of Pennsylvania Press.

Marriott, McKim (1955), "Little Communities in an Indigenous Civilization", in M. Marriott (ed.), *Village India: Studies in the Little Community*, Chicago: University of Chicago Press.

Martín-Barbero, Jesús (1993), *Communication, Culture and Hegemony: From the Media to Mediations*, London: Sage.

Mathieson, Clive (1998), "Village Loses Golden Harvest Action", *The Australian*, 14 July, p. 25.

McCargo, D. and Callahan, W. (1995), "Vote-buying in Thailand's Northeast", *Asian Survey,* vol. 36, no. 4, pp. 376–92.

McGuigan, Jim (1998), "What Price the Public Sphere?" in Daya Kishan Thussu (ed.), *Electronic Empires: Global Media and Local Resistance*, London: Arnold, pp. 91–107.

McNamara, D. (1992), "An Ethnic, Demographic and Socio-Economic Profile of the Thai Community in Australia", in J. Coughlan (ed.), *The Diverse Asians: A Profile of Six Asian Communities in Australia*, Brisbane: Centre for the Study of Australia–Asia Relations, Griffith University, pp. 85–122.

Miller, Toby (2000), "The NEA in the 1990s: A Black Eye on the Arts?", in Denise Meredyth and Jeffrey Minson (eds), *Citizenship and Cultural Policy*, London: Sage.

Mishra, Vijay (ed.) (1979), *Rama's Banishment: A Centenary Tribute to the Fiji Indians 1879–1979*, London: Heinemann Educational Books.

—— (1985), "Towards a Theoretical Critique of Bombay Cinema", *Screen*, vol. 26, nos 3/4, May–August.

—— (1992), "Decentring History: Some Versions of Bombay Cinema", *East-West Film Journal*, vol. 6, no. 1, January.

Morley, David (1992), *Television, Audiences and Cultural Studies*, London and New York: Routledge.

—— (1996), "EurAm, Modernity, Reason and Alterity", in David Morley and Kuan-Hsing Chen (eds), *Stuart Hall: Critical Dialogues in Cultural Studies*, London and New York: Routledge, pp. 326–60.

Mulder, N. (1992), *Inside Southeast Asia*, Bangkok: DK Books.

Mydans, S. (1997), "Thai Economic Dive Exposes Social Crisis", *International Herald Tribune*, 17 September, p. 1.

Naficy, Hamid (1993), *The Making of Exile Cultures: Iranian Television in Los Angeles*, Minneapolis: University of Minnesota Press.

Nacify, Hamid and Gabriel, Teshome (eds) (1993), *Otherness and the Media*, New York: Harwood Academic Publishers.

Nandy, Ashis (ed.) (1998), *The Secret Politics of Our Desires: Innocence, Culpability and Indian Popular Cinema*, Delhi: Oxford University Press.

Nederveen Pieterse, Jan (1995), "Globalization as Hybridization", in Mike Featherstone, Scott Lash and Roland Robertson (eds), *Global Modernities*, London: Sage, pp. 45–68.

Nguyen, Dang Liem (1987), "Cross-cultural Adjustment of the Vietnamese in the United States", in Truong Buu Lam (ed.), *Borrowings and Adaptations in Vietnamese Culture*, South East Asia Paper No. 25, Centre for South East Asian Studies, School of Hawaiian, Asian and Pacific Studies, University of Hawaii at Manoa, pp. 100–114.

Nguyen Trang (1997), Personal communications and research notes, June.

Nonini, Donald (1997) "Shifting Identities, Positioned Imaginaries: Transnational Traversals and Reversals by Malysian Chinese", in Aihwa Ong and Donald Nonini (eds), *Ungrounded Empires: The Cultural Politics of Modern Chinese Transnationalism*, London & New York: Routledge, pp. 203–27.

Nonini, Donald and Ong, Aihwa (1997), "Chinese Transnationalism as an Alternative Modernity", in Aihwa Ong and Donald Nonini (eds), *Ungrounded Empires: The Cultural Politics of Modern Chinese Transnationalism,* London and New York: Routledge, pp. 3–33.

Norton, Robert (1990), *Race and Politics in Fiji*. Brisbane: University of Queensland Press.

O'Regan, T. (1993), *Australian Television Culture*, Sydney: Allen & Unwin.

Ong, Aihwa (1997), "Chinese Modernities: Narratives of Nation and of Capitalism", in Aihwa Ong and Donald Nonini (eds), *Ungrounded Empires: The Cultural Politics of Modern Chinese Transnationalism*, London & New York: Routledge, pp. 171–202.

Pasuk, P. and Baker, C. (1996), *Thailand's Boom,* Sydney: Allen & Unwin.

Pham Duy (1973), *Musics of Vietnam*, Carbondale and London: Southern Illinois University Press and Feffer & Simons.

Pittam, Jeffrey (1993), "Media Representations of Ethnic Identity: The Vietnamese in Brisbane", *Migration Action*, December, pp. 29–32.

Pittam, Jeffrey and McKay, Susan (1991), "The Vietnamese: Representations in Brisbane's Press", *Australian Journal of Communication,* no. 18, pp. 90–106.

Prasad, Madhav (1998), "The Absolutist Gaze: Political Structure and Cultural Form, in *The Ideology of Hindi Films*, Delhi: Oxford University Press, pp. 75–76.

Pressman, D.H. (1993), Thai Modernity: A Study in the Sociology of Culture, PhD thesis, Brown University, USA.

Rajadhyaksha, Ashish and Willeman, Paul (1995), "Introduction", *Encyclopaedia of Indian Cinema*, London: British Film Institute.

Rajadhyaksha, Ashish (1987), "The Phalke Era: Conflict of Traditional Form and Modern Technology", *Journal of Arts and Ideas*, nos 14 and 15.

—— (1998), "Who's Looking? Viewership and Democracy in the Cinema", *Cultural Dynamics*, vol. 10, no. 2, pp. 171–95.

Rambo, A. Terry (1987), "Black Flight Suits and White Ao-dais: Borrowing and Adaptation of Symbols of Vietnamese Cultural Identity", in Truong Buu Lam (ed.), *Borrowings and Adaptations in Vietnamese Culture*, South East Asia Paper No. 25, Centre for South East Asian Studies, School of Hawaiian, Asian and Pacific Studies, University of Hawaii at Manoa.

Redfield, Robert (1956), *Peasant Society and Culture*, Chicago: University of Chicago Press.

Rex, John (1996), *Ethnic Minorities in the Modern Nation State: Working Papers in the Theory of Multiculturalism and Political Integration*, Houndmills/New York: St Martin's Press/Macmillan.

Reynolds, C. (ed.) (1991), *National Identity and its Defenders*, Chiang Mai: Silkworm Books.

Robbins, Bruce (1992), "Comparative Cosmopolitanism", *Social Text*, nos 31/32, pp. 169–86.

Rogers, Everett (1969), *Modernization Among Peasants: The Impact of Communication*, New York: Holt, Rinehart and Winston.

Rose, Nikolas (1996), "The Death of the Social? Re-figuring the Territory of Government", *Economy and Society*, vol. 25, no. 3, pp. 327–56.

Rouse, Roger (1991), "Mexican Migration and the Social Space of Postmodernism", *Diaspora* vol. 1, no. 1, pp. 8–23.

Safran, William (1991), "Diasporas in Modern Societies: Myths of Homeland and Return", *Diaspora*, vol. 1, no. 1, pp. 83–99.

Sansanee, J. (1997), "Women's Health: A Study Among Thai Women in Brisbane", Conference Paper, Australian Tropical Health and Nutrition Conference, 17–19 July, Brisbane.

Scannell, Paddy (1996), *Radio, Television and Modern Life*, Oxford: Blackwell.

Scarr, Deryck (1980), *Viceroy of the Pacific*, Vol. 2 of *The Majesty of Colour: a Life of Sir John Bates Thurston*, Canberra: Australian National University.

Schiller, H. (1989), *Culture Inc: The Corporate Takeover of Public Expression*, New York: Oxford.

Seagrave, Sterling (1995), *Lords of the Rim*, New York: G.P. Putnam.

Sheffer, Gabriel (1986), "A New Field of Study: Modern Diasporas in International Politics", in Gabriel Sheffer (ed.), *Modern Diasporas and International Politics*, London and Sydney: Croom Helm, pp. 1–15.

Silverstone, Roger, Hirsch, Eric and Morley, David (1992), "Information and Communication Technologies and the Moral Economy of the Household", in Roger Silverstone and Eric Hirsch (eds), *Consuming Technologies: Media and Information in Domestic Spaces,* London and New York: Routledge, pp. 15–31.

Silverstone, Roger, Hirsch, Eric and Morley. David (1991), "Listening to a Long Conversation: An Ethnographic Approach to the Study of Information and Communication Technologies in the Home", *Cultural Studies*, vol. 5, no. 2, pp. 204–27.

Sinclair, John (1992), "'Just Like Normal People': Towards the Investigation of the Use and Significance of Communication and Information Technologies in the Household", *CIRCIT Working*

Paper 1992/1, Melbourne: Centre for International Research on Communication and Information Technologies.

Sinclair, John, Jacka, Elizabeth and Cunningham, Stuart (eds) (1996), *New Patterns in Global Television: Peripheral Vision*, Oxford and New York: Oxford University Press.

Skrbis, Zlatko (1998), "Making it Tradeable: Video Tapes, Cultural Technologies and Diasporas", *Cultural Studies*, vol. 12, no. 2, pp. 265–73.

Smith, F. (1994), "Cultural Consumption: Cambodian Peasant Refugees and Television in the First World", in M. Ebihara et al. (eds), *Cambodian Culture Since 1975: Homeland and Exile*, New York: Cornell University Press, pp. 141–68.

Smith, Michael Peter and Tarallo, Bernadette (1995), "Who are the 'Good Guys'? The Social Construction of the Vietnamese 'Other'", in M.P. Smith and Joe R. Feagin (eds), *The Bubbling Cauldron: Race, Ethnicity and the Urban Crisis,* Minneapolis: University of Minnesota Press, pp. 50–76.

Srikandath, Sivaram (1993), Ethnicity and Cultural Identity in the Diasporas and Opportunities for Niche Media Marketing: An Audience Analysis of the Jains of North America, PhD thesis, Ohio University.

Srinivas, S.V. (1996), "Devotion and Defiance in Fan Activity", *Journal of Arts and Ideas*, no. 29.

Stevenson, Deborah (2000), *Art and Organisation: Making Australian Cultural Policy*, Brisbane: University of Quensland Press.

Stewart, Julianne (1993), "Television and Dependency: A Case Study of Policy Making in Fiji and Papua New Guinea", *The Contemporary Pacific*, vol. 5, no. 2, Fall, pp. 333–63.

Stratton, Jon (1999), *Race Daze: Australia in Identity Crisis*, Leichhardt: Pluto Press.

Studdert, M. (1996), *Thai — New Community — New Needs*. Paper presented at the Second Women in Migration Conference, 3–4 June, Sydney: Bureau of Immigration, Multicultural and Population Research.

Suntaree K. (1991), *Psychology of the Thai People: Value and Behavioral Patterns*, Bangkok: National Institute of Development Administration.

Thaweesak H. (1998), "The Perpetual Chronicles of Internet Events in Thailand", http://www.nectec.or.th/users/htk/milestones.html

Thomas, Mandy (1996), "In the Margins: Representations of Vietnamese-Australians", Chapter 6 of Place, Memory, and Identity in the Vietnamese Diaspora, PhD thesis, Australian National University.

—— (1997), "The Vietnamese in Australia", in James E. Coughlan and Deborah J. McNamara (eds), *Asians in Australia: Patterns of Migration and Settlement*, South Melbourne: Macmillan, pp. 274–95.

—— (1999), *Dreams in the Shadows: Vietnamese-Australian Lives in Transition*, Sydney: Allen & Unwin.

Thussu, Daya Kishan (ed.), *Electronic Empires: Global Media and Local Resistance*, London: Edward Arnold.

To Van Lai (1996), Interview with Tina Nguyen and Stuart Cunningham, Westminster, CA, May.

To Yiu-ming and Lau Tuen-yu (1995), "Global Export of Hong Kong Television: Television Broadcasts Limited", *Asian Journal of Communication*, vol. 5, no. 2, pp. 108–21.

Tölölyan, Khachig (1996), "Rethinking Diaspora(s): Stateless Power in the Transnational Moment", *Diaspora*, vol. 5, no. 1, pp. 3–86.

Tourism Authority of Thailand (1996), *Thai Tourism Journal*, June, p. 28.

Tran, Duc Danh (1995), "Vai net ve tinh hinh bao chi Viet ngu tai Uc" (Vietnamese ethnic newspapers in Australia), *Tuyen Tap Chuyen Gia 1995*, Melbourne: *The Journal of Vietnamese Professionals Society in Australia* II, pp. 32–34.

Turner, Graeme (1994), *Making it National: Nationalism and Australian Popular Culture*, Sydney: Allen & Unwin.

van der Veer, Peter (ed.) (1995), *Nation and Migration: The Politics of Space in the South Asian Diaspora*, Pennsylvania: University of Pennsylvania Press.

Vasudevan, Ravi (1993), "Shifting Codes, Dissolving Identities: The Hindi Social Films of the 1950s as Popular Culture", *Journal of Arts and Ideas*, nos 23&24, January.

Viviani, Nancy (1996), *The Indochinese in Australia 1975–1995: From Burnt Boats to Barbeques*, Melbourne: Oxford University Press.

Wallerstein, Immanuel (1991), *Geopolitics and Geoculture: Essays on the Changing World System*, Cambridge: Cambridge University Press.

Webb, Rod (Head of Programming, SBS) (1997), Interview with Joanne Clifford, May.

Williams, Raymond (1976), *Keywords*, London: Fontana/Croom Helm.

Wilson, Tony and Yue, Audrey (1996), "Australian Television/Chinese Audiences: A Postcolonial Dialectic", *Asian Journal of Communication*, vol. 6, no. 1, pp. 18–42.

Wong, Deborah (1994), "'I Want the Microphone': Mass Mediation and Agency in Asian-American Popular Music, *TDR (The Drama Review)* vol. 38, no. 3, Fall, pp. 152–67.

Yang, Mayfair Mei-hui (1997), "Mass Media and Transnational Subjectivity in Shanghai: Notes on (Re)Cosmopolitanism in a Chinese Metropolis", in Aihwa Ong and Donald Nonini (eds), *Ungrounded Empires: The Cultural Politics of Modern Chinese Transnationalism*, London and New York: Routledge, pp. 287–319.

Zizek, Slavoj (1993), *Tarrying with the Negative: Kant, Hegel, and the Critique of Ideology*, Durham: Duke University Press.

Zizek, Slavoj (1997), "Multiculturalism, or the Cultural Logic of Multinational Capitalism", *New Left Review*, vol. 225 (Sept–Oct), pp. 28–51.

Index